About the Author

A dynamic political activist determined to fight for a world free from prejudice and war. As a teenager, she worked as a waitress to put herself through college. As the wife of the Prime Minister of Greece, having lived through a coup d'état, she founded a grass roots organization committed to struggle for Women's Rights. Her inner conflict was between the feminist and the woman, her personal struggle, as described in her book, was love versus power.

Not pictured

Alpha Lambda, University of Minnesota Margarita Papandreou (formerly Margaret Chant), First Lady of Greece in the 1980s, has written a book called *Love and Power*. The book tells the story of the private woman behind the public face and documents Margarita's rise from waitress Margaret in America to the formidable Margarita, feminist campaigner and woman of style, power and influence. *Love and Power* is available on Amazon and at local bookstores.

Dedication

This book is written in fond memory of Andreas Papandreou, my lover, my husband, father of my children and Prime Minister of Greece.

It is dedicated to my splendid offspring, George, Sophia, Nikos and Andreas, and to my remarkable grandchildren, Andreas P, Andreas K, Margarita, Kostis, Andronikos and Phaedra.

Margarita Papandreou

Love and Power – A Midwestern First Lady

Copyright © Margarita Papandreou (2015)

The right of Margarita Papandreou to be identified as author of this work has been asserted by her in accordance with section 77 and 78 of the Copyright, Designs and Patents Act 1988.

All rights reserved. No part of this publication may be reproduced, stored in a retrieval system, or transmitted in any form or by any means, electronic, mechanical, photocopying, recording, or otherwise, without the prior permission of the publishers.

Any person who commits any unauthorized act in relation to this publication may be liable to criminal prosecution and civil claims for damages.

A CIP catalogue record for this title is available from the British Library.

ISBN 9781784558260 (Paperback)
ISBN 9781784558277 (Hardback)

www.austinmacauley.com

First Published (2015)
Austin Macauley Publishers Ltd.
25 Canada Square
Canary Wharf
London
E14 5LQ

Printed and bound in Great Britain

Acknowledgments

With very special warm thanks to those who stood by me always, my daughters-in-law, Ada, Alexia and Marianthi and my many special friends (in alphabetical order) Aliki, Aggela, Amalia, Anna, Aris, Avgoula, Christos, Didi, Dina, Elsa, Ely, Fotini, Gerasimos, Hara, Julia, Katerina, Kostas, Kostoula, Lefteris, Lila, Maddy, Mahasin, Maria, Marjorie, Mimika, Mireille, Natasha, Robin, Sotiris, Sou, Spyros, Tamar, Tasia, Thanasi, Theodore, Titina, Vasso, Yannis, Yota, Zeynep.

I would like to give full appreciation to my assistant, Venessa Leigh Daniel for her exceptional help on my book.

I would like to give thanks to George Kalofolias for the cover photograph from his periodical EXPRESS.

PROLOGUE

Just recently a new song came out written by two middle aged men about my father Andreas Papandreou. They had grown up during his period of political leadership. Their love for him dominated their lives. The song is very rhythmic, and I can see my father dancing to its tune as he often did to Greek music we played during our exile from the dictatorship while living in Sweden and Canada. We are all dancers in our family, but I am the only one with a York University dance degree. I loved our dancing sprees.

I would like, however, to hear a song about my mother. She was the person who finally persuaded my Dad to give up his successful academic career in the States and return to his home country as a potential candidate for the premiership. As a child of the Great Depression in the U.S., she developed a close association to the underdog, to the poor, to the discarded and discredited portion of the population. She grew up a natural socialist, without the flag of Marx, without the jingo of this ideology, but as a democratic socialist in her very being.

I asked her one day when I became tired of helping others why she brought us up to care for people. She laughed and said, "what do you want to care for – money?" Her attitude toward money was, first of all, that it was dirty. Second, that if you had it, you are obliged to share it as you must also share your time on behalf of others. She referred to our Greek heritage, pointing out that Socrates believed that being virtuous made you happy and that being happy guarantees a longer life. She never preached this to her four children, she just lived that way herself, and by seeing it, we absorbed her passion into our own way of thinking.

My mother was deeply in love with my father. She also recognized his leadership qualities. Once, during their decision making discussions of whether my father should take the big step to leave the University of California and his academic career, or play a political role in Greece, she told him rather dramatically "it is your destiny."

She worked as a baby-sitter and as a waitress during her high school years to put money in the bank for a university education. While a student at the University of Minnesota , she held many jobs, her "professional role," as she called it, as a bus girl clearing the tables in a cafeteria, as filer of books at the university library, as a hospital assistant, and as a riveter in a factory building airplanes during the Second World War, and on and on.

She was from an early age a natural organizer. At the age of 9 she organized summer carnivals in her backyard to earn money for a good cause. My Aunt Evelyn, my mother's sister, told me stories about the carnival. She got my grandmother, to sew a horse's outfit where two children could climb in through a slit in the stomach, one in the front toward the head, and one in the back toward the tail in order to give rides to the children who had paid 2 cents for admission to the carnival. Evelyn was in the tail end, and always remembered that the young children sat on her back. Both she and my mother earned money. My mom used her money to buy ice cream cones for the gypsy children living down by the railroad tracks.

Her political instincts were planted by her grandfather on her father's side, a person I never met, but to whom she gives credit for her own political interest and training. At the age of twelve she helped him conduct his campaign for a position in the Illinois State Legislature on the Socialist ticket of Illinois.

It wasn't too long after we returned to Greece at the fall of the dictatorship that she used her talents to build a women's organization called the Women's Union of Greece, the first and only grass roots women's organization in the country. Her achievements were many, some of which she describes in her book. Now, when she bumps into former members of that organization, she is told that the experiences they had under her leadership were like a university education to them. She helped them learn how to be active politically, how to set a goal and how to develop the steps, the strategy, to reach that goal. I have been told that their meetings had an exhilarating effect on the women. They realized that they could attack the sources of their repression if they joined together. This large organization has been credited with helping liberate women in the country.

I am glad she wrote this book, and I am glad she taught us through example to care. My mother has no pretentions, and being the First Lady of Greece never turned her head. She merely felt very proud, she loved Greece deeply. She is genuine, has a fantastic streak of humor, never complains. The one shot in her heart, along with the loss of my father, has been the attempt by opposing political forces as well as the establishment to debase the family with false stories of corruption. What she says is, "this too will pass, but meanwhile we must do everything possible to put the country back on its own feet."

Sophia Papandreou, daughter of Andreas and Margarita.

Chapter One

Could I have This Dance for the Rest of My Life?

When I was a little girl growing up in a small suburb of Chicago, I knew nothing about Greece. I barely knew that there was any other country than America. My third grade teacher at Washington public school, Miss Cohen, introduced our class to the Acropolis and the country that was called "the cradle of democracy." I remember being surprised about this because I thought America had invented democracy. When we finished the unit on Greece, she announced a competition for the best drawing of the Acropolis. Given what was already popping up as a characteristic of mine – to be somewhat unconventional – I drew it in all its glory spread out on top of blue Aegean waves. I won the contest.

In 6th Grade, I got my first introduction to politics. My grandfather Chant had been chosen by his Chicago plumber's union to become a candidate for the Illinois legislature. He asked me to help him. One of my responsibilities was to pass out pamphlets at his campaign speeches. After doing that, he instructed me to sit down with the audience to listen to his talk, and we would drive back home together. It was during the time of the Great Depression, and Americans, searching for a solution, were looking at the Socialist ticket where my grandfather's name was prominent. Mostly I got the impression that politics was about change; change for a better life for the impoverished citizens. Being a child of the Depression, I thought he was right when he rallied at the inequality of income in our society. I started imagining myself as a politician, an agent for change.

Then something happened that would give me that opportunity. In February, 1948, I first met Andreas, a University of Minnesota Associate Professor of Economics. He was twenty-nine, and I was twenty-four. Our meeting was in the unromantic setting of the waiting room of a dental office. The dentist was a Greek-Cypriot, and I was ghost writing his autobiography. While waiting for our work session to get underway, I laboured over the text of an advertisement for the rotogravure section of the Minneapolis Tribune as part of an account I had with a Minnesota Business School. Twenty minutes passed while I struggled to put together a sentence in French as an "exotic" component of an advertisement. The man sitting across from me looked foreign; or rather I should say that his shoes looked foreign – pointed and slim. I decided to ask him a question.

"Do you know French?"

His answer was a polite and cordial "yes," as he sat down next to me and easily provided the French sentence I needed.

At that point the tooth patient came out followed by Aris, the dentist, who joined us in the waiting room, explaining to "the foreigner" that he couldn't have dinner that night because of our collaboration on his book. He hesitated for a moment, then proposed that all three of us have a drink at the Radisson Hotel prior to work. The work never got started. The attraction between Andreas and me as the discussion progressed over cocktails glowed like the warm embers of fire, and Aris, in an act of nobility, suggested we drop the writing for the evening and graciously slipped away.

The two of us moved to the hotel restaurant and continued our discussion, talking about the things two people drawn together talk about – each other. He learned I was brought up in a small suburb of Chicago, the eldest of five daughters in a low-income family, and that I worked to put myself through the University of Minnesota's journalism school, doing odd jobs – waitress, bus girl, cashier, library cataloguer, burr bench girl on the assembly line for B-29 cylinder heads, riveter at Douglas Aircraft, hospital nurse's aide and others. I told him about my first job after graduation at the Hennepin County Tuberculosis Association, stirring my interest in public health. I explained that I recently left that job and was trying to succeed with my own public relations office.

I remember that I described an incident in my childhood – perhaps to show my character – or just maybe to intrigue him and bring him closer to me. I was five years old and in kindergarten. What happened placed me on the path of seeking justice as a key goal in my life. We kids were all sitting on the floor listening to each child stand up and recite a poem. One of the boys out of nervousness peed in his pants while trying to perform. Miss Peggy, our teacher, reprimanded him and put him on a chair facing the wall, tying his hands behind his back. When she returned to the circle, I stood up and said,

"You shouldn't do that."

She responded by saying, "Sit down, Margaret."

Still standing, I repeated myself, saying, "He didn't mean to do that – it was an accident."

Soon I found myself facing the wall next to the boy with my hands tied behind my back.

When I went home that day, I made an announcement to my parents.

"I am never going back to kindergarten."

They listened to my story, told me that I was correct in what I did, but that sometimes teachers make mistakes and I should return. They allowed me a couple of days' absence and then one morning my father said,

"I am taking you to school today." He literally dragged me to the car and when we reached the school yard, picked me out of the car and started carrying a struggling and screaming little girl toward the school door. We reached the door, my Dad stopped, and then put me down, kissed me on the head tenderly, and said,

"You were right, Margaret. Let's go home." This sense of justice may have been in my DNA, but the fact that my father ultimately justified my position made it stronger, I am sure.

Andreas listened carefully and reached over and patted my hand approvingly. Then it was his turn to tell me something about himself. He said "Since you have opened up to me, I can open to you. There was something I wrote when I was thirteen years old, and that my father gave me praise for. This was important to me because my father had left my mother when I was around three years old, and I saw him on rare occasions.

It went like this: "Ah! how I should like a world in which good men are met, in which the outside and inside coincide, a world in which a man would be free enough to show himself, and good enough to be worth looking at."

Now it was my turn to pat his hand.

He had left the dictatorial Greece of Metaxas in 1940 after leading a three year resistance movement against the regime. Late in May 1939, he was arrested at his home in Psyhico, a suburb of Athens and taken to jail, where he was beaten and tortured, sustaining a broken jaw. When he was released, he had but one thought: to leave Greece where freedom had been snuffed out and seemed destined never to return. Europe was largely totalitarian. Hitler had started his war to take over the continent, and America offered the hope of a free life and the pursuit of an academic career.

In the US Andreas enrolled in Harvard's Graduate School of Economics. His Harvard experience was truly "ivory tower," and not until he joined the US Navy did he learn about the Americans and their way of life. In 1946 he became an American citizen. When he was mustered out of the Navy, he returned to Harvard as an instructor in economics, giving supervisory sessions to teaching assistants. Soon these sessions were no longer needed because his students were talented, capable, intellectually powerful young men, future top economists of the country, such as Carl Kaysen, Thomas Schelling, James Tobin, James Dusenberry, Richard Ruggles and Glen Campbell. In the class a few years ahead of him and proceeding him at Winthrop House was a student named Jack Kennedy a future president of the U.S.A. And earlier than that, Kenneth Galbraith, who ultimately became a best friend. In 1948 when Andreas and I met, these names were unfamiliar to me.

I was two years out of the University of Minnesota, and had taken one course in economics. I told him I didn't like the subject. He smiled and said teasingly that I hadn't had the right teacher. Andreas was a warm and fascinating individual. He pronounced the word gigantic as "gijantic," twisting American colloquialisms in the most amusing manner, but otherwise his English was rich and eloquent. I was, to put it frankly, mesmerized. I was also tantalized by the fact that he was Greek.

When the music started and Andreas asked me to dance we went sailing off like Fred Astaire and Ginger Rogers. I knew something was happening that would change my life. We were dancing on the blue sea – the Aegean, of cause – we were soaring to the skies and gliding from star to star on the Big Dipper, our bodies bending and moving in tandem. I felt a delicious excitement spreading through every cell in my body. If I was mesmerized by him, it was obvious also that he was totally infatuated with me. Sometime later a country song came out that captured the feelings I had that night. It started out with the lines, "Could I have this dance for the rest of my life; would you be my partner ev-er-y night. When we're together, it feels so right..." Looking back, I realize I had always been waiting for the arrival of Andreas Papandreou, that one day my life would be dramatically different.

Everything would have been perfect except for one thing. He was married. His wife was finishing medical school in the East. Despite all my worries, good resolutions and determination to stay away from complicated involvements – I was falling in love.

After several months of a zestful and ecstatic relationship and a deeper and deeper involvement, I proposed we stop seeing each other until the problem of his marriage was resolved, one way or the other. It was the most difficult decision of my young life. Although he went East at Christmas to talk with his wife, there was no break-up of the marriage. I discovered I couldn't bear being in Minneapolis and not being with him, so one day I stashed my clothes in a couple of worn-out suitcases, locked the door of my office, and left the city, my home for seven years, as both college student and neophyte businesswoman.

I landed in Washington DC in early spring 1949, seeking a job with the US Public Health Service as a publicist. The job I held when I met Andreas was doing publicity for their public X-ray program that was carried out in the large cities to uncover early tuberculosis. There was no such official job title – it was just what I had been dubbed by the X-ray team in Minneapolis. Without a degree in public health education, the situation looked futile. With the help of a few friends I had met in the field during my work with them, I managed to get a temporary assignment on the government's national chest X-ray program, promising I would enroll in a public health graduate program as soon as a fellowship possibility turned up.

I spent three weeks in Washington for orientation. I was enchanted with the city (it was spring) and wandered through the streets after the lessons on weekends. My walks always included a search for the Greek restaurants where I would sip ouzo and eat moussaka, dropping nickels in the jukebox to hear songs Andreas had introduced me to such as "The Girl with Green Eyes and Blue Eyelashes" and "One Night When it Rained," most of them sung by Vembo, the husky-voiced singer of the resistance during the German occupation of Greece. I sat enraptured, yearning for Andreas, a long-legged slender American who puzzled the restaurateurs by seeming to know what Greek songs she wanted.

My first assignment was in Cleveland, Ohio. I organized neighborhood groups in order to speak to them and get their help in making the survey a success. In one meeting I went to

I met my first agitator, a man who shouted from the back of the room.

"You are promoting socialism; you are a socialist – we don't want your goddamn government survey here!"

I had never thought of socialism as bad; for me capitalism was the enemy. The Depression of 1929 through the 30s was the end of *laissez-faire* where the market was supposed to regulate itself. Roosevelt accomplished a marriage between socialism and capitalism, perhaps a much needed resolution for future economic crises. I argued with the man, by telling him this was a public health program that was good for the people and whether you call it socialism or reformed capitalism didn't matter. What mattered was its intentions, I didn't realize at the time that this was the beginning of a fierce debate, carried out vehemently by the "free marketers" who represented primarily the moneyed class. The manner of dealing with the economy became an international debate – and still is.

I affected the authentic diploma health educators on the project negatively. I was uneducated for the role, they complained. The fact that I was very successful in the job was a threat to their profession. After completing work on the survey in Cleveland, I was sent to Salt Lake City, Utah for my next assignment. In early September of 1949, just as I was settling in to enjoy the riot of colours in the mountain range which wreathed the city, and just as I was getting to know the community leaders in Brigham Young's Mormon territory, I received a wire from the Public Health Service to quickly prepare for graduate school. Funds had been found for my education through the Rockefeller Foundation. I applied to five schools, sending my college record that showed good grades, but inadequate undergraduate courses in science. I was rejected by all of them.

One university I had not applied to was the University of Minnesota. Reluctantly I made a telephone call to Ruth Grout, then head of the Health Education Department at the university, someone who knew me and knew my work in the health field. I was accepted. I had to promise to take two undergraduate courses in science while doing my graduate work. They could have given me ten undergraduate courses to complete. I was truly happy to get paid to go to school, but I had one reservation – the University of Minnesota was the last place I wanted to go. My great concern was that I might bump into Andreas on campus, and I knew the emotional upheaval that would bring.

Months passed, May came, and I was walking across campus one morning, feeling smart in my newly purchased yellow trench-style raincoat, experiencing the joy of youth and spring. My mind wandered to an earlier time in my undergraduate days when I was walking across campus with tears in my eyes, having just been told that Roosevelt had died. It was April 1945. I really admired him, but I was more attached to Eleanor, and concerned about her having lost the man she loved, and the title of First Lady, using her role to do remarkable things for the underprivileged.

I suddenly realized I was late for my morning seminar. I rashly decided to take a path I had been avoiding, a shortcut which led me directly in front of the economics building. So intent was I on making up time, I failed to notice a figure walking toward me until I was too close to turn and disappear down a side path. I knew the walk – a jaunty long stride with feet splayed out. I passed by silently, pretending to be engrossed in my own thoughts. I had gone four or five steps beyond Andreas when I heard the name,

"Margaret?"

My heart was pounding in my chest, but I turned around, put a look of surprise on my face, and said innocently,

"Oh, Andreas, is that you?"

The end result was our walk to my class together and several dinners out during which he indicated his marriage was breaking up. I remember thinking, *I've heard this story before.* The evenings with Andreas were exciting, a blend of anticipation and uncertainty. I tried to keep my emotions on ice so as not to affect my decision to marry Robert Hall, a fellow graduate student, in July. If Andreas had not left in June for a workshop in Maine, immediately at the end of the academic year, the course of events might have been different. On late June night after I returned to my rooming house, my roommate told me a long-distance call had come from the East. She did not take a message because the caller said he would call back. As it was, the days were passing by, my wedding preparations were underway, and on July 14th I got married. Robert and I left immediately thereafter for the training period in Los Angeles that I was obliged to do following the completion of my academic year in the School of Public Health. While I was doing my training, Robert took courses at the University of California to add credits for his PhD in sociology. He returned to Minnesota in the fall to continue his academic study. I stayed on waiting for my next assignment from the government.

One day, I spotted an article about the father of Andreas in the LA Examiner. It was November 1950. Impulsively I clipped it out and sent it to Andreas in an envelope that had the return address of the Southeast LA Health Center where I was located. Letters started coming from him which I read but left unanswered. What to say?

"You are out, Buddy. I got married."

In the winter of that year I was assigned to Albuquerque, New Mexico. By the following Easter after some hasty trips by Robert for us to be together in my new post in the south of America, I decided to get out of a situation that had become unbearable for both of us. We were not suited to each other.

Having made this decision I felt free to send my first response to Andreas' letters explaining that despite my feelings for him, I got married as planned, believing that our getting together again was a lost cause. I told him my marriage had failed. I thanked him for all his warm letters. I received a telegram immediately saying he was planning to drive to California for a summer seminar, and would take a detour to Albuquerque to see me. We spent five glorious days together. One evening while riding next to him in his car, I sang a song that went something like this "If I could be with you one hour tonight, if we could do the things I wish we might, then I'm telling you I'd be anything but blue, if I could be with you..."

He suddenly said, "Let's get married."

On August 30, 1951, after quick uncontested divorces, Andreas and I got married in Reno, Nevada in a civil ceremony. Following our marriage, we returned to the University of Minnesota, and in 1952 became active in American politics, inspired by the nomination of Adlai Stevenson for the Democratic Party's presidential candidate. Andreas became chairman of the Minnesota Stevenson's Forum Committee, and we watched Stevenson's defeat on election night at the home of Walter Heller, a man who subsequently became head of the Council of Economic Advisors under President Kennedy. A man of tradition, Walt had been initially hostile to me, believing marriages should last forever, and I was the home wrecker. That night he announced to me that he was happy with Andreas's decision to marry me because I provided balance in his life.

"I'm a Libra," I said.

I was delighted with this announcement because we were having the difficulty that many divorced couples have – friends take sides. In this case, many of Andreas's academic friends chose to stand by the ex-wife. One day late in the fall Andreas came home to announce happily that a professor he knew from the Agricultural Campus was coming for a drink with us that evening. I was the one who opened the door to greet him. I looked out at his car on the street some distance from the door, out of range of my clear vision, and said,

"Would you like to bring your wife in?" He looked at me quizzically, looked out at the car and said,

"That's not my wife, that's my dog." So the first opening to the academic community started with a blunder. This became a family joke in the future, with the members of the family debating which would have been worse – if the wife had been sitting in the car, and I invited him to bring in his dog, or the one that actually happened. We never agreed on the answer.

At the political level, we joined the Democratic-Farm-Labor Party, and both of us were delegates in 1954 to the Minnesota State Convention which nominated Orville Freeman for governor, a race he won. Here I renewed my acquaintance with Senator Hubert Humphrey for whom I had campaigned during college days in his Minneapolis mayor's bid. I introduced him to Andreas, who offered the Stevenson Forum Committee for help in his pending senatorial campaign.

Our marital life was warm and romantic. Andreas and I often held hands when we walked together, and he told me he had the need to communicate in a non-verbal way – something that couldn't be seen – but had meaning. Already he had resolved the problem. He would squeeze my hand three times and that would simply mean *I love you.* – Gooey, but we were still floating on cloud nine.

When we left Minnesota in 1955 for the University of California, we left politicking behind. Andreas became highly involved in university activities having been elected chairman of the Economics Department. I was equally involved in having my third and fourth child, and in running a home. Andreas's only brush with politics was to join a board of economic advisors for Pat Brown, governor of California. His various political efforts, however, were enough for me to recognize his leadership capabilities.

Our involvement in Greece came on gradually. It was for me in its own way a love affair, starting in 1959 when we arrived in Piraeus on a Fulbright fellowship with the four children and my mother-in-law, who lived with us. We rented a house in Ekali, just outside of Athens, built of pinkish rock, a color I was often to gaze upon through the years at dusk on the mountain of Hymettus. The pull of Greece was upon us. It was especially powerful upon me.

To Andreas, Greece represented the frustration and agony of living in an authoritarian environment with a powerful monarchy and a strong military, his memories still vivid of the dictatorial Greece he had left behind. He was less susceptible to the awesome hypnotic spell that Greece casts on those who visit her.

In the spring of 1960, toward the end of the Fulbright year, we were in a dialogue – Andreas and I, Andreas and his boyhood friends, Andreas and his father. The question was, should Andreas return to Greece to play a role in Greek public life? The pressures were great, not the least of which were mine. His father, believing that I was the key player in the decision-making, asked if I minded having my name changed to Margarita – much more Greek – from Margaret. I must admit that I liked the proposal. That was not, however, going to be a factor in our decision. Quite apart from having to give up a fruitful and successful academic career, Andreas believed the forces in Greece would never allow him a significant role in the development of the country. His independence of mind, his progressive ideas, his commitment to full democracy – all of these would make it necessary for the establishment forces to destroy him. My own position was that he had something special to give Greece: American know-how, knowledge and training in problems of economic development, modern methods, plus a political philosophy which would move Greece toward the left. He was unimpressed. At one moment of our debate, I made the dramatic statement that he was denying his destiny – his fate was to lead Greece. He gave me a tiny smirk as if to say, *my dear woman, are you out of your mind?*

We returned to California. The dilemma had not been resolved. However, a proposal had been made by the Karamanlis government – undoubtedly as a favor to his father, to establish a Centre of Economic Research in Athens with Andreas as the director. By the end of the semester, and with a grant for the Center from the Ford Foundation, we gathered our family again – George (eight), Sophia (six), Nikos (four) and Andrikos (one and a half), and headed for the San Francisco airport. We were soon soaring above the morning mist shrouding the Golden Gate Bridge, winging our way toward the Mediterranean, our mood shifting from elation to worry as we contemplated the new life ahead of us, full of uncertainties.

That winter of 1961 was not a happy winter. The adjustment for both of us was hard. Andreas was spending hours away from the home in an attempt to move the government bureaucracy to enable his Economic Research Center to start functioning. My anxiety confronting a new culture as a resident, not a visitor, caused me to lose weight. We had household help, which relieved me of household chores, but made my home more of a factory, employees and all, than a home – and a source of much friction.

In my free time I took lessons in Greek, did a lot of reading, and visited museums and historical spots in and around Athens. One incident that gave me a bit of comic relief was connected to my teacher of Greek. She had been a fighter in the mountains against the Germans in the World War. She was strong, tough, with the low husky voice that sounded more masculine than feminine. She asked me one day if I had any old baby clothes that I could give to a family in Piraeus who did not have the money to dress their six month old baby. My youngest child was two years old, and I told her that I did have such clothes and would be glad to send them to her. I went home that day and immediately prepared a package with outgrown clothes. I gave that and a bottle in which I had a specimen of dog doots that needed to be analyzed because of my dog's constant diarrhea. My driver was given instructions in my by now meticulous Greek to deliver the two items. About an hour later, I received a telephone call from my teacher. In her low guttural voice she asked me,

"Mrs. Margarita, why do you send me this shit?" I was taken aback momentarily, but understood quickly that my Greek was not so perfect after all.

However, I had to give her an explanation. Because I knew from experience that Greeks in general did not like dogs, something that was a result of their eating up the street garbage that humans sought in a period of vast hunger under the German occupation, I hesitated to say that we were treating dogs like human beings. Also, rabies had become an epidemic during that time. So I told her the specimen was from my son Nikos and that my driver had made a mistake in address. Once in the past when I was in high school, I had told a white lie that created more and bigger lies and from that experience had sworn never to tell a lie again. I was angry with myself that I had done it now. When I arrived the next week for my lesson, she asked me how Nikos was. I said simply, "fine now, thank you.

"What was it he had?"

At that moment I couldn't for the life of me think of a disease that would have created constant diarrhea. So I replied, "Pneumonia."

"Oh," she said, "you Americans are so strange. A child gets sick and you give him a complete health examination."

I left it at that, remembering my past experience with a lie.

Another feature of that grim winter was my lack of friends. I had difficulty developing friendships, except among a few women who had spent time in the US or any other Western country and had a value system and style of living closer to mine. Andreas and I didn't ask each other the question, but it was there, over our heads, like a hanging rope with a loop: had we made the right decision? In order not to dwell on this dizzying period in detail, let me say it took one more trip back to California to arrive at the final decision to make Greece our permanent home and the Center of Economic Research his first step into the world of politics.

Elections were scheduled again in 1964, after a brilliant campaign by Andreas's father. With the Research Center operating positively and productively, Andreas said a final good-bye to his Center and to his former academic career and entered politics, winning a seat in Parliament representing a constituency in the Peloponnesus. The next three years our lives were concentrated around political issues and the growing popularity of Andreas as the likely heir of his father's party – the Center Union.

Chapter Two

Confronting a Coup d'état

In April 1967 we faced a coup d'état, an armed invasion of our home by the Greek army. The experience was frightening and horrible. The next day I felt my two arms had been cut off. One represented Andreas; the other Democracy. Both had been torn away in less than half an hour.

Andreas and I were sleeping – it was after midnight, around 2 o' clock. A gunshot shattered the night. It was hardly a normal sound for the quiet wooded suburb of Athens where we lived. But nothing had been normal for a long time. I jerked upright in bed and heard sounds of breaking glass and loud voices. There was a loud pounding on our bedroom door. It was our in-the-house night guard, Manolis, who had run upstairs to shout at us.

"Mr. Minister, Mr. Minister, men with guns are at the door! What shall I do?" Andreas and I ripped off the sheet and leaped from bed like rockets from a launching pad. I threw on my pink quilted housecoat. Andreas pulled on his white shirt, wrinkled from its evening wear. We were trapped, and we knew it.

On my side of the bed was a buzzer wired to the house of Petros, a close member of Andreas's entourage who lived a block away. One long buzz was a signal to him to open his walkie-talkie and get instructions from us in case of an emergency. We had rehearsed it to perfection. I reached down and gave a long, hard buzz, then reached to the shelf under my night table for the walkie-talkie. It wasn't there. By then, George, my fourteen-year-old son, had awakened and was in the bedroom with us.

"For God's sake, George," I shouted. "Where is the walkie-talkie?" My natural thought was that the children had removed it. This turned out to be true. George ran to get it from his bedroom, but as the banging and shouting at the downstairs entrance increased; we abandoned the hope of reaching Petros. Andreas grabbed his automatic from the drawer next to our bed, and I heard the ominous click as he cocked it. I gave a frantic last three buzzes to Petro, which signified "Help!" and the two of us started up the stairway to the third-floor study. Going upstairs was instinctive. We wanted to get as far away as possible from the men smashing glass in their attempt to break in. Also, there was a telephone upstairs.

I was unaware of George following me, so great was my concern for Andreas, wondering how he could escape from the invading monsters below. I reached the phone and with trembling fingers, dialed Kastri, the house of my father-in-law, recently the Prime Minister of Greece. The phone was answered by the chauffeur who slept at the house. I shouted

"Yaney, Yaney, for God's sake send help. They are breaking the downstairs door!" He responded in a voice that sounded noncommittal and unperturbed. "Send us help right away!" I repeated. Then I turned to Andreas. "Oh, Andreas, he doesn't understand me. Tell him, tell him!" Andreas took the phone and repeated my plea for help. "Send everything you've got. And fast!"

I made another phone call to Petros. He had heard the buzzer and shouted, "I will help." Andreas talked to him.

"Do what you can, call our friends, the President, (This was what his father, George Papandreou, was called), Aris, Kostas, Spyros, and the others. Move fast!" Petros said something to Andreas, and I heard Andreas say he didn't know who it was, that it could be an assassination gang. When he hung up he told me,

"Petros says if it's the military, I should give myself up. I shouldn't fight, I will be killed." We stood for a moment, white-lipped, staring at each other.

We did not want to believe that the dreaded moment had arrived. For almost two years we had lived with threats – assassination, jail, military take-over. For almost two years, despite the dangers, Andreas had led a brilliant political crusade against the forces of power he believed were strangling the life and development of the nation, restricting the freedom of the people, and corrupting democracy. He had clashed with the Palace, the army, the economic elite, and the American Embassy, but he was the hope of the Greek people, and he refused to compromise in his fight against the establishment. His beliefs were progressive, those of an enlightened democrat. The establishment portrayed him as communist, or at least, a communist sympathizer. Now the establishment had decided to use more than smears and threats to stop Andreas.

We heard the shouts of men who had swarmed into the downstairs hall. They would soon find us. I had not even noticed the faces of my two youngest sons, Nick and Andrikos, whose beds were in the study during the visit of my parents from the United States.

"I'm going down, Andreas," I said. I felt that if I could ward them off for a while, Andreas might have time to escape. A frantic hope, but what else remained under the circumstances? My mouth was as dry as parched wood, but out of a need born of desperation, my mind remained clear. Barefoot, I moved with lightning speed down the steps. On the second flight, between the second and main floors, I confronted the intruders just as they were coming up from the first floor. This was a momentary triumph because there was no indication that I had been on the third floor. For all intents and purposes I had just awakened from sleep in my bedroom. At that moment the downstairs telephone rang, and I heard the bell interrupted as the cord was torn from the wall.

"We want Andreas!" screamed a short man in a helmet and battle gear, pointing a gun at me.

"Andreas is not here!" I shouted. They paid no attention. One soldier turned to George's room, just to the left of the stairway. The door was ajar and a quick look revealed that no one was there. The next door was the bedroom where my mother and father were staying. As the men kicked open the door, both my mother and father were coming out, in nightclothes, my father looking as if he wanted to tear the whole contingent apart. He shouted, "What the hell are you doing here?" and made a move toward the gun and bayonet being pointed at him.

I yelled, "They are my mother and father. He doesn't speak Greek. Leave them alone! They are Americans!" I tried to throw the fear of God in them. Americans! Masters and supporters of the Greek Army. At the time I did not know whether it was a coup, or a paramilitary group with the purpose of capturing Andreas.

"Dad," I said, "don't try anything. They will shoot all of us." My father, a fearless Marine in World War I, twice commander of the American Legion, THB Post 187 of Elmhurst, Illinois, believed that Americans could do no wrong, that fighting communism was the sole aim of American foreign policy, and that anyone who defied the orders of the American government should be put in jail. Yet these were guns supplied by the Americans being pointed at us, and he knew that not one of us was in any of these categories. By then the men were scrabbling through the bedrooms like hounds sighting a kill. They went in our bedroom, searched, and returned. They went into my daughter's room where Sophia and Andrea's mother were huddled, trembling, in their beds. They were snatched up and brought to the hall where the rest of us were gathered. Finally, the captain in charge sent two soldiers upstairs where my two younger children were still huddled. I screamed, "Don't touch the children!" While waiting for the soldiers to return, I kept saying, "Andreas is not here, he is in Kastri. Why don't you listen to me?"

The soldiers came down without Andreas. I was puzzled. Had he found a way to escape? The only side hidden from view from the outside of the house was a sheer, straight wall three floors down from the upstairs terrace. But even if he had managed to accomplish such an athletic feat, he would have confronted part of the contingent that probably surrounded the house. When I left him earlier to go downstairs, he was opening the doors of the study that lead to the terrace. What happened to him? Where was he? I felt a glimmer of hope.

By now we were all gathered in the second-floor hallway, four men guarding us with guns and bayonets. I said to the one pointing his weapon at me, "Why do you do this? We have no guns. Don't you see? Why do you keep us at gunpoint?" He was twenty years old at the most, tall and lanky, with dull gray eyes and a look of contempt.

"Because we like to, ma'am," he said in heavily accented English.

The captain disappeared into our bedroom again, then suddenly reappeared and pointed to me. "We'll take her!" Good, I thought. Andreas might, just might, have a chance to escape if they all left, taking me as a "hostage." At that moment, several soldiers came upstairs dragging Manoli, our night guard, with them. Blood trickled from the corner of his mouth.

"One moment this guy says Andreas is not here, and then he says he is here," one soldier reported in a loud voice to the captain.

"All right," said the captain. He turned to me spitting out his words: "What do you say to that?"

"If you would just shut up and stop your shouting, I will tell you where Andreas is," I answered. For a moment they looked as if they believed me, as if in terror I had finally decided to reveal Andreas' hiding place.

I repeated, "He went to Kastri. He is with…"

The captain cut me off, pointed to the closet door in the hall and gave an order that it be opened. One of the younger men took his bayonet and started prying the closet door open. Within a few minutes the lock was broken, and he then slashed his bayonet through the clothing hanging there. Had Andreas been hiding in the closet, he would have been cut to pieces. By now the other men in battle dress had come upstairs. The captain, in a "Special Forces" outfit with black beret gave orders. "Take that bedroom, you two there, you two there. Come with me," he yelled to four others, and they started up the stairs to the study.

This, then, was the moment. I followed them. As I reached the top of the stairway, I saw that the captain was kicking open the shutter doors leading out to the veranda. I rushed to get out with them. Huddled in the corner of the veranda was my son George. As it turned out, he had gone onto the veranda with his father and was the only means Andreas had of being boosted to the study-roof, since the wall was at least fourteen feet high. After boosting his father up, he was unable to get up himself. According to George, there was no place to hide, so he went to a corner of the veranda and squatted, and waited. He later told me that until the soldiers arrived, he was terrified. When they arrived, he lost his fear. When they discovered George, one put a gun to his head and yelled, "Tell us where your father is or we will kill you!"

George answered, "I don't know."

But right above, lying on his stomach, a gun in hand was his father, trying to decide whether to fight (and get killed) or to wait, or to give himself up. When he heard his son threatened, his decision was made. I wanted to find a way of telling him to stay where he was; I thought there was still a chance we might all escape unharmed. But my tongue was glued to the roof of my mouth, and I was afraid that if I shouted something in English, I would create suspicion rather than give help.

Andreas stood up, his hands raised slightly, and yelled, "Don't shoot! I'm coming down." He was a white apparition on a black, black night. He looked ten feet tall, a giant from outer space, who had landed on the roof and now towered over the earthlings below. The image was frightening and powerful, and I was afraid of the effect on the nervous gang of military. I thought they would shoot him. The captain became hysterical at the sight of the risen figure. "Get him, get him!" he screeched to one soldier, and the fellow made a desperate, clawing attempt to scale the sheer wall. At the same time, the captain shouted to Andreas, "Jump or I'll shoot!"

I was sure now he would shoot. "Jump, Andreas!" I shouted too. "Jump!" Andreas threw his gun down, and it hit to my left and clattered across the tile veranda. Then he jumped, and fell on his knees in front of me, virtually in my arms. Blood spurted from his knee. I put my arms out to help him, but others jerked him to his feet and with vicious jabs pushed him toward the terrace door. As they staggered and stumbled down the stairway, he told them, "Let me put on my clothes." They followed him into our bedroom. I pushed my way against a barrier of soldiers, and stood there helpless as I saw the blood still running from his knee. "You bastards!" I shouted, but no one heard me. He pulled on his trousers. They started pushing him toward the door of the bedroom. I grabbed his shoes and trailed after the contingent, by now numbering up to fifteen, trying to reach Andreas. I finally handed the shoes to a soldier, who took them. As he was being shoved to the door, I heard him ask the captain, "Where are you taking me?" and the captain responded, his face dark red and his voice rasping in his throat, "We have accounts to settle with you, Mr. Andreas," and they disappeared through the door.

For some reason, when I reached the door myself, having been briskly pushed aside by the soldiers, the door was locked. All I can remember is standing at the iron grill, my bare feet being cut by bits of glass, holding on to two bars like someone in jail, saying pleadingly to the rear soldiers turning down the street, "Please, let me speak to my husband. I want to speak to my husband. I want to say something to him." Two soldiers looked back, and later, remembering their faces,

I was certain they were sympathetic to my plea. They, as so many of the rest of us, were caught in a steel web which we knew nothing about, and could do nothing about.

I wanted to tell him that I loved him, that everything would be alright, that I would fight for him. But at the same time, I had a sudden image of his bullet-torn body, dumped in the field down at the corner of the block, beyond my help, or anybody's. The captain's remark, "We have accounts to settle with you" echoed and reechoed through my reeling brain as confirmation of my worst fears. I turned to my mother and started to scream, out of control, "They will kill him! They will kill him! Don't you understand?"

My mother grabbed me tightly, her arms a vice around my body as I fought to run out the back door, to cry to shout, to awaken the world.

"No, no, Margaret," she said. "They won't kill him." I was angry with her. Didn't she understand? Didn't she know what and who these people were? Didn't she realize that Andreas was hated by the Palace, by the Right, by the secret services, and that for months they had been trying to find ways to kill him?

Then I saw the faces of my children. They were gray with terror, and their eyes stared at me with animal fright. I merely said "Oh, my God, my God," and crumpled down in a hallway chair. Nikos said, "They won't kill him, Mommy, they won't kill him." I answered, "Don't talk to me."

In a few minutes I was up and running to the front door. I shouted through the iron bars, "Help, help! They've taken Andreas!" There was no answer. The neighborhood was completely silent. Not a door opened, nor a window. No light was turned on in response to my shouting. It was a ghost town. It was yawning abyss. It was the loneliest moment of my life. I told my father and George to run to Petros' house and bring him to me so that we could see if there was anything that could be done. But what? If there was a dictatorship, what to do? Fight it? If it were a special security battalion assigned to capture Andreas, then his life would be snuffed out in hours.

Just then I saw a police car driving slowly by. I raced to the door, and this time I managed to open it. I ran to the gate. "They've taken Andreas," I told them. "Can't you do something?" The policemen looked at me sadly.

"They've also taken Arnaoutis," one replied.

"They've done what?" I asked, astounded. Arnaoutis was King Constantinos' closest adviser and friend, his personal secretary. He, too, had been dragged from his house. Now I was truly confused. What did Arnaoutis have to do with Andreas, with the trumped-up charges of treasonable participation in ASPIDA; an organization the King's court had argued was established to be Andreas' method for taking over Greece. So how could they, the establishment, pick up a King's man? The arrest of Andreas must have been backed by the King, I reasoned, and yet...

I asked Elvira, my housekeeper, to run down the street and see if she could get Takis, a close political friend of Andreas who lived down the street, to come with his car. I was determined to go to Kastri and tell my father-in-law the grisly story. I was unable to cope with anything more than the brutal arrest of Andreas. The Arnaoutis information was a piece that didn't fit into the puzzle, so I ignored it. My thoughts were so focused on Andreas that I couldn't possibly imagine that a giant manhunt was going on all over Greece, and that others were experiencing this terror.

Takis came, with his driver, and I climbed into the back seat. The streets were ominously deserted. We met no car on the entire twenty-minute trip. At some point I thought I heard tanks rumbling along a nearby highway. Whether Takis felt this was a wild-goose chase or not, I do not know. He said very little, except things like this happened in Greece, and that he had lived through quite a few. This was some consolation. Takis, at least, was still alive. I leaned forward on the edge of the seat, buried my head in my folded arms of the front seat, and tried not to think of the worst. I held myself tight to keep from crying.

Chapter Three

They Cannot Defeat Us

An hour had gone by since that shocking moment when I heard the shot pierce the night. It was 3:20 A.M. I had changed into a skirt and sweater and light jacket, removing my pink bathrobe, which was blotched with blood. My feet were sore; tiny pieces of glass from the front-door pane were embedded in the soles. I remember feeling vaguely pleased with this pain, as if this mark of physical brutality complemented my mental anguish. We were approaching Kastri now. The only thought I had was that a barricade might be put up, and I would not be able to get in to see my father-in-law, former Prime Minister of Greece and head of the majority party. Although more conservative than Andreas, he was also a fighter for human rights and for the right of the people to participate in decisions affecting their destiny. He had fought almost single handedly against the fraudulent elections of 1963, winding up his speeches in all corners of Greece with the line, "Democracy will win!" At this moment, however, I was not thinking in political terms. He was Andreas' father and a source of help. The lights were ablaze when we drew up to the front gate of Villa Gallini, (Villa Serenity). I almost spit at the name.

Kostis, a night guard for George Papandreou was standing outside the gate looking red-faced and distraught. I barely noticed him as I bolted from the car and ran up the outdoor steps to the front door. Takis and his driver followed. The door was slightly ajar, and I pushed in. Standing in the front hallway were Dimitri, the chauffeur; Karambelas, my father-in-law's personal and trusted guard of thirty years; and Elena, the maid. I attacked Dimitri, shouting, "Why didn't you send somebody? Why didn't you do something when we called?"

"They came for the President," he said.

Once again, as to the police, I asked in amazement, "They did what?"

"Just after you called, they came and took the President." The President, Andreas' father, my one source of strength and hope. It came through now with harsh and cruel impact. Dictatorship. That ugly, intolerable word. This, then, was the event we had been dreading, yet expecting; fearing, yet hoping our fears were unjustified. Andreas had said it was inevitable. His father had said at the time King Constantine's removed him from office and made Panayiotis Cannellopoulos Prime Minister that "the worm was in the apple." So this was the end of a long and valiant battle for a democratic Greece, waged first by my father-in-law, then by Andreas. Or was it? Perhaps it was too early to say.

Elena's face was streaked with tears. I looked at her helplessly. Near her feet was a suitcase, sitting there impertinently, packed and waiting. "What's that?" I asked.

"The President's suitcase," she answered.

"What for? Do you know where they have taken him?"

"No," answered Karambelas, "but we will find out and send it to him.

It gave me a funny kind of comfort, as if George Papandreou had suddenly decided to go on a trip and had telephoned his maid to prepare his suitcase and send it on to him. "Did they hurt him when they came?" I asked. He was seventy-nine years old and had been in bed the day before with a touch of flu and fever. His heart was weakened by an attack in 1966. I wondered how he would be affected by a screaming, shouting band breaking into the house at 2:00 in the morning and hauling him off. Even while the thought crossed my mind, however, I was sure the "old man," as he was affectionately called by the people, had conducted himself with his usual aplomb.

"They rang the bell," Karambelas told me, "and while soldiers held the rest of us at gunpoint, two went upstairs to waken him. I heard the President ask them to step out into the hallway while he dressed, but they remained inside. After about ten minutes he came down fully clothed, and they walked him out the door."

"They weren't pushing him?"

The answer was no. We stood silently, Karambelas, Dimitri, Elena, Takis, and I. We were a pitiful-looking group, stunned, frightened, and tearful. Karambelas, trying to break the tense stillness into a positive fashion, said it wasn't the first time, and that it had happened before.

To my father-in-law, yes. He had been exiled and imprisoned five times during his fifty-year political career. This nonchalance was meant to reassure me, and it did, if only briefly.

"What shall I do? Should I pack a suitcase?"

He said I should. Then he asked about Andreas and I told him our experience in a few words, and that Andreas was bleeding when he left. I knew what they were all thinking. The President will probably be safe, although he may be sent into exile, but surely Andreas was in great danger. They didn't say it, but we were all aware that his life was at stake, if it had not already been blotted out by a firing squad. There was nothing more for me to do at Kastri. Then suddenly, Karambelas remembered something. "Hurry home," he said. "Find papers. Or whatever may be suspect. Get rid of them somehow."

"But I don't think I have any of Andreas' papers. They are all at his office, or wherever he keeps them."

"Never mind what kind of papers you have, whatever they are, get rid of them." It was something to do. There were guns in the house for our personal protection. Those I knew I should dispose of. There might be some of Andreas' papers in the locked cabinet in the third-floor study, a study that had become mine after Andreas entered politics. And when I remembered what a foul fuss the Greek press had made about a letter of mine the Novas government discovered and published, I decided that anything I had could be used, twisted, and distorted by these military minds.

I asked Karambelas to let me know if he had any word from the President, and he agreed to do so. His face was gray as I left. As we passed the iron gate, I saw Kostis, now a guard to a house empty of its moving spirit, inhabited by three desolate people with tears rolling down his fat ruddy cheeks.

My home was even more desolate and dreary. My father, George, and Petros had circled around Psychico trying to decide what to do. Then George remembered that Norbert Anschutz, charge d'affaires of the American Embassy, lived at Camellia Street, just five minutes from Guizi Street, where we lived. They found Mrs. Anschutz at home and awake. Norbert had been reached by the Embassy sometime earlier and had left in a hurry. She had been unable to reach him because her line had been cut. She suggested that they come back later in the day in case she heard something. In the meantime, my mother had gotten everyone at home to dress, simply because no one could sleep, and dressing was something to do. On his return home, George took pictures of the mess in the house at the suggestion of my mother, who tried to divert the children's attention from the horror of the experience they had been through. It was nearly five 'o'clock in the morning. As I walked in the door, I was startled by the telephone bell. One of the phones yanked from the wall was a plug telephone, and my father had reconnected it. The other was useless, its broken wires dangling from the wall. I snatched the receiver.

"This is Alexis, from Piraeus," the voice said. "You remember me? I publish a local newspaper." I said yes, but I didn't remember him. "They have taken your husband?" he asked. I said yes. "They are arresting thousands down here," he said in a whispery voice. "I am calling from a kiosk and must move quickly, but I am a friend of Andreas' and want to help." The first volunteer! But his next question threw me.

"What shall we do?" What to do, what to do, I thought amazed. "What should you do?" I shouted. "Tell the people to rise!" A lone appeal to an intangible something – the people, the only force that Andreas commanded. A large number of the people were ours, but they were ours at the ballot box, in a democratic society in free elections. Could they be asked to bare their breasts to guns and tanks, and to a ruthless use of armed power? When I look back at that moment I wonder who I thought I was, Joan d'Arc?

"I will try, Mrs. Margarita," he responded, "but I can't find any of our leaders. They have either been arrested or gone into hiding."

I told him to do what he could. "Remember, he said, almost whispering, "I am Alexis." I understood then that it was a false name, that he had taken the risk of mentioning his newspaper to identify himself, but that from then on he would simply be "Alexis." It was the beginning of a long list of false names used by friends over the telephone, in written messages, in letters, and eventually by me as we all adopted the methods of survival in a dictatorship.

After I hung up, I turned to Petros, Takis and his driver and beckoned them to follow me up to the study. Dawn would soon break, and I felt the need to hurry under the cover of night. We agreed that the essential task was to get the guns and papers out, away from the house, where they could be subsequently disposed of. I asked Petro's to bring me two empty suitcases from the upstairs storage room. Quickly we dumped in the guns, one from a locked desk drawer, one from behind a stack of books on the bookshelf, and one still lying on the terrace where Andreas had flung it down. I found bullets in a box behind the books. More ammunition was kept, I knew, on a top shelf above our bedroom closet. If there were more, I didn't know where Andreas hid them. I never liked guns, and I wondered how in the world they could be protection when whoever was breaking into the house would have his own guns. Then I started through the file drawers. "Correspondence – Andreas, 1964" – into the suitcase. "Key Posts in Government, 1964" – into the suitcase. "Outdoor Art Festival, 1964" – left in file drawer. "Social" – left in drawer. "Correspondence – Maggie, 1965" – into the suitcase along with "Human Rights." And on it went.

Takis' driver wanted me to dump everything, but I would have needed several more suitcases, and most of the material was truly innocuous. We moved fast, all of us feeling that a ring of the doorbell was imminent. Within fifteen minutes after we started, Takis and his driver disappeared down the stairs and into the night, lugging two suitcases with guns, ammunition, and files to their temporary hiding place. I felt relieved. Something had been done. Yet so little.

Downstairs my mother shoved a cup of steaming coffee under my nose. I sat down at the hallway table to drink it, and to think. My mouth was still dry, and my hands clammy… My body was taut, my stomach quivering with the sensation of a sudden elevator drop every time I thought of Andreas. I tried to guess where he was now. How was his leg? When would I hear of him? Had he been further mistreated? And the big question I tried not to ask myself: Was he alive? I talked to Petros – good, wonderful Petros – for years a faithful and devout follower of Andreas, a man who knew him as a boy and was always around to help. He had done the only thing he could do after that last frantic telephone call from us. He had started telephoning friends from a list Andreas had prepared for him for such an emergency with a prearranged message which informed them that something had happened and that they were to mobilize their people. After three such phone calls, his line was cut. He looked scared, and he had reason to be, as a political collaborator with my husband.

Two of the children, Nikos and Andrikos, had fallen asleep on the front couch, their heads in the lap of Andreas' mother, who sat staring into the distance, her face ashen white. Elvira, our housekeeper, had collapsed in a corner chair of the hallway, unable to return to her room, unable to work, and unable to talk. The rest of the family was floating aimlessly around, finding it impossible to remain still. I tried the phone every so often in a futile attempt to call out. The responding strange buzz told me the line was cut for outgoing calls. For some odd reason, however, my new-found Piraeus friend Alexis was able to call in.

"Alexis here. I have to keep on the move. I can't seem to do much."

"Won't anybody do anything?" I asked. "Is there to be nothing?" Where were the hordes of people in Syntagma Square, screaming themselves hoarse at my father-in-law's political speeches? Where were the passionate youths committed to Andreas who had pounded on our car as we made our way to local rallies? Where were those lines of cars which had followed our group to Lamia, Larissa, Corinth? It was a powerful force, I knew. Yet it was unorganized, leaderless, unarmed, and the communication system had been cut.

"If something happens to me, Mrs. Yannopoulos will call you," Alexis said. Another false name.

"All right," I answered wearily. It was nearly six 'o'clock and dawn had washed away the darkness. Through the gaping hole where the glass had been broken by the butt of a gun, I saw a figure standing at the low white gate in front of our house. It was a young boy, about nineteen, in workman's clothes. When he saw me at the door, his handsome suntanned face lit up, and he broke into a grin.

"Why do you look so frightened, Mrs. Margarita?" he asked.

"Don't you know what has happened?" I responded, opening the door and walking out. Although he had used my name, I didn't recognize him as one of the young people so often around Andreas.

"Don't worry. It will be alright. They cannot defeat us. We will help Mr. Andreas." Petros was behind me, when I asked if he knew the boy, he answered that he had never seen him.

"Thank you, thank you," I murmured. He looked strong and full of confidence and without fear. He was a new note in a night of horror and pain. He got on his bike which had been propped against a tree, and with the sun shining full on his face gave me an encouraging wave and pedaled off. Later in the morning, Petros reported to me that a young workman, in his teens had been shot to death on Vassilis Sophias highway, not far from our home, when he refused orders to halt his bicycle. I cannot say that it was the same young man, but I never saw him again.

Those hours of April 21, 1967, were the beginning of my nightmare in Athens. So here I was, a Midwestern American woman caught in the web of Byzantine politics and intrigue in the land of Greece, and now in the barb wired mesh of an army take-over. It was a true nightmare also for millions of Greeks who would live under the conditions of a dictatorship: fear, intimidation, uncertainty, distortion of human relationships, unwilling subjects of a dictatorial mafia, who, with their guns and war weapons had set themselves up as the representatives of the public will.

The next day I walked over to the house of Norbert Anschutz, the high official in the American Embassy, considered a friend of ours, but also considered the undeclared representative of the CIA in Athens. His wife met me at the door and ushered me into the living room saying, "Norbert is upstairs. I will have him come down right away." I sat down, nervously waiting, I remembered that Norbert had told Andreas a week earlier that he should pull back on his anti-American positions, and then added, "Don't you know you are a walking dead man?" When Andreas reported this to me, I asked him, "What is Norbert trying to do – scare you, and bully you into changing your political actions?" I heard the steps of Norbert arriving in the living room, and I wondered if I was looking at a friend or an enemy.

Without realizing it, I started the discussion with an accusatory stance. I plunged into a recital of why this was a monstrous, unforgivable mistake of judgment, that the

Embassy had misjudged Andreas, that they had misjudged the intentions of the party his father headed, that in their anti-communist phobia they were killing the only healthy, democratic forces in the country. Then back to Andreas, that he was not a demagogue, that he was not an unreasonable man, that he had done everything to try to prevent this insane thing from happening, including warning the Embassy and the State Department of the existence of the junta and its intentions.

Norbert tried to allay my suspicions that the Americans were behind this. I decided not to argue this political issue further. I wanted primarily to get an assurance that the embassy would do all in its power to save Andreas's life, a man who had acquired American citizenship after volunteering to join the Navy during the war. It was at this point, after leaving his house, that I started a determined battle to keep Andreas alive, that there would be no sudden execution. I turned for help to the economists in the U.S., and especially to Stanley Sheinbaum and Ken Galbraith, who both prodded President Johnson to take action. Shortly after that, Andreas was moved from wherever they were hiding him to Averoff Prison. The second step in my strategy was to debunk the high treason charge against him by planting adverse publicity against the dictatorship, thus undermining any acts the colonels might take.

Sheinbaum maneuvered an article in the magazine *Ramparts* with a front page of Andrea's face in a picture frame, entitled "The Framing of Andreas Papandreou." Other articles appeared in the international press, based on the information we were feeding to them. We emphasized the torture that was being used on people who might consider joining a resistance movement. I wondered at the time why information on torture was so easy to access. Then I understood that it was a method. The purpose was to scare others who might take anti-dictatorial action. Fear is a powerful weapon for affecting behavior.

After ten months Andreas was released, and the family went into exile, first in Sweden, then in Canada. The pressure we engendered played a role in his release: he had become a nuisance to the junta. But beyond that, I ceased being so naïve about the "goodness" of American intentions at the international level. It is a national myth that America goes into a country to protect or promote a democratic system. Or to promote human rights. There are business interests to take over and exploit the natural resources of a country. And there are military interests to control the territory. Greece had no natural resources of interest, but it was a good geographical place close to the Middle East for a military base. The president who felt strongly against interventions for these purposes – Jack Kennedy – was assassinated. I felt the coup would never have happened if Kennedy had been in power. I expected that when I had a chance to ask Andreas a question about the coup and the events leading up to the Coup, he would remind me of what he said when I was trying to persuade him to go into politics – vested interests would never let a person like him gain power. It was one of the first questions I asked him when he came back home. He looked at me as if I had touched a sore point but after slight hesitation, said, "I want to find a way to leave the country so I can carry on the fight from outside." I agreed. In Greece his hands and tongue were tied and he would soon find himself back in prison. For me, I could be a part of that struggle, a real partner in political action.

Our first exile location was Sweden. The progressive government there offered the post of professor of economics to Andreas at the University of Stockholm. They said they would also cover expenses for his political work. We rented a house in Solingen, where I began writing a book. I decided to try for a fifth child, even though I was in the upper forties, feeling that this was something I was successful at. Furthermore, I loved little babies and I needed a new creature to hug and kiss. We had an addition to the family that year, but I was not the mother. Andreas had strayed, trying, I believe, to assert his masculinity, but without caution. I must be just here: I am sure being locked up in prison is an emasculation process.

I called the child the "oops" baby, and offered to take the little girl in as one of ours, thinking I would relieve the rightful mother. It turned out she wanted a child, wasn't interested in a marriage, only that Andreas declare that he was the parent and by law had to provide monthly payments until the age of 16. Sweden has such a law. The family knew of her existence, but had no contact with her until a much later date. My youngest son Andreas got a temporary job in Sweden after his university degree and telephoned her, saying he was her brother and he wanted to meet her. She now is "one of the family."

While Andreas was teaching at Stockholm University, a job offer opened up at York University in Toronto, and, family in tow, we moved to Canada for the remaining five years in exile. Andreas formed the Pan-Hellenic Liberation Movement (PAK), and most of our time we spent in a liberation struggle against the dictatorship. During this time, I was totally involved in the anti-dictatorial movement, travelling, speaking, writing articles, lobbying, and editing the English version of the PAK Newsletter. My book entitled "Nightmare in Athens," came out describing the horror of going through a military coup and losing in one fell swoop all democratic rights and freedom. My appearance in a Congressional investigating committee hearing in 1973 gave me the opportunity to express my ire at U.S. involvement and support of the dictatorship. It also gave some hope to the liberation fighters back in Greece.

Chapter Four

Return to a Free Greece

We returned to a free Greece in the summer of 1974, following the overthrow of the junta. Andreas's father was no longer alive, and Andreas was free to form a new party consisting of the members of his father's old Center Union Party, and the Pan-Hellenic Liberation Movement. He named it the Pan-Hellenic Socialist Movement, written in acronym as PASOK. I was something of a bystander, having chosen not to be involved with party matters. I had another agenda which I will describe later.

With the dictators in prison in Greece, elections were called early by the temporary government headed by Karamanlis, former prime minister. From a liberation movement (PAK), the newly formed party of PASOK entered the democratic path to elections. In 1975 in the first elections the results for the party were unimpressive, garnering only 13% of the total vote. The next two years were used by Andreas for building his party and making contact with the people. He was running around the country for his purpose; I was running around the country for my purpose – to make contact with women in order to build a women's organization.

Elections were called again in 1977, and we garnered 26% of the total. Four years later, in 1981, we won elections with 48% of the total, enough to form government. The period of time from Andreas's arrest that horrible night of the coup d'état to this victory had been a long and arduous battle. I still have a keen memory of the family's beaming faces the night of the winning election returns.

Three days after the victory, Andreas and I rode in a government car for the official ceremony of his becoming Prime Minister. The street from our home in to the parliamentary building in the center of Athens was lined on both sides with cheering people. I experienced all kinds of emotions – pride in my husband, joy in seeing the happy faces of citizens along the way, gratification for a battle won, and also anxiety for the future. I was wondering about my role with the title of "First Lady of Greece."

The democratic system wants women who gain power by being the wife of an elected official to be accountable, to be under control. Tradition demands a back seat for the woman. In contemporary times, she has usually been not "just the wife," but a real participant in the political process which brought her husband into power and therefore feels entitled to share that power. I remember what Eleanor Roosevelt said about campaigning with a husband – "Always be on schedule, offer no personal opinions, remain undisturbed by the commotion, limit personal appearances, and lean back in an open car so the crowds can see *him*."

I made a comment to Andreas. "Running this country needs a very wise person."

"Mmmm," he said, his mind clearly elsewhere.

Then I asked a question, "I know your role as prime minister, but what is my role?"

While waving and smiling at the crowd, he answered casually, "I don't really know."

"Are there any rules?"

"Don't think so."

"I mean, nothing written?"

"That's it. Oh, look, Vassili with his family."

"Then I can write my own rules?"

"Yeah, I suppose so."

Within a few days of this conversation, I was told to get ready for our first international act – a meeting with the Ceausescu's from Romania. When I heard that, I fumed at Andreas, saying, "How could you possibly invite a dictator to come on a visit to Greece?" He told me that the invitation had been made by the previous Karamanlis government, and that according to custom, a new government is obliged to carry out whatever diplomatic decisions had been made earlier. The program indicated that Mrs. Ceausescu would be receiving honors from the auspicious Greek Academy for her specific work at the Romanian National Institute for Chemical Research. I was curious about this, and actually looked forward to hearing her speech of acceptance. I had heard many tales about the validity of her PhD, as well as questions about the authenticity of authorship on articles and books published under her name. I was secretly wondering what it would be like to be the wife of a dictator.

When we arrived at the airport, Andreas suggested I find the protocol officer to learn the procedure. I was told simply to greet the visitors. I would greet Mrs Ceausescu coming down the ramp of the airplane, wait for the introductions of the two presidents, then walk to the music of the national anthems. At the end of the red carpet would be Greek and Romanian officials waiting in line to shake our hands. I was to lead her to Car No. 2, put her in and climb in after her.

The two leaders started down the red carpet, and I took Elena by hand to follow. The protocol guy grabbed my arm and whispered, "Not on the red carpet." It had not been made clear to me that we were to follow the two important fellows *alongside* the carpet. I was disturbed by this distinction, so I walked along close to the carpet, Elena on the other side of me, with my left foot every so often landing on the red carpet. It was a minor act, but it alleviated slightly my anger at the distinction. By the time we got to the waiting dignitaries, it was raining. We were rushed through the handshakes and hurried to the line of official cars waiting for us. I found the second car, behind the first, rushed and opened the back door, literally pushing my guest in. She landed on the lap of a security guard. The car behind the No. 1 car was the security car, and didn't have a number. The third car, in other words, was the designated car No. 2.

Her speech had the theme "Peace." She spoke as if to a high school audience. Frankly I was embarrassed that such a serious organization as the Greek Academy could have been fooled or pressed into granting her honors. The experience didn't end there. A week later I received a call from the Romanian Embassy telling me that Elena had her birthday the next week, and could I send her a happy birthday greeting. I said "yes," with no intention of doing so. The Embassy called me every day saying they had not received the card of good wishes. As we drew close to her birth date, their pleas became stronger and almost hysterical. Then I figured that they were functioning with fear; fear that they might get their heads cut off if they didn't manage to accomplish this order. Deciding it was an act that no one would learn about, I sent a birthday greetings card through the embassy and left it at that. Years later a friend of mine paid a visit to Romania, and wandered around in the historical museum where she found a congratulations book of Elena's, who by then had been shot to death along with her husband at the fall of the dictatorship. In it was my card!

Next, the new government of PASOK sent our invitation to an international personality – Hortensia Allende, the wife of the former president of Chile. Chile had experienced a coup in 1973 that overturned a democratic government. Her husband, president of the government was killed. He was looked at by U.S. officials as a new breed revolutionist – socialist oriented. That year, still functioning as a liberation movement, PAK was among the first to castigate the coup as the work of the CIA, supported by the Nixon government. We were charged with being anti-American. Sometime later Henry Kissinger admitted that Nixon in September, 1970, had ordered him to organize a coup against the government of Salvador Allende. U.S government documents indicate that the CIA was involved. Many of us were beginning to understand the strategy of the U.S. for reducing the power of people-oriented parties and of maintaining the capitalist system no matter what the cost.

I was asked to be her official host. I was honored to do so. We were wives of those targeted, and that made us soul mates. She was a lovely creature, somewhat aristocratic in style, but very amenable and warm in her demeanor. She was knowledgeable about ancient Greece, and obviously pleased to be in our country. Although she had been officially the First Lady, there was no secret in Chile and elsewhere that there had been a "second lady" – a woman who was called "La Payita," and held the post of diary secretary with an office in the presidential palace. I was reminded of Lucy Mercer, also a secretary, and presumed lover of President Roosevelt. Hmmm…I wondered: "Is this a pattern?" Should I be wary of secretaries?

Hortensia was non-political. She did tell me one thing, however, that all of the "consultants" brought in by Pinochet, the dictator who replaced her husband, came from the University of Chicago Economics School. They were called the "Chicago boys" of Milton Friedman, the high powered and apparently charismatic professor of economics at the School. They were Chileans that had been given fellowships to study economics at the University. That explained Friedman's early visit to Pinochet – and presumably the School's interest if not involvement in the events leading up to the coup. Friedman was very much opposed to the New Deal of Franklin Roosevelt, despite its success in making big moves toward a fair distribution of income, or probably because of it. His "free market" concept was highly favored by the moneyed class who writhed at the shackles put on their transactions by a more managed society. His staff of conservative economists had been training for years the new generation of students in the worth of pure capitalism. The students he trained left the University with a religious zeal, getting high level jobs in the CIA, in the diplomatic core, in the Banks and in the corporate world, with the intent of proving their beliefs in actual practice. This cause, unfortunately, would change the course of the region's history for decades.

After my clumsy experience with the Ceausescus and a more favorable experience with Hortensia Allende, I decided it was time to do a little research on First Ladies, and how they handled their role. I was looking for a job description.

First I examined what women have gone through throughout the ages – the startling consistency of male fantasies – and their implementation – for controlling women in social and political life. Athenian and Roman men in the fifth century B.C. perceived women as a threat to male order and power, thus women had to be contained. If women dared to take political actions, strong, politically oriented women like Antigoni, Clytemnestra and Agrippina, they took them only under the condition that a male relative had consented. Otherwise they and others close to them came to a bad end.

Ancient Greek tragedies are full of stories of women who got out of control, out of their "proper place," with the end result of destroying the power of the male king, or male leader. Lysistrata, the liberated woman in the Greek comedy bearing her name, was saved because after organizing women to refuse sexual intercourse with their husbands in order to end a war, she and her followers went back to their kitchens and families. Similar examples occur in modern times when there are wars and national liberation struggles. Women in times of crisis are allowed to perform alongside men, even given decision-making powers. When the emergency is over, they are expected to return to their "natural" place in the home, and the men take over the governing and the destiny of the nation. In the last hundred years or so, political wives had the "perks" of derived power, but virtually no opportunity for independent exercise of that power. Well-known political wives of England, Lady Stanhope, Molly Trevelyan and Mary Chamberlain, while taking on political tasks, all conformed to the qualities of what might be called the "ideal political wife."

My own image of First Ladies had been formed, and I categorized them as follows: the "puppy wife" who trails after her man with tail wagging, silently and obediently, wherever he goes; the "adoring wife" who sees that she is present at big occasions looking with affection at her man when he speaks; the "reluctant wife" who prefers her own path and seems indifferent to the political world; the "ambitious wife" who uses every opportunity to enhance her image; and the "partner wife" intensely interested in politics, and most likely wanting to contribute to a better world. These categories were superficial and mostly formed with tongue in cheek.

President Carter's wife Rosalynn was castigated because she sat in on Security Council meetings and because she took on a diplomatic and political role in Latin America as the representative of President Carter. Called "Iron Magnolia," she openly declared it would be a shame not to take full advantage of her power as the wife of a president. Nancy Reagan got attacked for wielding power, especially in choosing the people her husband would appoint in high and sensitive positions.

Jackie Kennedy deplored the name "First Lady." She said it sounded like an entry in a horse race. Jackie was well liked as a woman with class who knew how to deal with her role. My attitude was that if there is a First Lady, there must be a second, and who would that be? In the Clinton administration, Hillary was bombarded with harsh questions like "Will the real Mrs. Clinton please step forward?" She was accused of creating unsettling new co-presidential powers. And she heard the familiar complaint, that she was exercising power without an official title and without the restriction of "accountability." She indicated early that she intended to be an active First Lady, and she specifically recalled Eleanor Roosevelt's style. I don't believe she anticipated the shower of objections that would pour down on her. Actually Eleanor had advice on that. "Every political woman needs to develop skin as tough as rhinoceros hide." Eleanor, Rosalynn, Nancy, and Hillary could all be considered strong political activists. It seems a First Lady who exerts any power will be severely criticized by those who resent women in politics. Patriarchal mentality has permeated deeply into societies, and, despite advances in the twentieth century, attitudes remain like suction cups on the membrane of society.

Probably the ideal First Lady in the eyes of the American public was Barbara Bush. She was the mother and grandmother of the nation. She kept out of the limelight, seldom expressed her opinions on anything controversial, did not tangle with the male decision-makers surrounding her husband, and carried on various humanitarian projects, with little fuss or fanfare. She made it clear she loved her husband, believed in him, pampered him when necessary, seldom criticizing him, but when she did, it was done gently and with humor.

That is what most men, and often women, expect a First lady to be. The political, more independent women are targets of ridicule, no matter how effective and how much of an asset to their husbands. They cannot play "the little woman"; they are motivated to "right" the world, their hearts with the outsiders, the citizens who bear the oppressive policies of governments and institutions. They want to build a political process that will be just and fair and all-inclusive. They compete in the arena of power, which is men's turf. And if there is not a political partnership between husband and wife, they are likely to gain the ire and protest of the husband as well.

In this short overview and description of first ladies, I have left Eleanor Roosevelt to the last – because she was something special, and I loved her, just as Hillary loved her. If I had listened to Eleanor a little more in my role as wife of a Prime Minister, I might have had a different pattern of life. But just as Eleanor Roosevelt did not follow dictates, neither did I, nor could either one of us have done so. We were both deeply political, and we needed an outlet for our political energies. Eleanor's humanism was the driving force in her political actions. Probably the same values, the same desire to help the underdog, the oppressed, were what motivated me. In my case, already a democratic socialist from childhood, and given the prevalent social movement of my era, I became a feminist. My involvement in politics was consistent with my feminist values; I believed in applying those values to my everyday life, public and private. It was impossible for me to play "the little woman," to return to my "rightful place" at the kitchen sink, even though the pressures not to break the conformity were immense. Particularly difficult was the fact that some of the pressure came from the man I loved, not as spoken admonitions, but in a myriad other ways.

I decided not to write a job description for the role of First Lady. I would simply try to become the Greek Eleanor Roosevelt.

Having given a brief review of my life up and through our election as government, I will continue with the subsequent story in more detail trying not to let my pain and my disappointment color what I relate. I am not sure I can succeed. What surely will come through is my tender feelings toward Andreas and my very deep commitment to him. This is a personal-political story about the life of a First Lady, and the conflict between ideology and emotion, between romanticism and reality, between the feminist and the woman, between political ambitions and personal needs. It is a tale about love and power.

On the day we left for exile, I vowed that when we returned, I would devote my time and energies to promoting social causes that would make for a better world. The first moment we planted our feet back on Greek soil after the fall of the junta I initiated the process of building a grass-roots women's organization. In 1975, seven of us – mostly women who had fought against the dictatorship – founded the independent non-party connected, "Women's Union of Greece" (EGE), an organization that ballooned to 40,000 within the next decade.

Our aim was to show women their situation in a way that would convince them that they could change it. I believed the best learning field was politics, starting with local community problems. They had to realize the "old boys" network would be a hurdle, and they would have to wrench power from ambitious and pugnacious opponents in a game designed by their opponents. They must expose the political behind the personal and challenge male supremacy and the patriarchal system. EGE would be a school for building self-confidence, for gender-perception and training in social change techniques. For the male-dominated PASOK, it was a problem: we were not under its control.

In the first two years of the PASOK government EGE managed to get several important and significant changes in the laws, first, by demanding the re-writing of the Family Code to give women an equal role in the marriage, to eliminate the dowry system, and to make civil marriage legal. Women could hold on to their maiden names and the last names of the children would be by a decision between the wife and husband. Farm women were accorded pensions; divorce could be gotten in a shorter period of time by consent. In addition to these very positive changes in the Family Code, we agitated for gaining more positions of power. Life was changing for the women of Greece. All of this created problems for the conservative Church. Meanwhile, I carried on my traditional duties as First Lady of Greece, attending receptions for foreign guests, appearing at ceremonial functions, responding to the many letters addressed to me, cutting ribbons for new establishments, visiting hospitals, schools, etc.

In 1985 EGE fought and won the legalization of abortion. All of the work preceding this was effective lobbying for change. The excitement and rewards were at the grass roots level. We toured the country, making contact with women in their various roles from housekeeper, farmer, teacher, factory worker to career woman. We urged them to join us in our big crusade. Our strategy was to spend one year teaching family planning through contraception methods thus reducing the number of unwanted pregnancies and hence, the number of abortions. We intended also to explain the reasons for the legalization of abortion. We noted the lack of sex education in the schools and pointed it out as part of our campaign on the abortion issue.

Our meetings were open to men, and we were surprised but pleased at the number who showed up at one of our first gatherings on the island of Mytelini. The woman who was more or less our specialist for speaking on family planning had been unable to join us at the last minute. I turned to one of our founding members, a rather conservative but capable woman by the name of Didi, and asked her to take on this duty. She was the one who castigated me at some point for not coming to Greece earlier. She liked my way of thinking, but claimed I had arrived too late for her to become a feminist and to change her form of relationship with her husband. About the speech she was reluctant because it included a rather detailed description of contraceptive methods. I was waiting to see her squirm on the podium, but after she warmed up she gave a hearty and unabashed delivery.

In the next phase for the legalization of abortion we gathered names for a petition, each one of us – whether true or not – declared we had abortions. This was a challenge to the court that was not prosecuting either us or doctors, according to the law. French women had used this method with success. We wanted in this way to create difficulties for the government. PASOK was not against the legalization of abortion; it was just scared of its repercussions – the so called "political cost." It needed a kick.

We arranged a meeting with the head of the institution we thought would be our natural opponent: the Church. As with the Roman Catholic Church, and certain other Christian denominations, abortion is unambiguously condemned. No one has the right to destroy human life. However, within the Greek Orthodox Church, flexibility on the question of birth control, equally condemned in the past, had begun to prevail. Many Orthodox theologians supported responsible use of contraception within the marriage; arguing that in itself is not sinful. How many children couples could have, and at what intervals, should be guided by their consciences. This more human approach is an element of the Greek Church not easily found in the Roman Catholic Church. This gave me hope in the coming confrontation.

Six of the members of our board were received warmly and hospitably in typical Greek fashion at the home of the Archbishop. After seating us, our host called for wine and a platter of Greek appetizers; fried squid, eggplant sauce, olives, feta cheese, accompanied by a basket of hot garlic bread. On formal occasions he seemed a formidable creature; this informal contact caused me to see a softer version, a good sign for our mission.

I looked around at the collection of women and experienced the warmth that comes from a sense of solidarity in a cause. Most of us were founding members of EGE. Sou, whose real name was Christanthi, and who had been designated to open up the discussion, was the most thoroughly socialist in thinking and acting of the entourage. She had an extraordinary resoluteness in her insistence on the viability of a socialist system. Brown-eyed, attractive, around thirty-five, and with a wild panoply of curly chestnut hair, she would have been a good companion to Emma Goldman had she lived in an earlier time and in a geographically different place. I turned to her for ideological support.

We got down to business quickly. "Your Worship," said Sou, who at that moment was the head of the Secretariat of Equality, a 1981 addition to the government structure at the insistence of women's organizations, "we have come to talk to you about an issue which is of great concern to us and which might come up soon for debate in Parliament. It is the question of the legalization of abortion."

The Archbishop didn't bat an eye.

She continued. "Abortions happen every day, and the financial benefit goes to the doctor. He charges enormous fees." Sou was now passionate. "Those doctors become rich on women's bodies. We are aware, Your Worship, that this is a sensitive issue for you, and most likely you will be opposed. Yet, if possible, we would like not to come into open battle with the church, and we believe we have some good arguments for this measure to pass." Sou, who was a lawyer, presented another argument the Board had discussed often.

"Abortions go on every day. The financial benefit of an abortion goes to the doctor. Because it is illegal, and he is risking his license, or being put in jail, he can justify charging enormous fees. Moreover, he will not report these payments, so all of his income is untaxed." Sou said rather passionately and vividly, "Those doctors become rich on women's bodies."

Sou turned to Maria Kypriotaki next. Maria, a gynecologist, was a committed member of our executive board, and the closest to actual experience with the problem. She was like a thoroughbred at the start of a race, raring to go, and eager to test her persuasive talents on a formidable opponent. It was fascinating to watch her speak, her voice going into higher and higher octaves as she warmed up, her face reddening, and her plump arms wind milling unsynchronized with the words. She mentioned the young unmarried girl from a village whose shame at getting pregnant is so acute she turns to desperate measures, self-abortion or even suicide, to find a solution. She declared that she performed abortions when women asked for them in order to prevent injuries, sterility and sometimes death.

Although we were on a serious topic, the atmosphere had grown convivial, and Archbishop Seraphim, sipping his wine slowly, appeared to savor the situation and the comments made by these very unusual guests. This approach to him on abortion by feminist women must have been a "first" in his tenure as Archbishop. When my turn came, I presented my favorite argument regarding the Church. If the Church was so much against abortion, it should lead in family planning and education about contraceptives. The vestibule of the Church should be stocked with pamphlets describing methods to avoid pregnancy and with boxes containing contraceptives. I doubt that His Worship had ever heard such an open and unabashed discussion of matters concerning sex.

He was silent for a moment and then said, "You know that abortion is excluded in our Church canons. As the head of the Church, I cannot take a different position on this. I understand the human side of the issue. During the time you were talking to me, I was wondering, as a village boy, what I would have done if my sister came to me and told me that she had inside her a growing baby and that it was impossible to marry the father." Although we had not raised the question in quite that fashion, it was clear that we had hit the correct chords to cause this elderly Archbishop to consider seriously the notion of stopping a pregnancy.

He continued, "You must understand that I do not control all of the priests. I cannot send a circular forbidding them to take a negative stand." He stopped at this point as if struggling with what he would say next. "The best I could do is not to give any orders…just to leave each priest and every church member to make a decision according to their conscience." This was the conclusion of a two hour discussion, and if there exists something like a collective sigh of relief, we breathed it at that moment.

Shortly after our meeting with the Archbishop, a member of the Executive Board of PASOK was sent to speak to me about all this. In my role as President of EGE, I was invited to Maximou, the headquarters of the government, to be confronted by George Gennimatas, Minister of Health. George, a conservative member of the party, had a black beard and full head of hair, penetrating eyes and a physically fit body. "Oh my god," I thought, "I am being confronted by Jesus himself." After telling me about the good work EGE was doing for the advancement of women, we got to the main subject.

"I have learned," he said, "that you are planning to raise the question as an organization about abortion."

"Yes," I said simply, then I continued, calling him by his first name to reduce the sense of importance "We are not raising the question of abortion. Abortion exists. We are raising the question of its legality. Our position is not based on any ethical rules. It comes from the fact that an unwanted baby and a reluctant mother do not bring something positive to society. A large percentage of those children end up impoverished in the slums of the city, or as drug traffickers or in jail. Those against have no compassion for that unwanted child once it leaves the womb. They never say they will find a good home for the child, pay for the cost of its upbringing, and provide a university education." I took a deep breath and added something that has always impressed me, "I seldom see these anti-abortionists parading in a peace demonstration, against war, where thousands of lives will be destroyed."

George waited for me to finish. All of this was a prelude to the key point of his asking to see me.

His first words were, "Of course you realize that this may cost us the elections."

"Are you serious?" was my reply.

"Absolutely."

"Abortions are done in this country every day, illegal or not. Nor is the doctor prosecuted for an illegal abortion. I have talked to women who have done as many as ten during their reproductive years. It is not the legalization of abortion that is scandalous; it is the hypocrisy and the exploitation of women and the denial of her right to choose. Scandalous also is the lack of education on methods of blocking a conception."

"All that you say is correct," he responded, "but there will be a huge reaction, and we have enough to contend with in the pre-election period – the Cyprus problem, the violation of our sea rights by Turkey, a huge public tax evasion…" The same old story. All the "small" issues like pregnancy, abortion, child care centers, farm women's pensions, the dowry – essentially women's nuisance problems – entail a "political cost."

I continued, "We have even had a dialogue with the Church, if you are considering a religious backlash. We have avoided it."

George had an answer for that, "Probably the Archbishop wanted to please you as the wife of the prime minister, but remember that there are many priests in the rural area who will fight to the bone to stop this law you are proposing." He hesitated for a moment, then said, not looking directly at me,

"Maybe you don't understand too well how people think in the rural areas." At last we had reached the crux of his argument. I understood what he wanted to say, "You are an American, and cannot comprehend the mentality of the Greek people." This was the line the Right opposition frequently used against me, implying that I introduced new ideas to Greek women, attacking traditions and overthrowing cultural values. Yes, that was exactly what EGE, being a women's organization, had been doing – seeking to cast out the traditions that kept women in the state of second class citizenship. Changing cultural norms is one of the most difficult changes a politician can make.

"There will be no negative reaction, and we will lose votes only if we don't comply to the party's written commitment," was my comment.

"I am very familiar with the rural areas," was his retort.

"Then I would like to ask you a question. During the speeches you give on behalf of the party – and I am aware you have been all over Greece, too – have you ever asked your audience about its opinion on abortions?" I knew I had cornered him. No male member of the party had ever raised this question. He didn't answer momentarily.

"Can't we at least wait until the elections are over?" he finally said, hinting that we were co-fighters in the same political party.

"The EGE Board does not wish to postpone the issue." I make it clear that we had our own decision-making mechanism. "We have decided on an action we copied from the French feminists. It is a positive political action, and we have the solidarity of other Greek women's organizations. We are particularly interested in a petition which has the names of personalities, well-known women, such as Melina, myself, your wife." When George heard the word "wife" his Adam's apple started going up and down, as if it was trying to swallow the fact that his wife had signed the declaration. Melina Mercouri could do whatever she pleased, without consequences – but his wife?

"I would also like to let you know that we intend to demonstrate in front of the Parliament, asking for legalization."

The member of the Executive Board of PASOK sighed. "Just think about it, Margarita, think about it."

Ten days went by and the leadership of the party did not make a move. One morning, while Andreas and I were having breakfast, I told him that we were going on with the protest demonstration. To his credit, with a soft sigh, he said, "Do what you have to do."

Women from almost all women's organizations took part in the march from the courtyard of Athens University to the House of Parliament, stopping traffic. Several authorized members went into the building and handed the government a resolution for the legalization of abortion. Two days later I got a phone call from a friend in Brazil. Her voice was full of excitement.

"Margarita, we saw you on TV leading a demonstration for the legalization of abortions. If you only knew how much that helps our own struggle." Yes, sisterhood is global.

Shortly after the demonstration and mostly to avoid such a trial, PASOK announced it would bring to Parliament a bill for the legalization of abortion. The date was after elections. What we achieved, however, was a public commitment for such a legislative action. The struggle, however, was not over yet.

I became a target of abuse. In the beginning it was because I dared to organize a women's organization separate from the PASOK party. Attacks on me were crude, juvenile and certainly patriarchal. My friends and I were advised to stop our political "talking" and look after our homes in order to give time to wash underpants and mend socks. We were charged with continually leaving our homes in order to run conferences and banquets and stick our noses in where they didn't belong. Our way of thinking and operating would cause husbands to abandon us, we were warned.

I was stunned by information that the President of Democracy, Mr. Sartzetakis, had stated his opposition to the legalization of abortion before the draft law was brought to the Parliament. This was contrary to the constitutional stipulation that he had no right to intervene in political actions. A newspaper actually supported us on this by writing the following:

"It is expected that there will be strong reaction by the women's organizations, such as the Women's Union of Greece, of which the president is Margarita Papandreou, the wife of the prime minister. This organization has taken a position in the past against Sartzetakis' opinion about women. It had then argued that President Sartzetakis considered women as "factories producing children," when he appealed to women to give birth to more children so that the demographic problem of the country would be solved."

The next move was a personal attack against me by a man called Psaroudakis in his party's newspaper 'Christianiki Demokratia.' It mentioned that "that woman" provoked the Orthodox beliefs of the people, and that she had developed a strategy to methodically quell all the popular opposition on the issue of legalization of abortion. The article ended with this appeal:

"Let the Christians overflow the streets and let them state in loud voice their convictions; their convictions that are being crushed, openly and in secret, because the aim is the total weakening and abolition of Greece."

I was alarmed by these severe accusations and the motives that were ascribed to me. I was accused for trying to destroy my adopted country. Without doubt, this time PASOK was concerned that EGE's attack against President Sartzetakis and the reaction of the Christianiki Demokratia party, the party collaborating with the government, would result in a cancellation of the collaboration and a reduction of the number of seats PASOK had in Parliament.

Democracy should be described as a form of governing with "cost." Political cost can be converted to social cost, because priorities are placed on the maintenance of power and not on decision making for the people's benefit. The system of representative governance – the best in an imperfect world – is in deep crisis. The system provokes corruption as long as political ethics are allowed to be thrown aside during and after a fight for power by its representatives.

Chapter Five

Plunging Deeply into Politics

Despite the abortion issue and the reactions of Christianiki Demokratia, PASOK won the elections for a second term in 1986. Just at that moment our attention turned elsewhere. We were confronted with an international crisis. Our concern in Greece was the possibility of a retaliatory action by Israel against Libya, because of a terrorist act at an Italian airport where many people lost their lives. I had the same trembling feeling I had in the USA in 1962 during the missile crisis in Cuba when it was discovered that the Soviet Union had placed installations for nuclear plants in that country. Back then, however, I was comforted by the fact that there were sane people in the Kennedy Administration. Now we had the Reagan Administration. I felt terribly insecure towards the people who would determine Israel's reaction. Was there any possibility that the Middle East could be the trigger for a local war which would lead to nuclear havoc? We were also afraid that the Americans would ask the Greek government to allow the use of their base on the island of Crete for retaliation, an act that would get us involved in the conflict.

Regardless of all the accusations against me, I decided to carry out my agenda as planned, and I attended a New Year's Eve party on the first day of the year 1986 at the Aegena Island home of Calliope Bourdara. Calliope was one of the more bouncy members of EGE, and also a member of parliament. Her parties were full of interesting people, warmth and good fun, combined with Calliope's sharp and usually snide remarks. Andreas had a "party" of his own, a new, or at least recent affair with a woman. Uncovering Andreas's affairs had its own fascination – in a perverse kind of way – especially the detective part of it, putting together the clues to create the picture. He is very transparent, but also ultimately willing to talk. I talk to him on the assumption that as long as I'm there to reprove him for his philandering, I reduce the clandestine nature which is the spice of a secret love affair.

Andreas was a faithful husband until we moved to Greece. I saw Greece as a macho society, dwelling between eastern and western values, with the men naturally choosing the eastern model in their relationships with women. The difference is that Arab men can marry three or four women and maintain them all in one household. Greek men marry one woman and maintain one, or a series, outside the home. In trying to deal with this, I was confronted with several factors: attitudes in Greece, that is, accepted practice, my own belief in the right of the individual to a certain degree of independence, and my further belief that philandering in a marriage is rather standard practice and does not have to affect a good relationship. Worst of all for me was Andreas's mesmerism with the woman he has become attracted to (and the fading of that attraction rather quickly after it lost its novelty). This "addiction" blinded him to reality, to responsibility, to argument. It is similar to the alcoholic – an addiction – how do you get an alcoholic to admit he is an alcoholic? Nonetheless, Andreas is aware of his vulnerability to women. He went to a psychiatrist before we got married to discuss it. The psychiatrist asked him if it affected in any way his professional career. When he answered, "no," the great doctor said he didn't need psychiatric help, another typically male attitude – it's the career and a male prerogative that take precedence.

When he got in this state in his first extra-marital affair, he actually asked me for understanding and help! I was so much in love with him I gave him both. The result was a short and quickly aborted relationship. This probably set the pattern. The next time around he asked only for understanding, and the relationship took longer to undo. At the beginning of this year, I was given a small tape recorder as a present making it much easier to keep track of my various activities. I will include portions of my diary entries in the story I am telling to bring more alive my mental state and actions at the time. Here is my first diary entry:

(Diary entry) *January 6, 1986 – Vouliagmenni, by the Sea*

We spent this day at a lovely hotel on the sea at Vouliagmenni, in the P.M.'s suite – one of those perks that come with the post. It is a perk that makes me uncomfortable because I dislike luxurious surroundings. They remind me of the unfair distribution of wealth. We got up at the amazing hour of 11 o'clock, taking advantage of a Sunday free of responsibilities. In the evening we went to the hotel night club with George and Titina Pantazi. Titina – a bright, politically astute, attractive young woman, once Andreas's secretary, but never a threat to the so-called sanctity of our marriage – has become a close and dear friend of mine. The day after the coup d'état in 1967, with tanks in the streets of Athens, with ominous radio announcements by the new dictators of Greece of shooting anyone on the streets, and with the knowledge that Andreas had been arrested during the night, she hitch-hiked to my house to be at my side. That was a public nightmare which I have described. There are private nightmares too.

Most of the first week in January, I was preoccupied with my speech for an NGO conference in Geneva. It gave me a chance to study the immense literature and understand better the complexities. What I read did not allow for much optimism. Maybe, if we could develop a worldwide mass movement, non-ideological and committed solely to the preservation of our globe and non-violent methods of resolving conflict, there would be a chance of surviving. This would mean networking with various social movements, the ones that have become the conduits for social transformation. Such a network would be a motley alliance of various ideologies, no doubt, but we could agree on a common goal. No more wars. Still, I wondered, could such a people's power type organization overcome the military-industrial complex that President Reagan so strongly cautioned us about?

In Geneva I spoke too long, almost an hour. The Greeks have a saying for this. Even though the language is gutter language, it makes the point which is appropriate here. "They told the fly to shit, and he shat his ass off." My eagerness in my baptismal appearance addressing peace organizations had me commenting on every conflict in the world! I even tried a little theater by going into a dialogue with Gorbachev and Reagan. I praised Gorbachev for his proposal that there be a gradual phasing out of nuclear bombs and weaponry so by the year 2000 we will be living in a nuclear-free world. I applauded his "new thinking." In truth I became a fan of his, liking his ideas and thrilled by his dedication to peace. I myself had a hell of a good time on the rostrum. I cannot speak for the audience.

I returned on Wednesday, January 22nd in time for our regular family lunch which Andreas and I set aside to spend with whoever of our four children was available, and whoever of our grandchildren was old enough to sit at the table. It wasn't always possible for both of us to be present, but we tried to ensure that at least one of us was there. This day we were both present along with our four children and Eva, George's wife, their son Andrikos, and Sophia's son Andreas. The rule: talk would be primarily with the kids at the table; political talk was forbidden until they all pulled themselves off their chairs and headed for play in the yard. On this particular day Eva said she would keep an eye on them, and she disappeared, tagging after the youngest – the two-year-olds.

It was rare for us to be alone at noon. Political life offers few opportunities for private talk. We had breakfast together, and we went to bed together at night, but neither one of these times was congenial to discussion. In the morning we read newspapers (Greek – as well as the Herald Tribune and Athens News.) Angela, the secretary of Andreas, started putting phone calls through as soon as we finished breakfast.

At night it was Andreas's habit to conk out when his head hit the pillow, but even if he stayed awake for a while, he didn't like serious talk in bed.

He asked about my trip to Geneva, clearly more interested in my impressions of the city and the countryside than in my activities there. Finally, he asked "How did your speech go?" I felt it was a perfunctory question, and I decided to give a perfunctory answer. "Smashing, but too long,"

"Andreas laughed. "I remember what President Roosevelt said, "Be sincere, be brief, be seated.'"

I laughed too "At least I did the first."

"You know I am preparing a speech for India, the Azad Memorial lecture. Angela is typing it up now. Would you care to take a look at it? I've covered all the important issues, I believe, but you might look at it for grammar and style." This was the Andreas of the days of the resistance against the dictatorship, and of his first term in government, asking me to critique his speeches. Those were our partnership days.

The quick shift to his speech meant that his attention span on my speech was over. I should have felt slighted, or ignored, but I guess I had become immune to that. This was a natural part of our marital experience- the spotlight was generally focused on him. And, frankly, that was right and okay with me. Now I was happy we were talking together as we did in former times and pleased he was asking for help. My help was not going to be limited to grammar and style, however. I wanted to know something about substance.

"Did you hit out at the Star Wars Program?"

"Yes, I argue that this is a militarization of space and it contravenes the Salt Agreement, and, in addition, it spells disaster for mankind. Actually, I talk about some of the things that Indira Gandhi and I talked about some years ago at this very table when we were putting together the "Initiative of the Six." I remembered that well. The Initiative was an example of exciting, creative actions that are possible when you have power. It was the brain-child of an American, an old friend of ours, Stanley Sheinbaum, who had fought to protect Andreas' life under the dictatorship, and then became the *eminence blanche* behind a lot of productive and positive ideas on the international scene. Stanley has been called a "fearless activist," who helped shape foreign policy In the States, influenced police practices in Los Angeles, and took tough stands to advance first-stage Israel-Palestinian peace negotiations. The six country leaders in this Initiative joined forces in a de-nuclearization campaign, offering both political and financial support toward this goal. The leaders, all in office, in addition to Indira and Andreas, were Olaf Palme of Sweden, Julius Nyerere of Tanzania, Miguel de la Madrid of Mexico and Raul Alfonsin of Argentina.

Indira seemed tense and nervous at the beginning of that lunch, until she fell under Andreas's spell, that special charisma which has a magic effect on almost all who came in contact with him. In Andreas's case I think it came from his ability to become wrapped up in the other person, to show empathy for whatever was being said, even comments which by most standards could be called stupid. He was a good politician because he was a good teacher. He was patient and tolerant, and always seemed to be submitting himself to the people. This is who I am, this is what I believe, and now you figure out what you make of it. With me he rarely bothered to turn on his charisma anymore, but now that we were talking about his work, he gave our conversation a flavor of intimacy and connection.

Andreas continued, "I talk about the arms race between two super-powers, the spending of scarce resources and how the Third World countries are also, in response, being forced to spend their resources on defense."

"It appears we are speaking the same language," I said. Andreas smiled and tweaked my nose. What's up here? I thought. These small demonstrations of affection always forewarned me of mischief ahead. He did something nice to lay the groundwork for something unpleasant, usually having to do with another woman. He changed the subject.

"You know there is a certain amount of talk going around about whether I will leave the office of the premiership and put my name in for the presidency when the next presidential election comes around."

"Why would you do a thing like that? Are you toying with the idea? You want my opinion?" He nodded. "It's not for you. You would go crazy in such a job. It has all the things you don't like: swearing in new ministers, presiding at national holiday events, receptions, church attendance, signing bills into law over which your opinion was never sought and so on. And even if it were sought, the party in power doesn't have to listen to you. It is a job with no power, a symbolic and ceremonial role….maybe when you are eighty and your legs are wobbly. Let's face it. You love the rough-and-tumble of political life, and the power to virtually dictate what you want. Why has this question come up? Does someone want to kick you offstage?"

"It's because of our plan to make some changes in the Constitution. Mitsotakis of New Democracy is asking the question." Mitsotakis was the opposition leader in parliament. Their intense rivalry started early in Andreas's political career. Both the same age, both capable in parliamentary debate, and both vying for leadership roles; they disliked each other with a passion. Neither one missed a chance to goad the other.

"But your changes would reduce the powers of the president."

"That's right."

"Then Mitsotakis has other motives; he is not stupid. If anyone knows you at all – and he surely does by now – he would know you would be increasing the constitutional power of the president if you were interested in gaining that post."

"It's probably a gambit to cause unrest or concern in PASOK, or to intimidate. I would be off the active political scene soon." He stopped for a moment, then said, "no way."

"That makes sense. I thought for a minute you were contemplating the idea."

"Not now. Who knows for the future?"

The lunch was one of the most relaxed we had had for a long time. Andreas was looking forward to the trip to India; he had formed a good relationship with Indira working with her on the global anti-nuclear project. Now, after her assassination, he was developing bonds with her son Rajiv. I was looking forward to it too and decided not to disrupt the serenity of the day by bringing up unpleasant personal issues. I was stimulated, as always, by my conversations with him when his mood was good. The sharpness of his mind, and the tone of his voice, his attention to what I said made me feel, well, special. This was what attracted me to him in the first place: his vitality, his sensuality, the aura of mystery, his intelligence. I felt certain that life with him would be full of turmoil, would, so to speak, be upside down, but given my own needs for excitement and drama, this was all very seductive. I guess I am saying in other words, "I asked for it."

The fellow across the table from me was still the same in some ways, and there were moments when we could be young again with each other, Andreas looking at me with playful desire. In order to see that, you had to peel back the layers of time and historical experience that had changed us both. I couldn't quite respond, as I had in the past, or as I remembered in my mind, with a flirtatious, soulful, sultry glance through heavy-lidded eyes. Nonetheless, when we connected with affection, the buried seeds of excitement were nourished.

I was no longer Maggie of Chant, Inc. the small public relations firm I had set up in Minneapolis after graduating from the University Of Minnesota School of Journalism, nor was he Associate professor of economics at the University of Minnesota. He was now Prime Minister of Greece, and I the First Lady. The title still gagged me. I often thought that no one called the husband of Margaret Thatcher the First Gentleman. In that country we could have given him the title "the First Bloke."

It had started to rain outside, and the grandchildren ran in for a good-bye kiss. The magic of the tete-a-tete was broken.

(Diary entry) *January 23rd, 1986*

Today Andreas and I had lunch with Angela and evaluated AGP's speech in parliament on the changes in the Constitution. I consider myself, frankly one of Andreas' best political advisers, a sort of savvy sounding board for his ideas and actions. Hopefully I will be judged as having played an integral role in his success. It is through his success, of course, that I am protecting my own turf, my own self-interest. If I calculate this derived power as useful to me, for whatever purpose, I will work to maintain my husband's popularity. I try to remember always, however, that he was the one who won the elections. This hardly sounds like a feminist statement. I am not taking a position. I am merely reporting what I observe from experience.

Tonight I carried out one of my official responsibilities by attending an exhibition of rugs and embroidery, tapestries, etc. put on by EOP and EOMMEX. Melina Mercouri spoke and cut the ribbon. Eppie Skiadaresis, one of our EGE members and a close personal friend, also spoke, very, very well – in fact, very eloquently, urging all benefactors who helped finance this effort to preserve traditional weaving skills to use the products in their offices and homes – as a further showcase. These two organizations used to be under the auspices of Queen Frederika and were named in those days as the Queen's Fund. The object was to give work to young girls who had "fallen by the wayside," or who were orphans or single mothers. They learned to make gorgeous items, were paid very little, and the items sold for thousands of drachmas. There was no public control, and no accounting. Now the old Queen's Fund is under the Ministry of Health and Welfare, which is much fairer to the workers. This is the human face of socialist type actions.

The most distressing news of that day concerned information about terrorist activity in Greece. A Palestinian, allegedly not a member of the PLO – but what Palestinian is not in some sense a member of the PLO? – A member of a unit of five (it seems this is the standard size of the present international terrorist groups – a leader and four "followers") was caught by our police entering Greece illegally from Yugoslavia. The leader was willing to talk, hoping to find asylum here, declaring he wanted to leave the terrorist game. The latter may be a ploy, but his information seems plausible – and specific. Not only is Libya training such "squads," but Syria and some conservative Arab states. Several things were disconcerting: Greece, he claimed, is used as a "resting place" between training and terrorist acts. Also there are targets in Greece, so we are not immune to attack. Yugoslavia harbors training camps; at least 50 Greeks have received training in one or another training camp, and there are connections among the Red Brigades, the Palestinians and other organizations.

This information coming from someone trying to please the authorities in order to get asylum in our country may be true or false. What concerned me most was what he says about Greece. The press in the U.S. has been arguing for some time that Greece harbors terrorists. I believe this has been concocted because of Andreas's support for the rights of the Palestinians to a homeland. Despite the fact that he asserts the right of Israel to a secure and sovereign state, his commitment to a Palestinian homeland aroused anger among powerful interests in the U.S.

The State Department, which often supplies such information to the press, recognizes how de-stabilizing this information can be. Such information can affect tourism, our largest industry, and make business investment difficult, thus damaging a democratic regime that is not always in tune with American demands. This way the U.S. becomes a player in the political life of another country by serving the powerful Jewish lobby.

(Diary entry) *January 24th, 1986, late at night, Bombay stopover*

I spent this morning of our trip to India in final packing. Most of it I did last night instead of watching a video Andreas wanted to see about a bank robbery by four Vietnam veterans. I called Sou to tell her to contact Kassimatis, the legal advisor to the government, for the wording of the latest version of the bill for the legalization of abortion. Andreas decided to drop the age from 18 to 16 when women must get permission from one parent, for an abortion, in other words to declare the age of 16 the age of adulthood for this particular circumstance. I am so accustomed to 18 being the age of adulthood that at first it seemed strange. Then I remembered that I was a working woman at 15, waiting on tables in a restaurant after school. Surely that made me an adult. So if it can be done, that's fine with me. I learned that Gennematas wants a meeting with Andreas, Sou, Kassimatis, probably the Minister of Justice, and me – to reach a final accord on the bill. That's also fine, except for my participation. I don't want to be in government meetings when I don't hold a post. I get enough hassle from the press for being head of a non-governmental organization; one can imagine the apoplexy if I start popping up in meetings concerning affairs of state – when I don't in any case consider abortion an affair of state. Andreas knows the subject well by now – my lips have not been sealed – so if he is there, I am there.

What they need to talk about is the government's public relations campaign to support the bill. On that I can help in my role as president of a non-governmental organization, and I will insist on sex education both for the general public and for schools. The Board of Directors of EGE had already developed a plan, the first step being to consult with Christos Lambrakis, the publisher of To Vima and Ta Nea, for articles in these newspapers supporting the legalization of abortion. Christos was not keen on the idea; I would guess because of his personal views. He proposed instead a newspaper poll to learn where the public stood on this issue, which I readily accepted. I was curious to see if my antennae correctly sensed general public opinion about this. I was correct. Seventy-four per cent of those surveyed nationally were in favor of legalizing abortion. In Athens, the figure was 80 per cent.

The trip was smooth. Much conviviality on the plane. Too much food. The "big shots," you know, Andreas and the First Lady, the Minister of the Exterior, Angela and Mihali, (assistant to Andreas), a few others from the Ministry – sit in the private first class section of the Olympic Airlines government plane which is curtained off from other government members, staff, newspaper reporters, television, etc. One of the hostesses is a cousin of George Lianis, the former Purdue professor who returned to Greece with Andreas after the fall of the dictatorship. I don't know her first name but she and her husband are putting together a series of TV shows on relations between the sexes – equality, communication, career choices, work in the home, etc. She is six feet tall with overly bleached blond hair and aggressiveness that even for me, a cheer-leader for strong women, found unpleasant. This was my first contact with the woman who was to become the home-breaker. I had not picked her out yet as the extra-marital creature in our life.

She asked me to get an interview for her with Rajiv Ghandi's wife, apparently for her TV show. I agreed to try. I suggested she interview Devaki Jain, a writer in the anthology put together by Robin Morgan entitled "Sisterhood is Global," where we both had articles. Devaki was working on a feminist approach to development for an organization called DAWN (Development Alternatives for Women) She had been collaborating with the Center of Research on Mediterranean Studies in Greece and shared a workshop with them in Nairobi at the international Decade of Women conference on the subject "Forward Looking Research Strategies." The Hostess showed no interest in an interview with Davaki. No glamour in that apparently.

(Diary entry) *January 25th, 1986, New Delhi*

A full day. After the ceremonies at the airport were over, we headed toward our residence. As we were travelling along the highway I was astounded to see a huge billboard with a gigantic photo of the couple Papandreou, and a sign underneath "A hearty welcome to His Excellency Mr. Andreas Papandreou and Mrs. Margarita Papandreou of Greece." The same poster was placed intermittently along the road. The photo was nice, and we looked very natural and happy together. That was my reaction. I didn't ask Andreas about his.

At the official dinner in the evening I was seated next to Rajiv Ghandi. At the beginning the P.M. of India and I talked seriously. He told me he was working hard to build a mass movement based on his Congress party's ideology. He believed in the inner strength of the people of India, and only with such a movement could the party be cleansed, and the nation. The country needed a politics of service to the poor. This was Indira's son who was considered the playboy, and whose love for flying seemed to be his only occupation before he inherited the leadership of the party, and the country!

After this somber discussion we talked fun. Rajiv told me about an official who had put notes in his jacket chest pocket for a speech he was about to give and pulled out by mistake a recipe for curry chicken – and started reading that. Then he told me about the head of state of another country who boasted about the talent of his speechwriter, who after explaining a few points to him was able to sit down and prepare a speech "the way he would have written it." In fact, Rajiv claimed that he had such faith in him that he often didn't read the speech ahead of time. On one such occasion, reaching page 11 of his text, a large written scrawl confronted him that read: "I GOT TIRED. YOU'RE ON YOUR OWN!"

Rajiv didn't have that problem; everything with his speech went well. And everything went well with AGP's speech until the last sentence. He paused, and apparently the man standing behind him, responsible for the table microphone, thought he was through. His arm reached around Andreas and snatched the mike away, and the last words disappeared – a mouth and no sound – lost to posterity. Rajiv and I both laughed, and realized we had another story to tell.

(Diary entry) January 28th, 1986, Olympic plane. Flying back to Greece

This morning was leisurely and moving. Leisurely because we didn't start our activities until 11 a.m. The ceremony at Nehru University was laid back, the academics wearing small capes and no hats. Andreas's speech, the one he asked me to look at, carried my imprint, particularly the somewhat poetic last paragraph It was moving because I saw my husband receive an honorary doctorate for his contributions to scholarship and peace and humanity. Today the Chancellor used the term "humanitarian" to describe Papandreou. It is a word I have always liked, and probably it ranks for me tops as a descriptive noun, even higher – now hear this – than feminist, which is actually a political position within the framework of a humanitarian philosophy. A humanitarian believes that man's (woman's) obligations are limited to, and dependent alone on, human relations; that a human being's nature is perfectible through his or her own efforts without divine grace. This could be a maxim for an activist.

Rajiv, on our last evening, was not able to attend the reception given by the Greek Embassy because of an occupation of the Holy Temple in Punjab territory – an incident that was similar to that which started a chain of events against Indira after she decided to attack the occupiers by force. More than a thousand Sikhs lost their lives in that confrontation, but ultimately, so did Indira. I asked Sonia in the car driving to the airport the next day what would happen in the still unsettled Punjab. She believes the moderate Sikhs who run the government will take action and there will be a civil war between the moderates and the extremists. She said this in a matter-of-fact voice, but she was visibly distressed.

I understood Sonia's feeling of vulnerability, both for herself and Rajiv, as well as for their children, and I empathized with her deep wish to be out of political life. When I asked her if she would give an interview to a TV crew from Greece, she said she never gave interviews. She had given one early in her marriage, before her husband was in politics, and she felt it had been so misconstrued, so unfairly critical, that she decided never to give one again. She is an attractive woman physically, a nice complement to Rajiv's own beauty.

I gained at least one kilo on this trip, which is enough to give me pause about joining Andreas on an official journey. Well, that's not the real reason. I don't have a problem with weight. The real reason is that I cannot be independent and do the things I would like to do. I did manage to see Devaki Jain at the Ambassador's house (and her wonderful, intelligent husband). I had an appointment with Margaret Alva, former head of the women's section of the Congress party and now director of the Department of Women's Activities in the Ministry of Human Resources. A sister worker who had been in the Indian delegation at the 1985 U.N. international women's conference in Nairobi was also there. She told me what an impact my speech had on the conference. (I continue to get compliments on that speech and continue to be amazed.)

What I wanted from Devaki was a general picture of the status of women, and where the official government forces put their emphasis, and their priorities today. This is where I act as someone on the inside of government, although I am first a representative of a non-governmental organization. This dual role gives me ammunition to develop a lobbying plan for our women's organization either pushing for or mimicking good ideas from foreign government programs or learning the pitfalls of new experiments. In India they are trying to overhaul their educational system to develop the critical and analytical capacities of children, rather than just learning the three Rs, or memorizing texts – in other words, a more American style education. They also are confronting the problem of not enough occupational schools for limited specialized training after high school as well as the mentality of parents and students – either you get a university degree after high school, or you stop. Consequently they have many college graduates who cannot find jobs, but no plumbers, electricians, mechanics and so forth.

I asked about textbooks on the issue of equality. Are they chipping away at patriarchal mentality? Most textbooks are written at the state level, and there is little uniformity from state to state, and up to now not much interference at the national level. Because of the centrifugal forces in the society toward autonomy for the states, the Rajiv government is trying to build a stronger central government, and this means, according to Margaret, more control over textbooks which the women's department intends to use for promoting the concept of equality. They are also encouraging the setting up of women's departments at the state level with which the central women's department can work. This is the same as Sou's concept of offices of equality in the provincial regions of Greece.

Devaki told me earlier she was satisfied that Rajiv has a great interest in this. He told her he believes he could almost be called a feminist; at least he understands the struggle women are engaged in and wants to support it, more so than did Indira. As a woman in a "man's job," probably she could not show a special sensitivity to the "woman question;" a common difficulty of women who climb up through the male hierarchy, or who have not had the consciousness-raising that occurs within a feminist organization.

I remember when we had lunch with Indira at Kastri. She wanted to disassociate herself from the word "feminist." She talked at that time about women doing charity work. The concept of a women's political movement was alien to her. I was happy at what I had learned subsequently that Indira had agreed to a campaign to teach women the secretion test for natural birth control. I am afraid the motivation, however, was not out of feminist concerns, but because of economic demographic reasons.

Chapter Six

Two Vagabonds

Back in Kastri Andreas and I each started preparations for separate trips, Andreas to the European Management Forum in Davos, Switzerland, and I for visiting tourist cooperatives on the snowy slopes of Molveno, Trentino, in Italy, later in the month. EGE was supporting a Secretariat of Equality program to help train women to set up tourist cooperatives in Greece. Andreas took off on the 31st of January, saying he would be back when the conference was over, the 2nd of February. My trip was scheduled for later so I would still be in Greece when he returned. It was customary for me to meet him at the airport, and I wanted to know the time of his return flight. He answered, "I'll let you know".

On Sunday, the final day of his meeting, he disappeared. He had checked out of his hotel without telephoning me. In an average family when there is such a disappearance only a few people would know. But Andreas was a public figure and in addition to the wife, the journalists and the rest of the country would know. The belief that one could hide such behavior is part of the feeling of invincibility that comes with power. Power puts men in a new dimension, on a plain above ordinary mortals. They begin to be annoyed by people who contradict them or challenge their authority. The unwritten laws of decency and consideration for other human beings are there for the mass of ordinary people, not the select few. A narcissistic self-esteem replaces a natural humility. I watched changes occur among many of those elevated to a high post and heard complaints from wives who claimed their husbands were no longer the same. There is a passage from Shakespeare's play "Much Ado About Nothing," that I like. The character Claudio said, "O, what men do! What men may do! What men clearly do, not knowing what they do."

On the 3rd of February several newspapers asked questions I was asking as well, "Where is the Prime Minister?", "What is he doing?" On February 4th I opened up *Eleftheros Typos*, a conservative newspaper with a penchant for gossip. I was reported as giving a stern order to my husband. RETURN IMMEDIATELY TO YOUR HOME." The article continued:

"Yesterday we wrote that Greece has lost its Prime Minister. And we are asking today where and with what purpose and with what person has Andreas hidden himself, somewhere in the land of William Tell. The official announcement indicated the Prime Minister would return to Athens on Wednesday, February 5, without giving any explanation about the extension of his stay beyond the end of the conference. Once in the past a deputy of PASOK disappeared in a similar way somewhere in the Caribbean. At that time Andreas ordered this deputy to gather his belongings rapidly and return. Now it is the turn of Andreas. After the fuss over his disappearance and undoubtedly the dynamic intervention of Mrs. Margarita, Andreas suddenly stopped his mysterious incognito and is returning today."

The newspaper '*Kathimerini*,' a more serious opposition newspaper headed its article with the title: "What IS the Prime Minister Doing So Many Days in Switzerland?"

I did not ask Andreas with whom he spent those unaccounted for three days. I was sure he would not give me a straight answer, and if he was prepared to tell me, I didn't really want to know. With all the publicity, he knew I knew. I preferred to let him manufacture a plausible story in anticipation of my questioning him. I was busy preparing for my trip to Italy, the subsequent trip to Egypt and also working on preparations for EGE's national conference in March. As always, I submerged my pain in work. I still didn't know the details of the trip. Nor was I, strangely or stupidly, suspecting the Hostess. What I do know is he had given the Hostess a recorded interview to be used to promote the TV series she had told me about on the airplane.

The Hostess, when I hadn't responded to her first efforts to engage me in being the courier for the series, sent me a copy of two scenarios. I was appalled by the lack of understanding of sexism and feminism, and the script's amateurish style. Sometime later I was furious to discover I was considered responsible for getting the show on the government TV station. How ironic and tantalizing a notion! The older woman naively offers the younger woman to her husband. One simple truth: I could never imagine Andreas being in any way attracted to her.

We left for Egypt on the 24th of February where Andreas and I were welcomed at the airport as the Honorable Guests, along with our load of about 20 – I suppose honorable – secretaries, ministers, physicians, special advisors and counselors, directors, aide-de-camps, interpreters, and what have you. There was also, unfortunately, the dishonorable Hostess. In addition there were about eight security guards, who were as far as I was concerned superfluous, since they neither knew the country, the language, or what people might be suspect. In addition, the host country had a tremendous responsibility to see that we were not killed while being Honorable Guests. A printed schedule, in excruciating detail, was given to each Honorable Guest as she or he arrived at the airport.

- H.E. Prime Minister Dr. Ali Loutfy accompanies the Honorable Guests to the Salute Point, the Guard of Honor presents Arms and the band plays the National Anthem of the Republic of Greece and the National Anthem of the Arab Republic of Egypt.

- Inspection of the Guard of Honor

- The First Chamberlain of the Presidency introduces the Head and members of the Mission of Honor to the Honorable Guests and also the dignitaries on hand to welcome Their Excellencies.

- H.E. the Prime Minister and Mrs. Loufty accompany the Honorable Guest and Mrs. Papandreou (it seems I've lost my "Honorable" title) to the Principal Drawing Room.

- After a short rest, H.E. the Prime Minister accompanies H.E. Mr. Andreas Papandreou to the talks hall while Mrs. Loufty and Mrs. Papandreou will remain at the Principal Drawing Room until bilateral talks are finished. (And there we are, two women outside the halls of power- waiting; waiting for our men to solve the problems of the world).

- 20:30 – Following the dinner, H.E. the President of the Republic and Mrs. Mubarak shake hands with the Honorable Guests and leave the Palace.

- END OF PROGRAM

With the general schedule was a page marked "Special Program for Mrs. Papandreou." This was for the morning of the second day. I had asked the protocol officer in Greece to arrange some meetings with heads of women's organizations. I also asked for a meeting with my friend Nawal el Sadaawi, a rare feminist activist in an Arab culture, fighting against clitorectomy. Unfortunately, she was out of the country, or so I was told. What I got was:

- 10:30 End of the visit to the Egyptian Museum. The motorcade of Mrs. Papandreou accompanied by Mrs. Sefain proceeds to the Islamic Art Museum.

- 10:40 Arrival and visit the Islamic Museum

- 11:10 End of the visit – the motorcade drives for the Citadel.

- 11:20 Arrival and visit the Citadel.

- 11:50 End of the visit – the motorcade proceeds to Tahera Palace.

My feminist agenda had been dumped. I was given a tourist program suitable for the "wife of." After a talk with our Ambassador, he invited nine women to the Greek Embassy where we had two hours of fruitful conversation on the subject that was dear to my heart.

As in many countries, women of Egypt have had their good times and their bad times. In ancient times, women had an elevated status in almost all areas of life, not just in the home. In the realm of the mythological deities, thrones were occupied by goddesses as well as gods. When the Greeks occupied Egypt three hundred years before Christ, women lost their favored position. This situation worsened during the Roman occupation. Under Christianity, the new faith which was presented as humanitarian, moral and ethical, the status of women hit the bottom of the barrel. Probably the best period for women occurred after the overthrow of the colonial regime of the British, when they obtained the right to vote, and to hold public office.

I was told that Women's rights took a downturn after the defeat of Egypt by Israel in 1967. As happens after wars in most countries, women were enjoined to "return home." The marriage law existing at the time of my visit gave men considerable privileges as well as full authority over their wives. The entire Family Code derives its canons from Islamic jurisprudence. Although the government passed legislation in 1970 against female clitorectomy (circumcision, or more correctly called genital mutilation), the custom continues in orthodox Islamic families. Nawal found herself in jail for speaking out openly against this practice. .

Before I left the meeting, one of the women gave me an article from Cairo's English language newspaper translated from the newspaper *AL AKHBAR*. Its title was "Wives Can Usher Husbands to Glory or Jail." She smiled and said "I thought you might like this for your leisure time reading." I told her I would read it on the plane, and consider carefully my options.

Diary entry – *February 25th, 1986, Egypt, 2 a.m.*

Greek Embassy tonight – music, belly dancing, part of the official visit. Around 10:30 p.m. we were suddenly ushered out. The explanation was that a "labor union" rebellion had developed and for security reasons, we had to return to our quarters.

When we left the Embassy in an armed car we were told "everything is under control." Already, however, we could sense the uneasiness permeating the Embassy personnel and the Egyptian security guard. It smelled bigger that a union protest. Having been through one coup d'état, I was not relishing confronting a second one.

When we arrived at our residence The BBC was reporting on an attempted coup in Egypt. It seems an army unit had joined with the rebellious police force, and the Cairo airport was closed. Soon after an Egyptian protocol officer told us cars had been ordered off the street by 1:00 a.m. We heard horns honking incessantly, apparently in desperate efforts by drivers to reach home before the curfew.

The atmosphere became more ominous with the passing of time. People were out on their balconies nearby our quarters watching developments. Andreas turned on TV. Normal programs were running; a romantic film was being shown. We considered that a good sign – no occupation of the television building. A decision was made to cancel the trip to Sinai the next day, explaining to journalists waiting on the floor below that Andreas would be having a session with Mubarak because of unfinished business. We felt we were helping create a scenario of "business as usual," of calm, not to give cause for hysteria, or contribute to the rumors that Mubarak was in danger of being overthrown.

In political life, much thought is given to what to tell journalists, how to keep them in the dark, or how to distort the news for one's own purposes. This is illusionary. People in power think they can control everything and everyone around them, but, except for those that are on the payroll of special interests and must comply to the demands of the corporate world, journalists have so many additional sources, and such an acute sense of fake news, that it is an exercise in futility. Nonetheless, it is done and the scenario builders feel their power and congratulate themselves on their capacity to be canny and clever.

The morning of our departure we spent one hour in the Mubarak home. A decidedly tranquil atmosphere prevailed. Mubarak gave us the official explanation of the events – a rumor had started within the police corps that a fourth year would be added to their three year stint. Apparently there is an obligatory police service, which is in truth their army service; in fact, one could say that they are soldiers in police clothing. Who started the rumor? That, he said, was the interesting question (which he didn't answer). He decided to take tough measures to prevent the spread of the rebellion. He said no civilians had joined the action, adding that one hundred per cent of the people were against the action of the police. So leaders skew the news, even when they are not talking to journalists.

"We speak frankly to the people, and we have already explained what happened." Mubarak said the measures would last for a few days and the incident would be over. Anyway, he had a speech on the 9th of March to present literary prizes, and he would use that occasion to speak frankly to the people. Apparently there were more "franklys" to be done, because he left the discussion for twenty minutes to record an announcement to the Egyptian people at the TV studio which was right next to his residence.

The discussion turned to international topics. He believes he has a good contact with Kenan Evren, the president of Turkey, and indicated he would talk seriously to him about our positions on Cyprus and the Aegean. About Gorbachev – he feels he is moving too fast, trying to make many changes and hitting vested interests. He is dubious about the length of tenure of the Gorbachev regime. As for Gorbachev's drive to cut down the consumption of alcohol, he finds it unrealistic. Mubarak said he lived for one year in Moscow and the winter demands alcohol. Now that's a convenient excuse for drinking.

Andreas inquired about his relations with the United States. Mubarak said he wanted to be friendly with the U.S., but they did things to humiliate him. They didn't understand the atmosphere under which he works. Reagan endorsed the Israeli raid of PLO headquarters in Tunis, which killed 68 Palestinians. This undermined Egypt's diplomatic ties with Israel, a situation already difficult given that Egypt was the only Arab nation to sign a peace treaty with Israel. The other nations saw him as a traitor to the cause. Just two weeks after the Tunis attack, the Americans intercepted an Egyptian aircraft heading for Italy carrying four hijackers said to be connected to the capture of the boat *Achille Lauro*. It was obvious that he considered this an assault on Egyptian pride and dignity.

After this discussion on international affairs, I spoke up. "Because of my interest in women's issues, Mr. President, I would like to ask you about changes you made recently in the laws protecting women's rights which seem to be steps backward." Before I had a chance to go further, Mubarak raised his hand.

"I know what you mean. To be frank with you, Mrs. Papandreou, we had to do something about the rising tide of Islamic fundamentalism in our country, something that threatens secular governments throughout our region. We are making a few compromises, not only concerning women's rights, but elsewhere, to placate Islamic demands, to take some air out of the inflated balloon. Of course, we cannot meet all their demands; it is not in the interest of our country. I hope, however, that we will find ways in the future to restore these rights."

"Then you know you are sacrificing women's rights at this moment." I looked over at Andreas who seemed to be shifting uncomfortably in his chair.

"As I said, temporarily," was the response.

I have observed that people use the word Islamic when they wanted to scare Westerners, instead of the less emotionally charged word "Muslim." If we perceive Islam as a threat to our way of life, then there can be no dialogue between Islam and the West. Under the pretext of this threat, many undemocratic and unsavory actions can be taken. I know governing is often a balancing act. The "balance" is frequently accomplished at a cost to women.

I am wary of decisions that attempt to make an old pair of pants, that is, the government, look new by putting fresh patches on it. This doesn't get to the root of the problem, that the pants are too old to be serviceable any more, that one has to consider a more radical step, say, a new pair of pants. Egypt suffers from unemployment, rising prices, overloaded schools, outdated school books, smelly alleys from lack of a good sewage system. The government is kept in place partly by United States support, no real opposition parties, and corruption. Appeasing the people by tinkering with laws is not going to work. Joining a religion which dreams of a better future and a more equitable distribution of wealth is a natural outgrowth of societal conditions. It's the conditions that have to change.

For the woman who sees a government with no values, no ideas, no vision, and who wonders how she is going to feed her children each day, simple patterns of religious conformity – a long -sleeved dress, a scarf over her head, going to prayers – may provide her with a sense of security, of comfort, of belonging. As a Western woman, as a political woman, I may not like this reaction. That is my cultural and political bias. I must say, however, that I don't consider a scarf the heart of the problem. Women's emancipation will take care of that and other features of slavery. Suzanne Mubarak, who is an articulate woman, remained silent in the discussion about restrictions on women's rights.

Still, I must admit I was attracted to her husband as a person. He was practical, down-to-earth, and essentially sincere. His body and face reminded me of the hard-working

Mid-Western farmers of my home state of Illinois, and displayed the same directness, simplicity and flinty realism. He was a contrast to the mercurial, sometimes unreliable Arab leaders of other countries. I could understand why he would appeal to the American State Department. He could be a moderating influence in the area and, like Sadat, could play an important role in the Israeli-Arab conflict.

It was time to leave. Both sides declared their love for each other, invitations were given to families for private visits, vacations, etc. At 4:50 p.m. we left for the airport. The streets were virtually vacant – soldiers here and there – a few civilians, possibly soldiers in civilian dress. People were no longer out on their balconies. Cairo appeared a dead city.

What were my feelings about the Egyptians? As a people they were friendly, very open, and gave the impression they were rooted in their past, proud of their history, confident of themselves. Their country, which had experienced centuries of trouble, despair, war, and glory, would always survive. There was no arrogance. They spoke well of themselves, in contrast to us in Greece. The native Greeks (as compared to me, a Greek out of love for Greece) seem always to belittle themselves, their character, their way of operating, their personal habits. Their relationships are permeated by suspicion, if not distrust.

On the plane I read the article by the columnist Mahmoud Abdul Moneim Mourad to see what power an Egyptian male believes we wives have to send our husbands to glory or to jail.

"Just as a wife can directly contribute to her husband's rise to greatness and glory, so wives can also be the main cause behind their husband's drifting to corruption. It is actually possible for a good and virtuous wife to play quite an influential role in guiding the steps of her husband toward success in life. By her proper conduct and sound attitudes, she can secure for him the calm, unperturbed life and thus create the conditions amenable for productive and creative work. In such conditions, the husband can easily excel and surpass others. But it is equally possible that an over-ambitious domineering wife imbued with a desire for the luxurious life can be the main cause behind her husband's deviation and corruption.

"Such a wife may even impel her husband to commit crimes and thus expedite his dismal end. Whoever scrutinizes cases of bribery, theft, embezzlement and other similar crimes will notice that in the majority of instances the main motive is the presence of a wife who dominates the husband, robs him of his quiet and equanimity of temper and asks him for comforts beyond his modest means. Such a poor man is usually forced to take to crime or to some other illegal ways of procuring the money required for satisfying her demands.

"A good wife is one who appreciates and fully understands the circumstances of her husband and therefore conditions her life to square with his limited income. She is always content with what her husband can earn. She does not envy other wives – for what they have got. Such a wife does not only serve her husband, but she also protects herself and safeguards her future. She provides the best safeguard for her husband's continued uprightness."

From now on, yes, I will be the guardian of my husband's uprightness. And if he is upright, he will go to glory; and if he is not upright he will go to jail. And I, the influential little wife, will have sent him there!

Naturally I wondered about my husband securing for *me* the calm and unperturbed life.

When we reached Athens we learned from a Reuters news dispatch what had really happened in Cairo while we were present. Fifteen Egyptians were killed and more than 300 wounded in riots by thousands of security police. It was President Hosni Mubarak's most serious crisis since he took power after Muslim zealots assassinated President Anwar Sadat in October of 1981. We had survived a serious attempt to overthrow the Egyptian government. In the meantime I was oblivious to any schemes to overthrow me. The Hostess was on the plane to Egypt, but I avoided her because I didn't want to respond to any questions about the scripts of two episodes of the TV series she had sent me. My honesty would have made it necessary for me to tell her that they were of extremely poor quality and essentially anti-feminist. Sophia, our daughter, was at the airport to greet us. Of the four children, she was the most deeply attached to her father, and had, in fact, chosen to study economics in order to further cement this connection. She was also concerned about our relationship and watched with anxiety any signs of tension, or indications that her father was engaged in an extra-marital affair. I am sure that the Davos disappearance and the publicity surrounding it raised her anxieties, although the two of us had not mentioned it to each other. Now she welcomed us in her shy, discreet way, having stood back while those who loved Andreas along with the political ass-lickers threw their arms around Andreas and the photographers' bulbs flashed. I have seldom seen Sophia display feelings or emotions openly, or boisterously, except when she dances. That is her outlet; that is her awakening. This is when she sparkles. She studied Fine Arts as her minor at York University in Toronto with special emphasis on dance. It should have been her major.

The three of us drove home together from the airport, security guards on motorcycles, security cars surrounding us through the streets of Athens. Sophia sat in the middle, her hand in her father's, and Andreas enjoyed the closeness. Having suffered the 1967 military coup d'état as a 12-year-old, having seen her father dragged from the house bleeding, in the middle of the night, the rest of us under gunpoint, she knew from personal experience what a military coup meant.

All of us had dinner together at the familiar old round oak table where we sat at as a family with George Papandreou, Andreas' father, every Saturday noon when the children were little. When he died under the dictatorship, he left his home to Sophia. Along with it came the furniture. The table was historic, not just because of family gatherings, but because of many long political conversations, and important political decisions made around it. Andreas had come here himself as a child, visiting his father and his father's second wife. Sophia felt it was the proper home for a prime minister and a first lady and thus offered it to us to live in when she inherited it. She herself lived close by with her husband and baby.

The evening was magnificent- much laughter, probably as a relief from what had turned out to be a tense trip. With that "good old times" feeling, and Andreas' warmth toward me, Davos faded in my mind, and I began to think about the activities in the days ahead. One was to finish an article for 'The Nation' which had asked me to do a piece for a special edition on anti-Americanism.

The next day, February 27th, was the funeral of Amalia Fleming, wife of the discoverer of penicillin, resistance fighter against the Nazis, and subsequently against the dictators. She tried to help Alekos Panagoulis, the would-be assassin of George Papadopoulis, head of the junta, escape from jail, only to be caught and put in jail herself. A courageous woman, she had become a deputy in parliament with PASOK. I was proud of her, as I always am of women with guts, and honored that she counted me among her friends.

Lunch the following day would be at Kastri with Andreas and Carlos Papoulias, the Minister of Foreign Affairs, who was also chairman of PASOK's International Relations committee, of which I was a member. Late afternoon was for gymnastics at a nearby gym, photographs for a magazine interview in the evening, board meeting of the Center of Studies on Mediterranean Women the following day, and in the evening a board meeting with EGE. Following that was a reception honoring the federal judges given by my opponent on abortion rights, the president of the country, Sartzetakis. Good, I thought. It would be interesting to hear how the judges respond to the legalization of abortion. Though I had numerous public and political activities scheduled in the days ahead, uppermost in my mind was a personal event, a decision I made with some difficulty months before. This event was a facelift. It was scheduled for the Monday after my talk in Argos. Old-face Margarita would talk about a renewal of hope in the international arena for peace in the world, and new-face Margarita some weeks later toward the end of March would address the EGE congress of women about the necessity for a dynamic struggle for women's rights. I knew of course what would be awaiting me from the staunch feminists in our organization – "Margarita – a facelift? What kind of feminist are you?"

During the next days I wrote my article for The Nation. It was entitled *"Anti-Americanism: Causes and Cures."* Because I think it is a valid and succinct exposition of this subject and reflective of my own views, I am including parts of it in this Memoir. It did not get published because it was "too long." There was no request for me to shorten it, however.

"One of the questions I am most frequently asked back in the States is why is Greece anti-American? The next two questions are. Will Greece get out of NATO? And will you keep American bases? In feminist circles there are also queries about our progressive measures toward equality for women. I seldom get questions about socialism in Greece, although if I happen to mention that we have a democratic-socialist government, the listener turns pale. No one, however, seems to be interested in our conflicts with Turkey, the Cyprus problem or our peace initiatives.

"The questions raised by Americans regarding Greece's intentions toward the North American Treaty Organization and the U.S. bases seem to reflect a keener awareness of national security issues in the States than existed during the years after World War II. But the question about anti-Americanism comes from the heart – people in the States are pained and puzzled by it. Some time ago Administration officials talked about launching a public relations program to dispel anti-American attitudes in Europe, a truly naïve idea. There are substantial reasons for such attitudes and feelings, and unless those reasons are understood and responded to, no media campaign, no exchange-student program, no cultural or scientific collaboration, will change them.

"Anti-Americanism does not mean hostility toward American people. Nor does it signify dislike of American culture. Blue jeans, rock-and-roll, Big Macs, films and television serials are generally popular and the United State most powerful ambassadors. The U.S. gets accused nowadays mostly from fundamentalist societies, as symbols of modernity, corruption and cultural intervention, but they are not in any way the cause of anti-American attitudes. Anti-Americanism is most prevalent in the underdeveloped and developing world. This is where people feel that U.S. economic forces have exploited them, military forces have tried to control them and political forces have supported unpopular, undemocratic establishments.

"Anti-Americanism reached its peak in 1974, when the dictatorship of the colonel's fell; it has diminished considerably since then, as the PASOK government followed a pro-Greek independent foreign policy that was grudgingly accepted by the Reagan administration. The Greeks watch what the United States does in the rest of the world and draw their own conclusions. During the dictatorial rule in Greece, when the United States was involved in the Vietnam War, a war which pitted a giant industrial military machine against a peasant society, even the colonels found it difficult to give open and enthusiastic support to the American side.

"Central Intelligence Agency intervention overseas, support for "friendly" dictators, the overthrow of the Allende government in Chile, Watergate, the efforts to overthrow the Sandinista regime, the nuclear arms buildup – all have served to strengthen the image of the United States as an aggressive, ruthless and unethical nation. For Americans to understand anti- Americanism they must take off their cultural blinders and see their country the way others see it. They must recognize that America's vast military and economic power does not give them the right to interfere in other nations' development or to frustrate their efforts to achieve independence. To the contrary, it antagonizes the people.

"This does not mean that millions of people in the world would not want to live in America. The American way of life, insofar as it applies to those who live in America, continues to be envied. America stands for opportunity and individual freedom. It means diversity, natural beauty, creativity, dynamism, vitality. But that is not the point, though it may be why Americans are distressed and puzzled about anti-Americanism. They are so convinced that their society is unique, just and good – and this is a conviction that permeates the consciousness of many who grow up in the United States – that they fail to understand criticism of their government's international actions.

"The way to fight anti-Americanism is with an enlightened policy of international relations that would seek to break down the global war system and establish a permanent peace; that would avoid intervention in the affairs of other nations but provide moral support for popular democratic forces; and that would reign in the military industrial complex, which affects so many things – the trade balance, the direction of industrial growth, the choice of technology, the rate at which natural resources are extracted, the status of women, even the culture, values and aspirations of people.

"These are not unrealistic proposals. One could make the case that they "advance national security interests." They are unworkable only in that there may not be the kind of leadership in Washington that wants to pursue them or that the vested interests opposing them are too deeply entrenched. But given the situation today – a world economic crisis, social unrest and turmoil; and an arms race that is driving the world to oblivion – these are the only realistic policies that will make it possible for the world to see the United States with new eyes."

Having done this, I turned my attention to preparation for the Argos talk. While my talk in Geneva was upbeat and optimistic, I felt I had to be either more pessimistic, or more realistic because of Reagan's response to the Gorbachev disarmament proposal. On the key item to eliminate all nuclear weapons by the year 2000, he claimed that Mr. Gorbachev had not made a good case for a non-nuclear world and had given no practical means for getting there. There does exist a practical way – stop testing. It was Reagan who resisted the extension of the existing ban on nuclear testing to include underground testing. Reagan wanted to be able to test for his "baby," the SDI, and other programs. Perhaps I was too impatient. But of one thing I was sure; if the super powers did not start destroying their nuclear stockpiles, and begin winding the nuclear clock backwards, they would never convince other nations to stop building their own nuclear weapons – and proliferation would go on.

Diary Entry – *March 9th, 1986 – afternoon at home in Kastri*

My speech in Argos went well, a packed auditorium and an enthusiastic audience. The various chapters of EGE are clearly progressing in their organizational skills and ability to put on a professional show. One of the most important functions of an all – woman organization is to give women the opportunity, in a friendly and non-threatening environment, to learn and practice the techniques of democratic methods. When a young woman from the countryside gets up before an audience and gives a short introductory talk that is better than mine, I feel much pride and gratification, as if they were my own kids.

That was yesterday, March 8th, International Women's Day. I have not told anyone in the organization, not even my closest friend Anna, that on Sunday evening – tonight – I am giving myself my own Women's Day gift, entering the clinic in a few hours in preparation for a facelift tomorrow. Will it also lift my spirits? Will it hurt very much? Will I like the result? The public reaction? My friends? And should I really do this?

Chapter Seven

The New Margarita

As I was coming out of the anesthetic the next day, around noon, I had a vivid dream. I was lying flat on my back in a canoe, going through a tunnel. The tunnel was very dark; I seemed to be having trouble breathing, and I thought to myself, "this is the tunnel of death" and I must have made the wrong decision. I was speculating on the things I had yet to do in my life, the need to contribute to making a better world, to watch my children's growth , to enjoy the companionship of my friends, to feel the excitement of political life and I was castigating myself for my stupidity. I was not frightened; in fact the gentle lapping of water as the canoe moved forward was soothing and produced the comforting thought that at least my demise would take place somewhere on the Aegean Sea that I loved so much.

I saw a gleam of light at the end of the tunnel. It became wider and brighter each moment and finally almost blinded me with its shiny sparkle. It enfolded me as I moved through it and produced what must have been a tight, happy grin as I made out the face of Dr. Foustanos right above me.

"I'm glad to see you," I said, "and get out of that tunnel." I was asleep when I was wheeled back to my room. My friend Effie, the only one who was with me at the clinic, told me I looked like a fat-faced teen-age cherub when I arrived. I kept that image in mind for a few days before I dared look in a mirror.

The news was out. Opposition newspapers attacked me. One reporter wrote:

"In the beginning I had some doubt. Is it possible? Here the people are burning, Greece is drowning in the noise of PASOK's statements of nonsense, and Margaret, yes, yes, Margaret, entered the clinic to do...'lifting.' To 'stretch' her skin, to vanquish her wrinkles, to make EGE more beautiful! The world is on fire, and Margaret is fawning! Look now at the sacrifices done by one woman in order to put limits on her husband's misbehaviors!"

Another one carried the title:

"Maggie Leaves the Clinic Today with a New Face"

"Twenty Years younger – Margarita!" This tongue-in-cheek article published two pictures which they named "before and after" in which I looked twice as good before and something resembling a witch afterward.

Trying to give me support, a friendly newspaper, '*Avriani*', with the title "SHAME" wrote the following: "Public opinion respects Mrs. Margarita Papandreou, not only because of her discretion and simplicity but because she doesn't get under her husband's feet and has never exposed or humiliated him. We regret the unacceptable attacks on her and do not forget that the upper echelons of the party of New Democracy do not use Greek doctors, but go outside the country for their medical treatment and operations."

My coming out, my first public appearance, was at the bi-annual EGE Congress held March 22nd and 23rd. I was their President, I was up for re-election and although I was not fully healed, I felt compelled to make an appearance to talk to the organization and to preside over the debate on our action program for the next two years. I wanted also to give an explanation, to justify my decision to do facial surgery – to hold it up to the light and look at it from my point of view.

When I took the podium, I got a warm round of applause which encouraged me to say what I wanted to say. I asked first that the hall be cleared of any males. There were some photographers and a few reporters as well as janitors and electricians. I told them I wanted to talk "woman to woman." After the men left, I asked that the auditorium doors be closed. This was all part of the drama I used sometimes in order to draw a higher interest. I have a touch of the theater in me. It created an atmosphere of hushed expectation.

""Before we get down to business, I want to say a few words to you about all the fuss and hullabaloo created, by me, because of a personal decision I made about myself.

"I want to tell you, confidentially, that when I went into the clinic I gave my doctor three choices: that he make me into a Katherine Hepburn, or a Sophia Loren, or Marilyn Monroe.

"Instead, he gave me back the same face, a little rounder, a little fresher, less rumpled, and a little more spirited. Okay, I didn't get a new face. But there is a change and even that is something, and I am pleased.

"In any case, I want to assure you that the feminist-socialist Margarita is still with you- completely – and with a strong appetite for struggle. Who said that if you are a feminist you are indifferent to your appearance, or you cease being a woman? And who says that once in a while you can't do something just for yourself? According to your mood? Even if it's crazy. If you are okay with your conscience, if what you do does not hurt another person, then you should make the decision YOU want – and the hell with gossip!"

My speech got tumultuous applause; in fact, the women were on their feet. I had touched a nerve. I had said do something you really want to do and tell your critics to go to the devil. I had not had a facelift to please others, but only myself. I had made the point often that criticism and slander are political tools which are used against women, not just because of macho mentality but because men – and women – know we are raised to conform, to want to please, to keep, in other words, a slave mentality. And when we crawl back into our cocoons because of criticism or gossip, we are giving up the struggle for our independence and liberation, and making it harder for those who are still willing to stand up and fight.

I went on to give a short pep talk about our work, our organization, our power, my still swollen eyes hidden behind dark glasses, and my mouth feeling the tightness of my skin as I talked. I didn't get 20 years back, but I could see I had retrieved between 7 and 8 years. That would hold me for a while. It was a tremendous boost. It was fun. I was euphoric.

"This Congress is decisive for the future of our organization!" I told them dramatically. "Our proposals must be short and simple, clear and understandable; no getting caught up in secondary issues, or details. We must turn our attention to the most significant themes, the key themes of our times – make sure our proposals are consistent with our ideology. And our beliefs must be followed by actions."

I mentioned our two enemies at the international level: the world economic crisis which will create a more unequal division of income, and the growing religious fanaticism.

Before I closed I commented on an important development – the introduction in Parliament of the bill for the legalization of abortion. "After years of battle, with many difficulties, the correct step has been taken and it authenticates the right of women to decide when they want to have babies and when they don't. Without the international women's movement, this bill would never have existed. And I can say something further. Without EGE, this positive result would never have happened."

I ended with a plea to everyone to join the struggle for peace during the "1986 International Year of Peace." Perhaps facelifts and peace are strange bedfellows. Nevertheless, I put them together, and it seems to have worked. While the response to me and what I said was good, we had not gotten yet into the nitty-gritty of three days of discussions, ideological debate, strategy decisions. Each EGE chapter, I had discovered long before, had its own character and dynamics. In addition there was a tension between city and rural chapters and a particular competition between Athens and Salonica. It reminded me of the ancient days of the city-state, and I wondered whether historical memory was in fact a reality. Or was I actually present at those events, now reincarnated into the president of EGE? Was I once a maid of Sparta spurring my loved one into battle with Athens? Or, more likely, a Lysistrata withholding sex to make men stop war?

(Diary entry) *March 25th 1986 – Kastri*

Days of loneliness – starting Sunday evening through Monday. First, because I felt depressed with the Congress. From a positive and upbeat start, it deteriorated into squabbling, back-knifing, pettiness. I wondered what we built all these years to have such a tense, acrimonious meeting. Second, because I was not told by AGP that he would be away for two days, another unexplained absence, leaving me without any arrangements for company. I realize the need for company is very Greek. Well, I have become Greek. I like to have people around.

Monday, yesterday, I invited Anna Panagopoulou for lunch at Kastri, knowing that she would give me an honest assessment of the conference. Anna was my solid friend. In my collection of friends she was my brick, my hunk of marble, my rock. She liked to say "we are a 'paketo,'" meaning we were a package, moving together, thinking together, eating together, and most important, confiding in each other. She gave me a more optimistic picture of things – as had, in fact Anna Diamantopoulos, our young prefect from Kozani, who reached me toward the end of the Congress and told me she thought the quality of the statements from individuals and the reports from the chapters were very high as compared to the past. Since I sat in on only a few of the sessions, I was not aware of this, and she was the only person who told me. All others were reporting on the intrigue, the criticism, names of chapters threatening to withdraw from the organization, etc. The fact that we have elections at the end of the two-day Congress, while we try in the meantime to discuss substance, creates an atmosphere of competition, enlivens ambitions and antagonisms. It makes the meeting a focal point for power struggles. I vowed to propose that we schedule times for our serious work separate from the hectic conditions of an election campaign. And perhaps I should be more cautious about my faith that women can work together better than men.

Because of the U.S./Libyan air clashes, the pending arrival of George Schultz, U.S. Secretary of State, had created a tension about his visit. Word was that the Libyans had downed three American planes. I called Andreas on the orange phone – the personal "hot line," and his information was that two Libyan missile ships had been sunk. All of this was unconfirmed, but what concerned me was that any violent action against Libya would make targets out of all American installations in the Mediterranean. Imagine sitting in Athens discussing American bases in Greece with Schultz and having one blown up in our faces!

(Diary entry) *March 28th, 1986 – Kastri*

I took Mrs. Schultz and the American ambassador's wife (my friend, Louise Keeley) to lunch with several minister's wives. Female talk and laughter. The Libyan issue has settled down, and in any case, since we were women in non-decision making positions, it didn't concern us directly. Even if it had, we were only in a position to express opinions to the decision-makers. Perhaps that's one of the reasons women's conversations dwell on personal relationships; this has been the primary means we have for influence.

A day or so after Schultz's visit, Greece came close to war with Turkey. Turkey had sent a research ship, Sismik I into the Aegean, presumably for discovering oil reserves, and declared that any attempt to bother the ship by Greece would be considered cause for war. Andreas's response was "We are ready for war. We will sink that ship." For at least twenty-four hours, until the situation was defused, the country was on alert and the people palpably worried. How important, I felt, for all of us to work for the elimination of crisis situations and the peaceful settlement of disputes.

I realize now that Andrea's reputation as a renegade, a formidable figure in confrontation, were positive elements in such a crisis situation. Andreas actually is a sensitive person, very just, with a fine set of values and good personal relationships. He understood that a leader must care for the nation and must sometimes take tough actions consistent with national goals.

Many years later during a Turkish/Greek dispute over an island, I met a spectacular Turkish woman by the name of Zeynep Oral, formed the organization WINPEACE, to build understanding and friendship between our populations. One of our projects, a summer camp with adolescent children from Turkey, Greece, and both northern and southern Cyprus, conducts training in conflict resolution. The head of the training chooses an international conflict situation, and has the participants play the roles of the two sides to determine a solution. Their own conflict situation gets deep reflection and some often fantastic realistic proposals for solution. A large number of these youngsters developed such interest in the project that they have gone on for university degrees in peace studies.

(Diary entry) *April 2nd, 1986 – Kastri*

I have reduced my political and social activities until our departure for China, and this gives me time to play with my grandson Andreas, Sophia's boy. Before little Andreas was born, about twenty-five years after my last child was born, I had an ache in my arms. I honestly, truly felt my arms had a need and were complaining – they wanted to hold a baby again. My first grandson filled that emptiness, that void. I love to bathe him, powder him and wrap him in clean – smelling nightshirts and blankets and then sing all the songs of the 1920s my Dad taught me, or which I learned from the scratchy 78 records piled up in my cousin's summer house in the Indiana Dunes. Lullabies were for the birds. I preferred to sing "Take Me Out to the Ball Game," or "Casey Would Waltz with the Strawberry Blonde," or "It's a Long Way to Tipperary." My second grandson is also named Andreas. I asked my youngest son Andreas when he was going to produce a baby girl that would be named Margarita. He told me, "Mom, don't get your hopes up. Dad will want to name her Andreanna."

My contacts and conversations with Chinese women were disappointing. It is time that I accept that travelling on an official visit with the P.M. forecloses opportunities for a deeper understanding of the status of women in a foreign land. I can accomplish that only when I am invited as head of a women's organization and the program revolves around the subject of women. The only positive feature of being on an official trip, especially when we have with us the general secretary of the Secretariat of Equality, Sou Laiou-Antoniou- is that we use our informal contacts, dinners, receptions, etc. to discuss the role of women with members of the government who would otherwise not talk about it. Also, we do some "internal" work with our own travelers from Greece…mostly men.

I had one accomplishment after my trip to India. Traditionally a report is prepared by the Ministry of Foreign Affairs for all members of a mission on the country we will be visiting: their history, economic situation, international relations, cultural heritage, Greeks living in that country, education, etc. Nothing is written on the status of women. This time, on our trip to China, with the help of Sou, a section was included. Despite the fact that it was, of course, put at the very end of the report, it was by far the most interesting.

My most useful conversations in China took place in the car travelling from place to place with the woman interpreter and my official hostess, the wife of the Minister of Mineralogy. We had developed a warm enough relationship so that she agreed to let me tape an interview with her in the car. The last question I put to her as we were going to the airport was one she did not quite understand, although her views on the "woman question" were close to mine. I asked her what she, or the women's organization, or just ordinary people thought of feminism.

She was puzzled. I tried to help.

"People in the socialist world, for example, the Women's Federation of Cuba, consider feminism a bourgeois reformist movement." She was still uncertain.

"How would you describe feminism?" she asked me.

I decided to keep it short and simple. "Feminism requires first a conviction that women are oppressed in all parts of the world, and that sexual inequality was one of the first injustices from which stem many of the others. It argues that in terms of social and political power and control, we remain less privileged than men. It requires, also, that to be a true feminist you must struggle to change the status and situation of women, that is, to have a vision for women as full and equal participants with men in societal life, which means," of course, transforming society."

"Yes, there is no doubt that although societies differ, women have a lower status than men."

I pushed a little further. "The criticism of feminism is that it does not attack the system, that is, capitalism, that it is trying to alleviate and improve women's condition within the capitalist system. These critics argue that this is not revolutionary but reformist and will not accomplish the goal that has been set."

No immediate reaction. Then, "Men and women are different, of course. They can't do the same things."

Ooo, I thought. How did this get in here? I believed we were on the same wave length. I dropped the ideological argument and told her how I and my organization looked at these issues. "We are biologically different – we can get pregnant, give birth and feed milk to babies from our bodies. Perhaps another difference, is a difference in muscle strength. The latter, with machines doing heavy work and requiring only the push of a button, is becoming less and less relevant. The first is a given and apart from the substitution of other milk for breast milk, will take a long time for technology to undertake a pregnancy outside the female body.

"After subtracting these biological characteristics, men and women are equal and must be recognized publicly as equal. Equal does not mean alike. It means equal opportunity and choice. What is called 'mothering,' the nurturing and protection of the physical and emotional development of the child, can be done also by men. And all the public tasks men do, business, medicine, construction and politics, can be done by women. What is required is a new organization of society which truly makes division of labor equal."

She slowly nodded her head. "You mean we need to change our concepts of masculinity and femininity." She said this thoughtfully, uncertainly.

"We need to transform the entire web of psycho-social relations in which gender is formed," I told her.

She was puzzling over what I had said, and now that I think back on it, had not exposed her own thoughts or ideas on this subject, nor had she answered my initial question about feminism. I wanted to tell her more, – that feminists believe the personal is political, that public behavior and private behavior must be based on the same set of principles and values, that what goes on in the bedroom is related to what goes on in the halls of power, that you can't have a private face different from your public face. I also didn't raise the question that stumps me. Is that man inherently given to violence? Does he feel the need to assert himself through brutal actions? Is he somehow wired for war? But I decided I had given her enough to digest.

We reached the airport. We had become friends and sisters, and this turned out to be the most significant profit of my trip.

As far as Andreas was concerned, the trip was successful, if not earth shaking. Greece, with its nine million people, could be tucked into one corner of China and fall into oblivion. But Greece, tiny in terms of land and population, has a magic and charm which emerges from its ancient history, its culture, its once important role in the world, and its contribution to western thought. It seems that almost every third or fourth grade student in the world has studied ancient Greece and Egypt. The ages of 8 and 9 are the stage of impressions, when the child has gone past the rudimentary learning of reading and writing and arithmetic and has begun to open its mind to the wonders of the world. Whether in Brazil or Sweden, in Algeria or Nairobi, the mention of Greece brings excitement and respect.

The press release put together by the press officers of the two prime ministers could have been written ahead of time, as was the case with most good-neighborly type official meetings.

It started: "Views were exchanged on East-West relations, North-South relations, military relations" – everything but relations between men and women. Apart from hanging on to male privilege, most men in powerful positions feel squeamish about the question of equality between men and women. Talking about great BIG issues like gun traffic, the economy and war and then talking about "the woman question" demeans them. Declarations of everlasting friendship and good relations were not the sole reasons for the visit; the government of Greece had come for a significant purpose – to boost business and investment. We have an active private sector in our democratic socialist regime. We had taken with us on the government plane a number of Greek businessmen who wanted to develop projects with China, or export to China – what a market!, or develop schemes that would be profitable to them, and, hopefully, to Greece.

And speaking of schemes, I wondered if any of them had noticed The Hostess's behavior during the journey on the plane. Sou gave me a rundown of her antics later. She took advantage of her position as stewardess for the official plane. I was exhausted from the trip and my recent surgery. On the plane The Hostess went to Sou, head of the Secretariat of Equality, who was in the back seat behind us, and she begged, cajoled, flattered and finally wept in her attempt to convince Sou that it was imperative to secure another eight episodes of her TV show *Miso-Miso*. It was ruining the tranquility of her home, she said.

The government television board had contracted for eight episodes of *Miso-Miso*, the first of which was soon to air – including an interview with Andreas – and was debating a proposal for another eight episodes. Most government funds are given to private projects through what in Greek is called "ta mesa" that is, influence. So this was not an unfamiliar dramatic scene. Because I am hostile to the whole idea of patronage and political favors, I was seldom approached anymore. The Hostess had tried me once. My silence was the answer.

Sou was repelled by the theatrics and finally told her to take the case to the Prime Minister, who was accessible. You might call that an understatement. Then she watched in astonishment at what happened next. After lunch I fell asleep in the aisle seat next to Andreas who sat at the window. The Hostess, after her talk with Sou, went to the cockpit and soon appeared in the doorway newly painted, blond tresses pulled down from the austere bun she had been parading in, the scarf around her neck removed and her white blouse opened to the middle button. She was carrying a tray with a liqueur for the Prime Minister, which she could only serve by leaning over me and placing it on the table in front of us. Sou says she lingered for some time in that position, her bosom virtually hanging in his lap (or mine) close enough to show its rich glory behind a parted blouse. It was a call to arms of sorts – his "arms" or my "arms," but I was comatose, and instead of just relaxing, I was undoubtedly dreaming up my next action for saving the world.

A Greek opposition paper described me for the duration of the trip as Madame Lee Fting, referring to my facial surgery. This bit of humor made the trip a partial success. The trip had not been satisfactory for me, and if I had known the above scene had taken place, I would have described it as a disaster.

(Diary entry) *April 7th, 1986- Kastri*

Yesterday family lunch, relaxed and full of good spirits. Today lunch with my youngest son Andrikos (a diminutive for Andreas), and his Harvard physicist friend Petros, whom he met in army service. After basic training and 19 heart-stopping (for me) parachute jumps, Andrikos was assigned, along with Petros, to do research for the Defense Ministry at the Pentagon. Whenever I hear the word "Pentagon" I think of the States and the war machine, but Pentagon is a Greek word, so the Greeks are certainly entitled to use it. In Greek it is pronounced Pen-TA-go-no, with the accent on "TA." The P.M. and Petros swapped Harvard stories. I have heard my husband many times, but he is a good story teller, and I usually laugh all over again.

I had a full schedule in the afternoon and evening. At 6 o'clock gymnastics in Nea Erethrea's, local health club. At 7:30 a visit with Anna Lea, here from Washington, D.C., my "agent- friend" in Washington, and at 9:30 a reception in the Grand Bretagne for the Syrian Arab Republic's National Holiday. I am fond of Mrs. Mandani, the wife of the Syrian Ambassador, who is politically astute, and as much of an activist as she can be in her position. She marched with us on a number of women's issues, rare for an Ambassador's wife, and also, naturally, when we did things in solidarity with Palestinian women.

Earlier this month Andreas and I discussed where we would go on PASKA, or Greek Easter. This is a holiday I love very much – lamb on a skewer over a bed of charcoal, potatoes baked under the coals, a crisp green salad with Greek olive oil, and lots of feta cheese as well as retsina wine. It's a time to be out in the countryside, or on a Greek island. Andreas suggested the island of Rhodes; I suggested the mountain village of Kalentzi. He told me the names of a few good friends in Rhodes for us to enjoy.

"I'm sorry," I said. "I don't relish the notion of joining you and the people you mention for Easter. It's not my idea of fun. I'll make my own arrangements for Paska." This will be the first Easter we will be separated since the one in 1967 when Andreas was in jail.

I called Melina Mercouri the next day and told her I would be alone for Easter, and wondered whether she and her

American movie director husband Jules Dassin had any plans. Melina asked no questions but immediately invited me to their summer home in Epidaurus. She and Jules had built a lovely, simple house on a hill overlooking the bay of Epidaurus, and close to the ancient theater where the ancients gathered to see some of the remarkable plays that became the foundation of Western drama: Antigone, Lissistratos, Medea, Ornithes, The Frogs, and others. Jules, a dramatist, screen writer and director, and Melina, a theater and movie actress, and Minister of Culture in the PASOK government, had found a spot harmonious with their souls. I needed a spot like that, but I was keenly aware that the souls had to be in harmony first. Then they could locate their geographical paradise.

Chapter Eight

Out with the Americans

I had several activities before I could join the Dassins for Easter. One was an Executive Board meeting of EGE. I was still smarting from the dissension within the organization at our Congress. Am I too obsessed with overcoming divisions? It seems to me a basic feminist principle is our connection: we are a part of each other. Why then do we have such confrontations among ourselves? I began by saying I would be much more austere with the organization and the Board. In Board meetings I would absolutely not allow everyone to talk at the same time, which was a common occurrence, and I would impose a fine on anyone who was late or talked out of turn. I barely recognized this as an autocratic approach. I know only that it came from being pissed off. When I asked why we engaged in battle rather than worked together, I got the answer that arguing was natural among Mediterranean women.

"What is natural," I told them, "is that conflicts of interest and struggles about method crop up when we are trying to transform patriarchal practices. It is natural that women choose different strategies. We must understand something about the power dynamics among us and discuss our differences with seriousness and a sense of responsibility. We must remain committed to the ethic which rejects personal aggrandizement because we intend to bring this ethic to the center of public life. If we don't cement the bonds among us,

EGE will fail in its mission...and don't tell me it is natural for women to argue."

Our administrative job at this meeting was to select from the women on the Board which ones would be the coordinators between the Board and the various work committees that were part of the organizational scheme of our central office. Those selected would report to the Board on each committee's activities, problems, proposals, etc. Despite everything I had said, the selection of these coordinators became a power struggle. Several members wanted to be the coordinator of the organization committee, which is the link with the regions outside of Athens. This person gains contacts with women all over Greece, and can develop a loyal constituency, a political base for future aspirations in the mainstream political arena. I did not object to the motivation; women have a hell of a time building a name and a base for themselves.

The problem was elsewhere. Several women pressing for this position were not appropriate, either because they were from a rural town themselves, thus setting up a potential for regional jealousies, or because they did not have the skills required. Some women highly exaggerate their abilities. I suppose I should be happy. This is superior to the traditional reluctance of women to assert themselves and their normal insecurity and lack of self-esteem, but it is a superficial approach to our struggle for equality. The equality we are searching for is to be equal one to the other, woman to man and woman to woman, in terms of opportunities and responsibilities. Once we have equal opportunities and gender is not an issue, we still must compete on the basis of capabilities.

How to deal with this in a democratically functioning organization and board...should we vote? It was clear to me that the board members would vote as if it were a popularity contest and would choose the most inappropriate candidates. My need for an effective Board was overshadowing my commitment to democratic procedures. If we didn't have an effective organization, our political clout would be nil.

So what is my role as president? I knew I had power, both as president, and also as the wife of the Prime Minister of Greece. In this authoritarian culture, I could just point out the person I considered best, and the task would be done. But I was trying to demonstrate feminist, non-hierarchical methods of decision-making. Put your money where your mouth is; practice what you preach, and all that jazz. It is not my style to dictate. I grew up in a democracy, was brain-washed, if you like, in the ideals of the American system – and I am not bad-mouthing this – they became a part of my value system. When I was sixteen I was named by the American Legion THB Post 178 as the girl most representative of American ideals, and was sent for a week to Girl's State in Southern Illinois. That establishes my credentials for those in the States who call me anti-American!

Finally I proposed for each work committee we would choose two links, or co-coordinators; a woman from Athens, generally my candidate, and one from the countryside. I knew full well who would have the last word. This was readily accepted and the issue was resolved. Without a vote. And democratically?

Following the EGE meeting was a reception for the prime minister of Australia, Bob Hawke and his wife. I changed to cocktail dress in a room at EGE headquarters. This was becoming a pattern. I moved from the dress of an activist (mostly skirt, blouse and flat shoes) to my formal attire with the alacrity of a rabbit. Changing my mindset and demeanor took more time.

Andreas had sent a message that he would be delayed slightly. I stood in the reception line alone with the Hawkes, obliging me at one point to shake hands with Mitsotakis, the opposition leader. Fresh in my head was his nasty attack on Andreas in Parliament a few days earlier, and I had difficulty greeting him. I told Mrs. Hawke that political passions run high in this country, and although I am less fanatic, I did feel repulsed by Mitsotakis. In 1965, he collaborated with the King and the Right to overthrow Prime Minister George Papandreou, even though he was a member of my father-in-law's party at the time. His unpredictability and arrogance, and his "walk over grandmother" approach to power made him a dangerous person in a leadership position.

Since Mrs. Hawke and I were both from progressive parties, I asked her if she felt she could instinctively guess where people were on the political spectrum, just by looking at them, greeting them, and shaking their hands. I explained that I was certain that there was a link between political views and body and personality type. She laughed and said "perhaps."

"Why don't we play a game, Hazel?" I suggested. "After each invitee passes through the line, you tell me where you think he or she fits politically – to the left or to the right. And I'll give you a secret clue that will help in some instances. If the person addresses me as Mrs. Margaret, that's a signal of the Right. If the person addresses me as Mrs. Margarita, that's a signal of the Left."

"Can you explain that?" she whispered to me as we continued shaking hands with our guests.

"The rightist newspapers want to emphasize that I am a foreigner, that I don't belong – I'm not one of them. The progressive papers have accepted me as one of the family and refer to me by the Greek version of my name, which was given to me by my father-in-law who considered it more Greek and obviously more "family."

We played this game of "ours" and "theirs" for a while. As each guest disappeared from Hazel's handshake, she would very discreetly out of the side of her mouth say "left" or "right" and sometimes "can't figure that one out." Even when she didn't get the secret clue, her intuitive senses were perfect. Her judgment was 80% correct. This game would be more difficult in the States, I believe, but still possible to some degree to pick out Republicans and Democrats. Could the central difference be class distinction? Or, as I liked to think, people who were power – oriented versus those who were human – oriented?

(Diary entry) – *April 26, Kastri, Early morning*

Last night I had an unexpected dinner out without my husband. Andreas arrived late and took my place in the reception line so I could mingle with the crowd. With all the hullabaloo about my face lifting, people were eager to see and judge the "new me." It was pleasant to get positive reactions. Normally we have a snack with close friends after such a formal occasion. At some point I saw Angela and asked her if she knew where we were going to eat after the reception. She informed me she thought Andreas was "occupied." I went up to Andreas and asked him directly if we were to have dinner together. He said "no," but gave me no reason for the change.

Angela found an alternative for me that evening, and it turned out to be a lovely alternative. Along with Karolos Papoulias, the Minister of Foreign Affairs, I was with three professors, two from the U.S., and the third from Sweden, now director of the Center of Mediterranean Research in Athens, would be my companions. We went to Xinos in Plaka, the old Athens area under the Acropolis, a place that always takes me back to my early years in Greece. It was the very first tavern I ate in during my initial trip to this country in 1953 with my recently married husband Andreas. Three guitarists were still the standard; who knows, maybe the same three from way back. In any case, they played and sang the old traditional songs, and generally off key – something else I remember from the past. Without asking, they sang my favorite song "Green Eyes with Blue Eyelashes." Tonight it had a bittersweet flavor.

When I finished dinner at Xinos, I returned to Kastri and was reading in bed when Andreas arrived around midnight, looking both flustered and euphoric. He told me he would not be going to Rhodes after all for Easter. When I asked him, out of curiosity, what had made him change his mind, he said he'd rather not get into that. He told me he knew I was staying with Melina, and if I didn't want to change my plans; he would take a hotel room in Nafplion, about half an hour from Epidaurus, and we could drive back to Athens together on Saturday when we were obliged by custom to attend midnight mass at the Metropolis Church. I suggested he might drive one day to Melina's to join us for lunch. He suggested I might drive to Nafplion for the same purpose. He appeared happy and eager to be with me. Puzzled by this turn of events, I neglected to ask him where he had disappeared to for dinner. I was certain it had some connection to this change of plans – but what?

On Wednesday before Easter Andreas and I attended the funeral of Spyros Moustouklis, the courageous resistance fighter against the junta dictatorship who had been tortured so badly and hit over the head so severely that he could barely walk afterwards, and could hardly talk. He was an army man who would not go along with the overthrow of a democratic government, and started organizing acts of sabotage, and received his reward from the hands of his own colleagues. He was a hero who after the fall of the junta and the return of democracy came out to all national events and anniversaries of resistance actions, such as the uprising of the students at the Polytechnic, despite his physical disabilities, walking in agony with a cane, saying hello, and virtually nothing else, to people he recognized. He was a striking figure on such occasions, and a stark reminder that fighting for freedom and democracy has high costs.

After the funeral I left for Epidaurus and several delightful days with Melina and Jules. Jules recalled the period of time when we all came back to Greece after the fall of the dictatorship, and Andreas was campaigning for a victory of his new party PASOK. It was a period of time when he encouraged the Greeks to stand on their own two feet, so to speak, and move away from the control of the Americans. Before the war Greece was the baby of the British. At Yalta Churchill turned it over to the Americans. The Greek Civil War at the end of World War II set nationalist forces against the Communist Party which had been active in the mountain battles against the Germans. The Americans came in to deal with the problem – and to remain as new "parents."

One of the campaign slogans was "Out with the Americans." In the recent campaign for elections, Melina Mercouri was a candidate for deputy in Parliament from Piraeus, the location of her very successful movie *Never On A Sunday*. She had joined Andreas for his speech in Salonica where a huge crowd had gathered. Jules Dassin, her husband and also an American, was on one side of the platform slightly behind the curtain, and I was on the other side. The people were chanting loudly this important slogan. Jules got my attention, pointed his finger at me and then at himself, and threw out his arms as if to say "what the hell are we going to do now?" Both of us Americans felt slightly uncomfortable hearing thousands of people demanding our departure. A cartoon later showed me with my suitcase moving toward an open door. Andreas was sitting in a chair looking up at me from behind a newspaper. The title was "Where are you going, Margarita?"

In their home, we played backgammon, watched old classical films from Dassin's extensive collection of video tapes, and read newspapers and books. I often just gazed from their hilltop veranda at the sea cove spread before us in majestic, pristine beauty, the area not much changed from ancient times. The sea has a hypnotic effect on me, tugging on that eternal longing to go back to a prehistoric connection with the earth, with the elements. Shirley McClain says she was once, in times past, an elephant. I would have been a fish. Or, more elegantly, a mermaid?

On Friday Andreas arrived and we ate the sparse but tasty lunch for semi-dieters, those who do not follow the Orthodox tradition of fasting on Good Friday. Andrikos, my son, arrived with his girlfriend Vaggy, and Nikos from the States after passing his orals for his PhD in economics from Princeton University. On Saturday I joined Andreas and the kids in Nafplion for a boat ride in the Argosaraniko gulf. It had been decided that we would attend the ceremonies for "Big Saturday," as it is called in Greek, or the Ascension night, at the Church of St. George in Nafplion instead of the Athens midnight church service.

On Sunday morning we left for Athens to do our usual Easter rounds of military bases, spending most of our time hitting together hard-boiled red painted eggs with the young men of the army, navy and air corps, but also with the fire fighters, policemen, and the training school at Ikaron. The objective is to crack the tip of the egg of your counterpart which is nestled between his thumb and forefinger. You can say "Christ has risen," or "Happy Easter." It is a friendly competition and must have a religious origin, which no one has been able to explain to me. At each stop we were offered plates stacked high with hunks of spit-broiled lamb and truck driver portions of potatoes and shredded fresh lettuce lightly covered with olive oil. It was an insult to the hosts to leave food on your plate. I left a lot of insults behind.

A friendly newspaper described me as being stylish and impressive. "Our Margarita consistently appears in attractive, colorful, but simple clothes, radiating the spirit of a Greek woman." At last – a newspaper compliment!

The opposition newspaper *Eleftheros Typos* took this occasion to blast me for pushing my husband to make Maria Kypriotaki, the gynecologist formerly on our EGE board, a deputy minister. It is true I wanted more women in decision-making positions. Maria, member of Parliament, looked like a good candidate for the Health Ministry, but I had ceased to trust her, because of her fanatic need for power, and also because of her limited capacities in management, administration and organizational skills. It saddened me not to be able to promote her with all my heart. I do not believe in working to get women in governmental or political posts just because they are women. This is using our bodies as a determining criterion for what we can do. For positions that concern the future of a country, and of our children, I am not interested in the fact that there is a vagina; I want to know what's going on in the head. I want her feminist ideology to be the criterion, along with her capacities. In any case she got the job – and I was given the credit, or discredit. Putting these two newspaper descriptions together, I guess I come out as a strong, pushy advocate of women, beating my husband over the head to get what I want, but wearing the right clothes, and radiating.

If lovers are supposed to spend April in Paris, then perhaps they should spend May in Greece. Whether it is April, May or June, springtime in Greece is a feast for the eyes, the nose and the ears, a tantalizing recipe to engage the senses. Spring sunlight plays on the yellow-green leaves of the grape vines, on fig trees, daisies and poppies. Wild flowers, pines, oleander and the smell of thyme and sage intoxicate the air. Birds start singing and tree leaves rustle softly in the breeze. Greeks are considered to be good lovers, and it does not emanate just from the Mediterranean blood in their veins. I believe the explosion of bodily senses from climate and topography induces the expression of emotion and feeling, and creates an atmosphere of romance, mystery and sensuality. It happens also to us, to women, to non-Mediterranean women exposed to the red cliffs, the lilac slopes, the sheeted fields of poppies, the blue sea. This spring I longed for romance in my life, a new romance. The old seemed irretrievable and corrupted by the power game, the competitiveness, the headiness of walking with the gods of the establishment – and "goddesses" outside the establishment.

I hated to leave Greece at this time of year, but I had a number of speaking engagements in the States, visits with activist friends, contacts with new persons working in the women's and peace movements and meetings with members of my scattered family – sisters, cousins, and, most of all, my dear mother. As it was, the trip turned out to have a great impact on my life, both public and private, indirectly and directly. When I left on May 18th, the gonad tropic influence of Greek spring was acting as a stimulus – for whatever awaited me.

Andreas and I spent the day before my departure at Vouliagmenni in the lovely suite held for the Prime Minister. I looked forward to the day with him, but he was occupied with political discussions – a few of which I sat in on, and preoccupied with several phone calls, the kind where one says, "Yes, yes, one second, I'll transfer this to the other room," and then the conversation carries on for ages behind closed doors. I can attest to the fact that this has a devastating effect on one's stomach and adds poison to a souring relationship. If nothing else, it made me feel glad, after all, about leaving the next day. There are several ways of dealing with a crumbling marriage, depending, of course, on the individual circumstances and possibilities. One is to explode, which may be therapeutic, but is seldom effective. Another is to sulk, which is self-defeating. A third is to develop indifference, which lets bitterness creep in. The fourth is to escape, at least for a while. The ultimate escape, to get out of the marriage, well, I was not ready for this – yet. In fact, I was clinging to what may have been a self-deception: I loved him.

Andreas rode with me to the airport to say good-bye. At the airport he bought me candies and periodicals for the trip, and actually said to take care of myself, that he would miss me. I couldn't read this. Salve for a sense of guilt? Relieved that I was leaving? True feelings, dormant, but there? We had not made love for some time. Maybe when I returned?

During the period of my "first ladyship," I travelled economy class (which I paid for) on the principle that I was not an elected official, just an ordinary citizen like the rest. Despite this, I was generally put into first class; another one of those perks that spoils the hell out of you. This was the case for Olympic Airlines, the government-owned air service. It happened frequently as well on foreign airlines. I would present my passport and my economy class ticket. The passport was a diplomatic one stating that I was the wife of the Prime Minister. The agent would look at it, declare my upgrade, then usher me in to the VIP lounge. I wonder if anyone ever said, "thanks a lot, but I have only paid for an economy class seat, and so I will remain with the proletariat." Somehow it never crossed my mind to say that.

I did not, however, agree to travel with a security guard. That was true also within Greece. I did accept a driver, providing I could use him to drive my own car. This was granted. Only on official occasions did I ride in one of those overly pompous long black Mercedes. I dislike any outward display of power. I was raised to believe that those in government are servants of the people.

First class on Olympic Airways, a sixteen seat cabin at the top of a winding staircase, is ideal for work: reading, writing, and thinking. On this particular trip I did little of any of this. I sat next to a man who had been a high level officer in the French army under NATO command and who was now giving speeches for the European peace movement as a member of an environmental organization. His concern was nuclear weapons and the sloppiness and irresponsibility of the nuclear command section of NATO. He was convinced a nuclear war could be started just out of incompetence, by accident, with great environmental and human damage.

I told him about opening the International Year of Peace for non-governmental organizations with my speech in February in Geneva. He wanted to know what issues I highlighted. I wanted to know all about what goes on within the belly of the beast. How does it feel to work for a nuclear military bloc with humanity-endangering missiles pointed at the other side while the other side's missiles are pointed at you? I told him I had been impressed by Gorbacov's full page ad in the New York Times in February proposing to eliminate nuclear weapons by the year 2000. I said I thought this was an excellent goal for the peace movement.

"Yes, I would agree with you," he said, "and I believe it is a top priority for a variety of reasons, let alone the destruction of the human race. But the knowledge of how to build them remains. I think we have to ask deeper questions."

"I know what you are going to say, like what are the causes of war."

"There is no one cause," he went on. "Perhaps if there were, things would be simpler. What pushes nations to turn on each other?"

"I've thought about it, and I know all the standard explanations like oil, money, control of land, etc. I do have one simple answer: FEAR. I think that explains man's early attempts to find protective gods as magnified parents – a sense of helplessness and uncertainty. The people, while being a powerful force, do not have the means to stop a war. The powers that be use fear as a method of control. Can we eliminate fear? Can we develop trust?" Strong political leadership committed to peaceful actions could manage this, but it is also hampered by special interests."

"The problem," he said, "is one thing leads to the other. The gigantic military build-up of the U.S. Administration certainly creates fear. Too few arms leave people feeling unprotected, and too many in the hands of the 'enemy' makes them feel vulnerable. But surely you have put your hand on a key element in human behavior."

We had a rich debate. At some point I started wondering how a guy like this ever chose to go into the army in the first place. He was articulate, thoughtful, and sensitive – and had a marvelous sense of humor. He had been in Greece at the invitation of one of our peace organizations, and he mentioned people he had seen. I did not know most of the names. In Greece, all organizations to survive have to have their "party connection." Every aggregation – trade unions, cultural organizations, women's organizations, the lawyers' and medical organizations – has its particular party affiliation.

"Did you know we have this disease in Greece? This disease of 'partyism'?" I asked him.

"I learned about it when I made my first trip."

"It's even worse than that. The main parties in Parliament have their peace organizations but there are parties without representation in Parliament, and they have their peace organizations too. The network gets larger, and the string of organizations longer, but they are all tied to one source – A PARTY."

"Someone told me that people buy their bread according to the party color of the bakery," he said in some wonderment.

"I call it a disease because I believe it has infected our thinking and our actions in a negative way. Our thoughts have become captive of an ideology, or worse than that, of party policy, which is mainly interested in the struggle for power. We cease to examine our values. We want canned or prepared stuff. We allow the party to intervene in our lives in such a way that the party determines what neurologist, or heart specialist, or pediatrician we choose. A democracy requires informed citizens, with independent judgment and freedom of thought."

My friend smiled. I will call him Pierre. That is not his real name. "You sound passionate about this, and it becomes you."

"It's not the only thing I can be passionate about."

Pierre was quiet. No response. I was teasing – perhaps he thought it was a come on. Perhaps it was. I felt awkward and wondered if I had crossed a boundary. Had I given some meaning to our discussion that was not there? Was the champagne talking? Was it Greek spring?

"Would you tell me something about flexible response, the NATO defense doctrine?" I was scrambling to get away from my feeling of embarrassment. And I thought at my age nothing could embarrass me any more. But then maybe it wasn't that. I was feeling an unexpected attraction to him.

During that ten hour flight to New York, in addition to learning about NATO strategy, Tactical Air-to-Surface Missiles (TASM) – their survivability and flexibility, the Nuclear Planning Group, etc., I learned he was married with two sons, started out to become a history teacher, switching to engineering somewhere in the middle of his university career. He loved swimming (right on!), sailing (okay), and scuba diving (not for me). His wife had her own jewellery shop, disliked travelling or anything very physical. He studied

English in high-school and college, but got his real chance to use it when he was a post-doctoral student at Columbia University in communications, and in the several subsequent years in Washington. He was vague about Washington, something to do with the military. I didn't press for details.

The political picture in Greece he knew quite well. He had not known the P.M. had an American wife. By the time we reached New York, we each had a resume of the other's life history, had explored issues concerning feminism, the military, the international scene, the environment, books we liked, the Reagan administration, and baseball. According to the age he was when America entered the war against Hitler, I calculated he was 10 years younger than I. Whether he had figured I was 10 years older than he, I couldn't say, and it seemed irrelevant. I smiled with the thought that when I "sculptured" my face, I neglected to invent a new timetable to go with my reduced years.

(Diary entry) *May 18th, 1986, Atlanta, Georgia, late night*

I am beat from air travel, but I must make a brief entry. I met someone on the plane from Athens. We will be in Washington at the same time later in the month, and we agreed to attend a baseball game together if the Washington Senators are playing at that time. By landing time, I was heady with the hours I spent with this engaging man. I am feeling, well, like a femme fatale. I wonder if he had formed the right image of me: provocative, bold, risk-taking, mischievous, wild. In New York he caught a plane to Cleveland. I caught one to Atlanta. Here I am with my college roommate, Ruthie, and her husband, Phil, for a few jet-lag recovery days with two old pals before going on to the National Convention of American Women in Radio and Television in Dallas. Although we had promised a baseball game together, I doubt I will see Pierre again. I am fighting with the idea that I want to.

Chapter Nine

Women in the Army

I met one of the Golden Girls of television fame at my speech in Dallas. If I had the talent to entertain, to sing, for example, imagine what I could offer to society. Instead of grubbing around for grants to set up a conference on peace, or to do research on nuclear proliferation, or to produce pamphlets on environmental protection, I could give one whopper of a concert and donate all the profits to a cause! And enjoy myself at the same time. What an exhilarating experience that would be.

The woman I met was Jean Arthur, a key character in the TV series *Golden Girls*, She was a speaker, along with mc. And she was funny. I try to be funny, still insisting on using humor despite my earlier experience, but it is difficult to find the right kind of humor about war, nuclear devastation, hunger, violence. It isn't glamorous to take a gun; it isn't comical to kill people. Is there the right kind of humor? At the beginning I threw in a few humorous stories, mostly relating to me, and they did provoke laughter, while not bringing the house down. Then it was all work and no play – and I hoped, not too dull. For some reason, after telling them their responsibilities, scolding them for being remiss – I got huge applause, and at the end a standing ovation. Maybe this is a lesson in public speaking. Scold people, make them feel guilty, remorseful, shamed, belittled. Found: The key to successful presentations.

The evening prior to this, my sister Evelyn was waiting for me at the designated spot at O'Hare airport. We joined Everett, her husband, at a Chinese restaurant. Her marriage was not going well, and she was thinking of getting out of it. I wondered if perhaps we could form a duet.

I stayed in the former bedroom of her son Greg in a house not too distant from where we five girls grew up. The next day we picked up Nana, our mother, who was in a nursing home, and took her to lunch. I looked forward to smothering that sweet, old familiar face with kisses. The next morning Evelyn and I lingered over a long breakfast, catching up on our personal lives, and in my case, my public life. She wanted very much to hear my speech, and it didn't take much persuading for me to read the main parts of it to her, which I include here:

"..... The media can play an important, catalytic role in reshaping attitudes, in pointing the way to a more just, more tranquil, more secure society beyond war. You are, I know, the oldest continuing professional broadcast organization in America. You have interests of a professional nature concerning the electronic media. Your goals, however, are not only inward – toward your profession – but outward, toward serving as a medium of communication and idea exchange, and involving yourselves in community interests. Today the community is not only local or national, but international, and given the impact you have in other parts of the world, you bear a heavy responsibility toward understanding the concerns and interests of other cultures, other nations, and in what way those interests are linked to U.S. interests.

"The message the U.S. sends out through its communication network does not demonstrate strong interest in PEACE concerns. I give you the picture from the other side of the ocean, as I experience it, and as citizens of other countries experience it. And yet I know the American people are committed to PEACE. I myself would like to see the U.S. take the lead in the struggle for PEACE. Its leadership in the world after World War II gave it this possibility to be a strong

moral force against war. Its capacity to influence human behavior through its global communication network makes it effective in building trust and confidence, in encouraging more and more communication between people of the world so we no longer have the polarization between the 'we' and the 'they.'

" America's role in the world gives it the possibility to work for real change in the global system- to support those movements which work for change – the feminist movement, the peace movement, the ecological movement, the movement against hunger, the movement against poverty – as a matter of survival of this earth and its children.

"Now, more than ever in this age of nuclear extremism, we people treasure our earth, we love our planet. We want you – who have a voice, and I speak now as a resident of a foreign country, as a feminist and peace activist – to fight to protect all the living creatures who make their home here; to sing the song of life, not the dirge of death and destruction. That is the song we would like to hear sung – truly – from the 'land of the brave and the free' – and we would like it beamed through the airwaves to every citizen in every corner of this earth."

One thing I didn't bring up was my concern about the business world gaining power by buying off the communication system. Enough is enough. Another time.

Evelyn and I picked up our mother around 10:30 and drove first to the cemetery where Dad and our sister Pat were buried, a lovely vast area of greenery, tall oaks and elms shading the grass, a place offering tranquility, beauty and repose. Old tombstones, silent symbols of personal histories, jutted up in one section of the ground. We placed a thick bunch of daisies in the vases at Dad's and Pat's burial spot. Mom's flower choice. She said they were "plain, simple, but beautiful," and I think that was how she saw herself, her life, her soul. We stood silently for many minutes when Mom said, "I can't believe Doug is down there." "He's not," I responded, "he's here, in our hearts."

Afterwards we drove to a small, pleasant restaurant on York Street. I needed a real American meal. Mom wanted mostly our company. We wanted hers, partially for selfish reasons. She was our fan club, always boosting our egos, giving us confidence in ourselves. I brought my tape recorder along because I wanted to record reminiscences. I must confess I also wanted my mother's voice on tape. I had many photos of her, and quite a lot of 8-millimeter film, but no sound recordings.

"Mom, Evelyn and I would like to ask you questions having to do with our family history. Do you think you can squeeze in your answers between bites?

"Oh, sure. I don't eat much anyway." The voice was soft and melodic, with a touch of mid-western twang. I asked her how she met our father, Douglas Chant. She was delighted to talk about her past.

"Because there were so many girls in our family (seven girls and four boys) we knew about young, single men in the neighborhood. Your Dad lived on a farm nearby. One day everyone heard he was going off to war, so my sisters walked over to his house to greet him and to wish him well. I didn't go. I was afraid I might be looking at a dead man. I hated the idea of war. When the girls came home, he walked back with them. Doug had a date in town that evening, and my brother Lee suggested he take him there in his horse carriage. I piled in with everybody and ended up sitting next to Doug. He told me before he got out he wanted to see me the next evening. I said okay, and then, just before he got out, he turned and kissed me on the cheek."

"Wow! A daring lad!" This from Evelyn.

"Soon after this meeting, Doug joined the marines and was shipped off to Haiti. I never did understand why he was in Haiti and not on the German front," my mother said.

"That was one of the U.S.'s nice little occupations to maintain its economic dominance," I felt the need to utter.

"We wrote to each other constantly. I remember the mailman coming down the road in his horse and buggy. He would shout, 'Hulda, Haiti, Hulda, Haiti!' and joyfully hand me the letter. Finally the war was over and your father returned. He couldn't find a job. He couldn't go back to the university because there was no money. My brother Paul told me not to marry 'that fellow', but I went ahead anyway."

"It would be appropriate for all of us sisters to say you made the right decision, Mom." I told her, "I will always feel indebted to his sister Margaret. She took me into her home in Minnesota when I started the University. I don't believe her husband Herb liked having me live with them. The truth of the matter was I saw the inner workings of a family and a wife-husband relationship very different from yours. I considered it very oppressive and wondered why Aunt Margaret didn't just walk out. I guess women didn't do that very easily in those days. Anyway, my dear mother, you gave all of us a very warm and cozy childhood." My mother gave a big smile accompanied by tears in her eyes.

The conversation continued with each of us girls prodding for more details. At some point my mother turned to me and said, "You had a good connection with your father."

"Yes, indeed. As the first of five daughters, and very active athletically, I kind of became the 'boy' in his life. I was a bit tomboyish anyway. I remember especially the period when we were both working the late shift at different factories. It was during the Second World War." My mother was eager to tell the story and she said, "You would return from your defense work on the burr bench around midnight, and I would drive to the end of Clinton Street to pick you up. Then Doug would come home from his defense job, and I would go to bed while the two of you sat up and ate and talked."

"Mostly we would have a couple of beers. We were factory workers, and we talked union talk." At this point Evelyn pointed across the street to a church we could see through the large picture window of the restaurant. We talked about our attendance at Sunday school when we were young kids. It was our mother's church.

"What I remember, Mom, was the two styles of living of the members of your family, the Pfund clan, depending on their commitment to the Church of Christ. When we had a family event, the drinkers, card players, and dancers would be in the basement; the 'Christians' on the upper floor with juice and tea. For a while I was a member of the upper floor assemblage, not because of conviction, but because of age. When I came home from my first year of college I decided I had graduated to the basement. I walked down the renegade's stairway with great excitement. Do you remember those parties?"

"I sure do. I was always busy trying to hide the fact to the upstairs that shenanigans were going on downstairs. I guess they always knew, but didn't want to make an issue of it."

Mom turned to another subject. "When you were around nine years old you organized circuses in the summer in our back yard on Niagara Street. Once you used my brother Rob as a side attraction, and he played his banjo for a penny from each one of the customers. I'll never forget those days. You were always the manager, and you got everybody else to do the work for you. Evelyn and the girl down the street put on the elephant costume I had made and gave little kids rides while you collected the money and led the elephant around the yard."

"That's right, Mom," Evelyn said, pretending anger. "And not only was I a part of the elephant act, I was the rear end, and all the little kids sat on my back for their ride! She turned to me and said, "you took all the profits and treated the gypsy children living down near the railroad tracks to ice cream cones."

"All I can say, Margaret, is that you never wanted anybody to tell you anything. You were a very stubborn and independent child."

"What about the father of our father – Grandpa Chant?" Evelyn asked.

"He was a quiet person, rather reserved. He always stuck up for me in any disagreement that occurred in the house. That

I appreciated. He was in Alaska when Doug was born. He went there in the 1890's during the Gold Rush. He was hoping to hit the big time, I think. He came back penniless."

"The great American dream. Somehow it affects all of us," I mused. "Do you know that that Grandpa introduced me to politics?" He was running for the State Legislature from Du Page County. He had been active in the plumber's union and became a candidate through Union activities. Norman Thomas was the leader of the Socialist Party at that time. Gramps told me he would like to have my help, that I was 'educated.' I was in 6th grade. I told him I didn't know anything about politics, although I suspect that even then it was in my blood. I was clearly an organizer, and had already run for class secretary. He explained what I was to do – the writing of pamphlets, statements, letters to the editor (particularly the Chicago Tribune), and passing out literature at his campaign rallies. One letter I wrote for the Tribune was published under his name – George Chant. When I saw that letter in the newspaper, I was a proud 12 year old. This experience truly got me hooked on politics."

I spent the next five days in Elmhurst, mostly with my mother. I can't say that I had a premonition that I would lose her soon. I think when a person has reached the age of 93, one assumes any visit might be the last one. I put my arms around her often and realized how slight she had become, her shoulder bones protruding sharply under her dress – no longer the plump soft body I got wrapped up in as a child.

On May 28th I left for Washington, and the next day I had a meeting with women who had participated in the trip to Geneva at the time of the summit meeting between Gorbachev and Reagan. They entitled their effort "Women for a Meaningful Summit" and saw themselves as a lobby for keeping the leaders honest and "on track" so to speak. The title was a way of saying "We don't want demagoguery or hypocritical statements or meaningless, self-serving propaganda. We will be your watch birds and intend to chirp, squeal, whistle, shout and fight to make this a nuclear-free world. Although we are outside the decision-making process on such important issues as disarmament and peace – we are not going to remain silent."

The American initiators of this effort wanted to internationalize "Women for a Meaningful Summit." They asked if I could take on the responsibility of doing this. This was a monumental task, very challenging and interesting I considered it an honor to be asked. To be responsible for such an effort we would have to have clear objectives, and a complete understanding of the manner in which we would carry out our goals. They agreed to this and suggested another session for further discussion. After checking with the Ambassador, I wrote on my calendar, "Strategy Session – Women for a Meaningful Summit," Lunch, June 4, Greek Embassy.

Meanwhile, I was trying to make arrangements to attend a baseball game with Pierre. He had, after all, called me. I discovered there was no Washington team anymore. I checked the Baltimore Orioles schedule. Their games were out of town. On Sunday, the day we planned to spend together, I woke up with a whale of a toothache, and with the help of the Ambassador's wife located a dentist. It had been difficult to find one with most dentists unwilling to give up their Sundays. I suffered through two hours of probing, drilling and pounding. I was unimpressed by this Sunday emergency doctor, and wondered if he made his living by jumping at sad, sudden cases like mine which no doctor on his weekend would touch. When I looked at the bill, I understood. Sunday was a money making time.

I called Pierre when I got back and told him the most I could do that day was meet him for a drink around 6 p.m., assuming my legs held up. We met at a small bar not far from the Greek Embassy. The Ambassador didn't like the First Lady wandering the streets on her own, but I told him it was nearby, and I would return before it got dark. I indicated my "friends" would walk me back. I was learning the tricks of clandestine operations. In fact, it was quite unnecessary. I could have invited Pierre to come to the Embassy and introduced him to everyone around. My age, my maturity, my reputation made me an unlikely prospect for arousing suspicion or for conduct unbecoming to my role.

We were only about an hour and a half together, but it reinforced my feeling that this was a very special guy. His face was chiseled, the bones strongly delineated, a square jaw with a dimpled chin, light brown eyes, brown almost reddish hair with streaks of grey, ruddy cheeks, a good-sized mouth with a smile displaying plenty of teeth. Very masculine. I was not generally attracted by this type face. My idea of handsomeness was Montgomery Clift, Robert Taylor, Jimmy Dean – sensitive, fine features, perhaps pretty. I was looking at a Kirk Douglas, a Cary Grant, maybe even a Schwarzenegger (at least above the neck). I wasn't complaining.

We spent most of our time telling each other what we had done since we separated at Kennedy Airport. Already we were a couple bringing each other up to date on our activities. He walked me back to the Embassy and left before the door was opened by the doorman. Our need to be together was not satisfied, and we arranged to have lunch the next day.

In the morning I had breakfast with Andy Athens, a Greek-American from Chicago whose name always struck me as a prime example of nationalistic fervor, or love of homeland, and although I was curious as to how he got it, I never asked him. I knew the stories of immigrants. I think the Greek can actually pine away and die from nostalgia. Andy was active in supporting Greek causes in Washington, and although a Republican, he would work with any American or Greek government to support a just Greek cause, something I admire very much.

Lunch at Nora's restaurant consisted of exquisite fresh fish and gorgeous properly chilled California white chardonnay wine. What was most gorgeous was the man himself. We laughed a lot. In Greece few people appreciated my sense of humor, nor did I appreciate or understand theirs.

Pierre's humor – was it French? – tickled me immensely. He would say, "I gave my speech in Cleveland, and it was superb. In fact it was one of my best. It was a piece of perfection. Next to me, it came in second." He told me he felt from the beginning there was something between us. "I saw your revulsion, but I felt it was something I could build on." His style was to present himself as clever, bright, always in command but it was not arrogant. In the end, this self-promotion was his fantasy, and indirectly, a put-down of himself.

My style was to poke fun at myself, as if I were a stumbling country bumpkin, or a dumb, half-witted blonde. Or I would say something that was not true in a very serious tone. "Pierre, the Ambassador saw you last night. It appears he was looking out the window when you walked me to the door. He called me into his office this morning, – and said he has a responsibility to file a report, and he is obliged to describe what you look like and what clothes you were wearing. He wanted me to tell him whether your suit was blue or green." Pierre gulped, and then he laughed.

What kept us at the table for two hours was a discussion we got into about women in the army. Pierre started the debate. "You know, I'm a little confused about women in the feminist camp who cry out for equality, yet don't want women to join the army. If you want real equality with men, you should be willing to defend your country in the same way men do."

"And kill, the same way men do? I do not want to see women stand equal with men in command centers, on the battleground, in war rooms where deaths of thousands are being engineered."

"Well, yes, that's part of it. It's not the only thing going on in the army, however. There is training, learning discipline, comradeship."

"You think those qualities can't be learned anywhere else? School? Home? Sports?"

"That's true, Margarita, and I don't really claim one should join the army just to develop these qualities. And that, in any case, gets me away from my line of reasoning. Women are asking for power, or, at least, a sharing of power. I think they can never get equal power if they do not participate in this important institution, the military. Whether you like the military or not, it is an entrenched institution in all societies."

"A friend of mine once said that war is too serious to be left to men."

"That's a good feminist remark," he said, laughing.

"Seriously though, Pierre, "I am really intrigued, that you, an army man, are making arguments for women's participation in the army. This challenges men's power in society to monopolize licensed killing. Anyway, if we examine several ancient societies, we find that what you are saying is not a given. Take the Minoan civilization in the second century B.C. on the island of Crete. All evidence from archaeological diggings indicates that this was a peace-loving society, without an army, without weapons of violence, or scenes of violence in their art work. This is also true of many American Indian societies, as well as those in South America and those in the South Pacific."

"Oh, come on now, those were different times, different conditions." Pierre moved his head around causing a piece of hair to fall onto his face, almost covering an eye, making him look very young and lovable. Were these maternal feelings I was sensing, or man-woman sexual feelings? We women can often get the two mixed up, or they are so blended in our emotional world we could not easily separate them. I believe I have that problem.

"Still, they were people living together," I said. "Perhaps we can learn from our history, examine what made these societies peaceful. Anyway, I won't belabor this point, because I think we will be talking more about war and peace, and less on the role of women in an institution based on the use of violence. Or her non-participation in same. I am playing with you because I want to hear all your arguments before I come out with my counter-arguments."

Pierre looked at me with a half-smile on his face. "Then you are in that class of feminists that is against women in the army? To be truthful with you, emotionally I would like to think there is something in women that would not be touched by the brutality, the carnage, the vulgarity of war."

"Well, well, well, interesting declaration. I haven't stated yet whether I am for or against. I want to be a devil's advocate."

"You're too pretty for that." This was the first straight forward compliment, playful though it was, I had received from him. It felt good. I realized it was a long time since I had heard an honest compliment. I heard flattery every day by the power seekers; that was entirely different.

I pretended to be stern. "This is a serious interchange. Go ahead."

This time he smiled his broad, infectious smile. "Yes, ma'am," and he held up his glass of wine to be clinked with mine. "I'm saying you can't struggle to win rights and privileges and not expect to have to take on the duties of a society."

"Let me respond to that one; I guess I will not be able to hold back to hear all of your arguments. Don't you think we women have enough burdens and duties in society already? And unpaid at that. I'm talking about the caring for children, the housework, looking after the older relatives, running to doctors and hospitals for the sick in the family, the long workdays and often nights up with a restless child. It is taken for granted the kids are our total responsibility. Have you heard of a man who comes home from his job and says he has a meeting in the evening, but he wonders who will take care of the children? He may help with the house and child care tasks, but he does not think of the kids as part of his job, as a shared responsibility, even when his wife works outside the home. Do you realize what a heavy physical and emotional burden this is?"

"So what you are saying is that until the man splits the domestic tasks..."

"It is not a question of division of labor; it is taking responsibility."

"Okay, responsibility – until then, a woman should not take on army service."

"Wait a minute. This is not the sole reason, just a response to your argument. Go on now. Do you have others?"

"Are you becoming aggressive?"

"No, my dear friend. Just intense. Give me more wine to quell the fire." We both laughed, and I decided to tone down my feminist ire.

"I have always held the thought," he continued, "that by going into the army women could work at humanizing it, and it could have the effect of increasing the rights of women on the outside."

"I don't know how it would affect the rights of a woman outside unless you argue that the more rights women in general claim as theirs, the more this would produce a kind of domino effect, to use a military expression. To infiltrate would be a political decision, made by feminists, and carried out by feminists. We would have to join in large numbers with a clear strategy of what we want to change, and how we would connect with each other in the process, the timing of certain acts, etc. It's a fascinating idea. But I don't think it could be organized – it wouldn't work."

"I'd sort of like to see you try. Remember I quit the army because I thought it needed change."

"Come on now, General, not the changes we are talking about. Society has traditions long embedded. Society has to be changed."

"Okay, but what if it would change the attitudes of army men toward women? They would see that women are loyal and dependable and capable to handle all army jobs, too. Since you talk about the military as being the repository of sexism, wouldn't this be a great education for the guys?"

"You really think that men in the Army can see women as something other than sex objects?" Unfortunately, there are reports that an awful lot of unwanted sex goes on in this institution." I didn't give him time to respond to this accusation. "Anyway, we don't believe we can change the army by joining it. You yourself didn't stay when you failed to accomplish what you thought was important. You quit. We disagree with the main ideology of the military. We are ready to defend our countries, although we even disagree with the concept of borders – right now we have to accept that reality – we would like to defend, not by copying men in the use of violence, but through other means, peaceful means."

"My dear Margarita," Pierre took hold of both of my hands. "Aren't you living in a dream world, some kind of utopian fantasy?"

"No. I know reality. And I am not talking about today, or tomorrow, but far in the future. We need a global ethics of care. We must begin new ways of operating, of de-militarizing our international relations, while having at times, unfortunately, to fall back on traditional methods. If we were, for example to put more emphasis on human beings and welfare, not on power and profit, we would engage in less killing. Anyway, we've got to start. I think Gorbachev's new thinking is in that line."

"I would like to hear your methods."

"I will tell you on our next cross – Atlantic trip – and I'm not just avoiding the question. I just want to say one more thing now. We are asking for equality, but that doesn't mean we want to become men. We want to play a role in the fate of our countries, of humankind. We have something to offer. We have a tradition of nonviolent fighting, even though that sounds like an oxymoron, and we represent a force for peace. We would destroy this tradition if we became integrated into the army. We challenge the institution of the military, and this we must do from without. The peace movement must continue to grow and become strong. Undoubtedly we must, in a parallel fashion, move into political positions of power, so there is also a strong force from within the establishment to complement the social change forces of the people. Now I've given my speech to a one-man audience and I shut up."

"Margarita, I sense in you an embarrassment, or a shyness, when you talk about your beliefs. You have an acute sensitivity to the wrongs, the inequities and injustices in the system. You shouldn't be ashamed of wanting to improve the world, of the possibility of perfecting the world. What you are saying is you think militarism can be overcome. I may not be ready to believe that, but I like to hear someone who does."

I was surprised by his perspicacity. It is true I feel uncomfortable when I talk about saving the world. It is such big talk. I have an image of someone on a soap box preaching to her followers. I fear sounding naive, or as a figure flying off with the doves with an olive branch in my mouth. It may be an inculcated sense of unworthiness or incapacity associated with being female. We have not been raised to believe we can save the world, or what we do or say on issues of global consequence are of any import or interest to anyone.

Chapter Ten

A Lysistrata Scenario

On my calendar for the next few days was a reception for me by the organization of "American Women for International Understanding." The list of women who were invited to meet with me was impressive, including: Carolyn Ahmanson, former chair of the Federal Reserve Board of San Francisco, Betty Thomas, a writer, Ann Nelson, C.B.S. Production Managing Director, Barbara Waterfall, News editor, SCIENCE magazine, and a name that puzzled me, Ambassador Robert Oakley, Director, Office for Counter-Terrorism and Emergency Planning. I wondered if that had anything to do with the myth propagated by the State Department that Greece was a "terrorist country." Other activities included a meeting with the peace activist, Betty Bumpers, a Senator's wife, and Eleanor Smeal, president of N.O.W., members from the League of Women Voters and a session with women of the press interested in discussing women's and peace issues. In addition, and most important, was my strategy lunch with "Women for a Meaningful Summit."

The next evening I had a dinner engagement with Anna Lea, my close colleague and Washington link, and Dick and Barbara Westebbe, he of the World Bank, and she of the world. Barbara took on all causes and seemed to accomplish what she wanted to do in each of them. Andreas and I had become their friends when Dick was the American assigned to work with the Greek Minister of Coordination as foreign trade advisor, and on matters of the economy in 1959. Greece was moving away from its client-state status under the Marshall Plan and the Truman Doctrine. Dick was a remnant of that control.

We recalled at dinner a marvelous incident. Once in the early 1960s, Barbara asked if I would like to see her become a lesbian. This threw me off momentarily, but it was such a tantalizing prospect that I agreed. The story is that she had been active in bringing clothing, foodstuff, school materials to the small town of Molivos in Lesbos, and the town council decided to make her an honorary citizen. They organized that a color guard from the sixth fleet anchored off-shore could take part in the ritual. So the U.S. Navy was implicated in her becoming a Lesbian.

I left Anna's dinner party a little early in order to meet Pierre. I telephoned from the lobby of his hotel, and he suggested I come on up. I was fatigued, buoyant, perhaps overly charged up from a long day of exciting activities, and I literally bounded into the elevator at his invitation. He had arranged the coffee table in his room with a bottle of red wine, a nice spread of cheese and crackers and slices of apple. He took me by the arm and led me over to the table.

"I would have made it champagne," he said, "but somewhere along the line I remember you said champagne gives you a headache."

"Thanks for remembering. You would have made it awkward for me if I had found a bottle of champagne sitting on the table."

"That I don't believe. You are awfully damn direct in your way of dealing with issues. You would have said something."

"Yeah, I would have said, 'Take your fuckin' champagne and get me a real drink.'"

Pierre gave a tiny bleat of laughter. He was wearing a green short-sleeved polo shirt. He looked rested and relaxed. "You're wearing the color of PASOK," I told him.

"Should I take it off?"

"No special reason. I'm not anti-PASOK, you know."

"Yes, but I remember our conversation in the plane. You didn't like the political party determining every action in your life, including, I presume, what clothes one wears."

"Well, that hardly applies to you. Unless you want to join."

"I find it a conceivable proposition," he said with a wry grin.

I plunked down in a comfortable chair, pulled off my shoes, remembering my mother's admonition when I was a young girl never to take off my shoes when alone with a man because it signals future undressing – and accepted a glass of wine from his hands.

We talked about political events of the day, and our meetings. Pierre was seeing American peace activists and people from his NATO past. After describing my meetings, I returned to our conversation about women in the army, told him I had been thinking a lot about it and was impressed with his highly thoughtful position. "You did say something during our discussion about your emotional wish that women would be untouched by the brutality of war. We were really discussing at the intellectual, theoretical level, but I was wondering whether there might be a schism between the intellectual and the emotional, in this case."

"Meaning what, exactly?"

"Well, I happen to believe men who accept the concept of equality between the sexes intellectually, then become uneasy when this concept is extended to the military, and to war, and, I might add, to themselves. That is, they don't see women as equal partners in battle. They prefer another image, a softer, more helpless image. Your remark opened a tiny streak of light on the window to your soul. These were your feelings. Am I right?" Pierre hesitated. I sensed the reluctance that comes when you ask a man about himself, about his inner feelings, his private world. I decided not to probe but to generalize.

"You know, we were talking primarily about women in our last meeting together. Why don't we talk about men?"

"Don't tell me you are interested in men." Yes, I thought, humor is a good way to cover awkwardness. "Well," he continued, "toying with me. "I can tell you about one man, a man of great courage, spirit, intelligence and wit. Now this guy...a little more wine?"

I would not be de-railed. I realized I was on a verbal binge, expressing scattered thoughts, plowing on, despite cues I was getting he wasn't interested in either a serious discussion or a discussion on the subject I had chosen. What was compelling me to continue?

"Let me start with a presumption, something I truly believe: all men have a deep need for maternal compassion and approval." God, what was I getting into? It was midnight, and I was ranting on about men – all men.

"Anything wrong with that?"

"Yes, when it's being asked of women other than a mother."

"Now wait a minute. I'm certainly not asking that of you."

"I didn't want us to personalize this," I quickly retorted.

"You mean we are doing a general psychoanalysis of men?" He looked at me in surprise, if not disdain.

I was beginning to doubt this conversation would get anywhere. "Sort of. That's what I had in mind, mainly to help me, to give me more insight into your brand of creature. If I am going to be an effective peace activist, I have to know more about the other half of humanity, not just my own half. So can we get back to our analysis of men."

"You call it 'our' analysis. I haven't analyzed anything yet." Pierre was still teasing me, and I was about to give up, when he said I was wrong.

"You mean about men's needs."

"Yes. Those are childish needs, perhaps even adolescent needs. They are not needs of a healthy, grown up man."

"Perhaps it's in the subconscious."

"How the hell would a man know, then? I mean, we won't be able to psychoanalyze a man unless we get into his subconscious, so how is this conversation, or my ideas about my gender, going to help you?"

"I thought maybe I could gain insight through a conversation with you. For example, what would a man expect from his mother?"

"You mean what would a boy expect from his mother?" Pierre was maintaining his notion of a difference between the boy-child and the man. "He'd expect approval, I presume, and understanding and forgiveness when he did something wrong; probably he'd expect comfort from her no matter what."

"But isn't that what you expect from a woman, from your wife or lover? She will forgive your cruelty, understand your vulnerability, be flexible to your moods, whims, idiosyncrasies?"

"Sure, but those are the things that make up a relationship between man and woman. They are not necessarily maternal attributes, Margarita."

"I think they are, and I think men look for these things, and expect these things. I don't think a woman expects such things in a man, although she might be very pleased to discover them there. I saw a piece of research once which I thought was quite revealing. The study was on alcoholism. How long did one partner tolerate living with the alcoholic? It turned out the average amount of time a man would stay with an alcoholic wife was little over a year, and for the woman it was around seven years."

"Wait a minute, wait a minute. There are undoubtedly other factors here – her economic dependence, children." Pierre got up and started walking up and down in the hotel room, not agitated, but thoughtful and a little troubled by the subject matter.

"I think it is more than that, I conjectured. "I think it has to do with expectations, the expectation that the woman will play the maternal role – most likely expectations on both sides. The man takes advantage of that and feels free to behave according to his rules, because the wife-mother will understand. And if she doesn't understand, he won't hang around for long."

"I don't really know what you're getting at." Pierre appeared a trifle annoyed by now. "Especially I don't understand how this is going to help you in your peace activities!"

"Let me try a line of thought. Men readily join the army in time of war to protect country, home and family. They will return heroes to the warmth of their hearth and the ever lovin' embrace of the little woman, who will offer them admiration, comfort and understanding. What if they knew when they come back they would be called knuckleheads for going in the military in the first place, and were forbidden to spread the microbe of violence to the children, and should take their stinkin' blood soaked bodies off the premises. Do you think that would reduce man's drive to fight?"

"You are developing a Lysistrata-type scenario. If you want to play games, I can concoct some too. But isn't it a little late to be talking so seriously?" Pierre looked at me almost beseechingly, like 'let me out of this, please.' I was about to say something when he put up his hand.

"Wait, wait. This has nothing to do with your peace activities. You said you didn't want to personalize the conversation, yet I believe you have. This is not a general analysis of men. It's about one man, about your husband."

I shut my mouth. The words tumbling out so easily up to now were clogged in my throat. I had cloaked a personal story in philosophical, psychological gobbledygook, all the time thinking how clever I was about men. It was Andreas I was analyzing. It was Andreas who was on my mind. It was Andreas who was eating at my soul.

I stared for a while at my empty glass. "Oh, god, yes," I said, not looking at him. "I'm so sorry. Please forgive me. I really don't know what got into me."

"Don't worry about it. I don't mind your talking about your husband. I don't mind a personal conversation. I just couldn't get a fix on this one in the beginning. Anyway, the kind of personal conversation I would have preferred would have been about you and me. Should we open another bottle of wine?"

It was past 1 o'clock. "My Ambassador will be pacing the floor," I answered, remembering that I was staying at the Embassy, not a hotel and suddenly realizing this was a moment of choice. The opportunity was there. Pierre had set the stage, and had delivered the opening line. I found myself unexpectedly in an internal game of tug-of-war: stay-go, go-stay, stay-go. I knew perfectly well when I came up to his room I would face this decision. I simply put it out of my mind, or had I? Perhaps the flow of words in addition to covering the real issue was also meant to foreclose an intimate experience that night – my gabbing expressed the nervousness of a first time sex experience in an arranged marriage.

I looked at him. He was winsome, he was charming, he was fun, and I had abused his hospitality, if nothing else. As I looked at him holding the unopened bottle waiting for a more explicit answer I realized he had re-awakened something in me which I thought was lost forever- desire. I was a faithful wife for so many years it had become a habit. If I did go to bed with him, would I be doing it out of revenge to Andreas, "you do it, so I can do it too?" This I always considered was absolutely the wrong reason to get involved with someone else. Would I be able to make good love, or would I feel guilty, would I be betraying a person I was still emotionally connected to? Can you betray someone who has betrayed you? That special intimate oneness was gone – or so I thought. That sublime space belonging just to me and Andreas had been invaded by female terrestrial beings.

"I'm ready to conk out, Pierre, and tomorrow I have a meeting at the Embassy which may give me an important role in the Peace Movement. I had an absolutely beautiful time because, I suppose, you let me rave on, and that became therapeutic." I was now standing up. Pierre took my two hands and held them, looking me straight in the eye, and I felt warm sparks of electricity dancing through my body.

"We have just gotten started, Margarita. Do you mind, by the way if I call you Maggie?"

"You prefer that?"

"It suits you. It's more down to earth, more familiar."

"It's what my closest friends call me."

"Then you are Maggie for me." He lifted my hands to his face and kissed each one, then, European style, kissed me on both cheeks. I floated out of the room, down the two flights of stairway and out into the cool spring night air of Washington, that power center of the world, now competing with my own newfound center of chemical energy.

Chapter Eleven

A Personal Loss

At the strategy session lunch in the Embassy following my welcoming comments to the 15 people gathered, Karen Mulhauser gave a description of me which sounded like I was to become the savior of the world, the banisher of all wars and evil, the fearless leader who would take hordes of women into the halls of power. She ended with a strong proposal suggesting I head the internationalization of the committee which had been at the first historical summit meeting that had met in Geneva the year before. The proposal, couched as it was in such flattering language, was hard to refuse.

I asked first how many of them had been in Geneva (about seven), and then asked if someone could describe their experience there. A revealing bit of information- they managed to get the meeting with Gorbachev only when they collaborated with Jesse Jackson and included him on the list of names requesting an audience. That would have been a fine ploy, if then they were given a chance to talk, to express women's views. Apparently Gorby was so delighted to meet Jesse, and vice versa, the majority of the time was spent in a dialogue between the two. So women had moved from the halls to a room, and were still merely observers. A step up? Or another humiliation for our gender?

The women used the rest of their time sensibly tracking down journalists and demanding coverage, interviews, photographs, what have you, to get out messages of concern about nuclear weapons, the East-West conflict, arms traffic, world peace, etc. They were the women's brigade of 1985, similar to the suffragettes of 1915 who crossed the English Channel to reach The Hague and demand no force be used in settling the burgeoning world war.

Bella Abzug, the combustible ex-congresswoman from New York, was in the brigade, wearing her usual wide-brimmed hat and thundering. The peace activists in 1915 were called "petticoats," "hens" and other derogatory names. Had there been such titles this time? Or had the modern women's movement succeeded in halting this form of debasement?

I was honored by the fact they considered me the person who could do the job saying I felt it was necessary to hold an organizing meeting with delegates from the seven key regions of the world to state clearly our *raison d'etre*. Rather than just set up one more international peace organization, we needed to determine what was unique about ours, and also create a strategy, a plan of action, as well as a loose structure. I wanted to have an endorsement from those we were going to be working with. Would this be a network? An association? Would it be comprised of a number of organizations, or individuals, or both? Where would we find funds to operate?

I suggested the meeting be held in Athens because I was knowledgeable about setting up conferences there, and because I was sure we would get support from the Greek government. At least we would get moral support and fewer obstacles. Greece as one of the members of the Initiative of the Six was ideally suited to house our conference. My time until November – a date I proposed – was going to be taken arranging this meeting. I was thrilled and excited. I sincerely felt we could be a factor in the East-West peace process.

After a brief stay in New York I headed West to Colorado, but since I had a few days before my speech, I arranged my travel plan to go to San Francisco to see Bea Bain, a woman whom I met as "wife of" the economist Joe Bain when we joined the faculty at the University of California in the mid-'50s, but who was far more than that.

She was a warm, all-embracing, hearty, strong female who could listen tirelessly to everyone's woes and inevitably pick up their spirits. Bea had the compelling grace of a person who was secure in the knowledge of her identity and values. She taught mathematics, but was really a teacher of life, and now she was dying from cancer. I told her not to meet me at the airport, but she was there, hobbling from the disease which would conquer her, and shouting "Maggie" as soon as she saw my head appear in the entryway of the airport waiting room. When we hugged each other I felt she was giving me the energy and optimism I had come to give her.

We talked for hours in her apartment. At one point tears welled up, and I felt my cheeks quiver as I fought to keep them back. I wanted just to embrace this old friend, to tell her I was crying because our fate is one, but I hoped also she understood the tears meant I cared. She completely ignored my show of emotion. She gave me the impression that having constructed a full life, she was facing death as a new adventure – and this was not out of any metaphysical religious conviction.

After seeing old friends in the Berkeley area, I took a sentimental drive past our former home on Corona Court. Many thoughts came up as I gazed at the familiar front door facade. I had brought there my last two newborns, Nikos and Andreas, from Kaiser Hospital in Oakland. The scenes were very vivid in my mind. I remembered stepping gingerly out of the car with my last baby Andreas cradled in my arms, the older children ran up with excitement to stare at and ultimately poke the new arrival. Remembrances were both pleasurable and painful. Family life was full and rich, and although I was often fatigued, I was proud of the children and of their father.

I headed for Colorado and the NOW conference. Anna Lea from Washington was waiting for me in Denver. Evelyn was flying in from Chicago to hear my speech. My university roommate, Ruthie, flew in from Atlanta to be with me and her daughters who lived in the area. The next day I expected two of my nieces, Marcia and Kathy, to appear thus making the NOW event an occasion for a family and old friends' reunion.

That evening around 11 o'clock, my sister took a phone call. Our Mom had died in her sleep in the old folks' home. She had slipped away quietly, so like her, not to make a fuss or create problems for others. I thought I was prepared for it, but I wasn't. I had the illusion she would go on forever. She was beside me physically or spiritually all my life. She was a solid entity I could lean on; I could turn to when life dealt its ugly blows. She was a precious piece of my history, and she would take much of it with her, unrecoverable now. These, as must be understood, were all selfish reasons for my sadness. When someone dies, the only ones who can feel the loss, or feel anything, are those left behind. Mom nurtured her five daughters; we were her career. She was our pillar, our safe harbor. And she asked so little of us in return. I was sad also for her. She still had spunk and life in her and was able to enjoy her children for whom she had made so many sacrifices.

I went in to tell Anna, then sat staring at the floor for a full five minutes. Evelyn had disappeared into her room. The tears were now coming, and I excused myself. I needed to be alone to freely let out my sorrow, and, yes, to talk to my mother. I wanted to tell her how glad I was we had spent several wonderful days together in Elmhurst, that she was a beautiful soul, warm, funny and very lovable. That I appreciated everything she had done for me, and all the sacrifices she had made, that the emotional security she gave me was worth more than any amount of money she could provide. She was always unhappy Dad and she were not able to assist me in my quest for an education. I wanted to tell her I hoped she didn't feel too lonely and abandoned in the home we put her in, although I knew she did. And I said, "Mom, I should have come back through Elmhurst to cradle you in my arms and carry you back to Greece with me." I was sure she said to me, "Don't worry, Margaret, I understand, and I know you loved me very much."

We called Marcella in Los Angeles, then our youngest sister Joanne in Indianapolis and cried on the phone together. Joanne said she would go to Elmhurst the next day to make the funeral arrangements, giving me the chance to deliver my speech, and to be able to keep Evelyn close by. After that Evelyn and I sat together on the bed holding hands and remembering. We talked about Mom's lovely singing voice and wondered why she hadn't passed it on to any of us, her delicate painting of flowers on vases and plates, gardening, her days of canning – chili sauce, beans, tomatoes – her coping with any crisis. When we went through her capabilities and talents, we realized she could do anything.

My speech was unimpressive. It was about women and power, whether women in the feminist movement were ready to seek and achieve formal political power, and how we would use this power to make the social changes important to us. I was drained from a sleepless night and a deep sense of loss. At the end Eleanor Smeal, the president, who could bring an audience to its feet, made a very tender and moving statement about the loss of my mother the day before. This touched the women at the conference who stood up and clapped respectfully, while the tears poured down my cheeks. I was saying all the time inside me, "Mom, Mom, look, this is for you." She seldom got the attention or kudos she deserved. Now when over a thousand women were standing in her honor, she wasn't there. The next day I flew back to Elmhurst, not to take my mom to lunch, but for her funeral. We buried her next to Dad, in the same cemetery we had visited only ten days earlier.

As soon as I returned to Greece I started the preparations for the International Assembly meeting of WMS and wrote a welcoming speech for an international gathering on women's studies to be held on the island of Spetses. The first five days I spent quite a bit of time with Andreas – lunch, dinner, two days at Vouliagmenni. He was affectionate and seemed pleased to have me back, but there was a detachment. He was absorbed in his own thoughts, thoughts which I could only muse about. Sometimes I asked what was on his mind. He would stare at me as if to say, "What an odd question," then usually reply "work problems." Whatever they were, he made it clear they concerned him and not me. My hopes for greater intimacy, ever present and raised a bit when he drove me to the airport on my departure from Greece, were not to be realized.

Now there was a new element in the picture – Pierre. It was hard not to make comparisons. My time with him had been playful, fun, adventurous. I suppose that's how a new affair feels, like something remarkable is going on in one's life. I didn't really want an affair though. I was deeply attached to Andreas. But if this attachment was no longer mutual, if really Andreas had ceased to want me, to need me, to be interested in me, what was the point of hanging around? I was wondering whether having an affair would make it easier to bear the hurt. I was wondering whether we would become one of those couples with a special arrangement, a legal commitment showing us married on paper, but in reality free birds, emotionally independent, emotionally indifferent. He would have his fun and I would have mine. We would share the same roof, but not the same bed. That stinks, I thought.

Chapter Twelve

An International Intervention

Soon, however, I became occupied by another goal: to go to Syria to speak to the president of the country, Hafez Assad, about the hostages in Lebanon. During my stay in the States I recognized more international pressure was needed for action to take place. Because I had gotten so much outside help in my campaign to free Andreas from jail during the dictatorship, I knew what such efforts meant to relatives and how ultimately they play a role in the release. I believed it was my duty to help, not only for the Americans, but for all the hostages. It was my way of saying thanks for the human and moral support I received. I did not have the illusion that my contact with Assad would accomplish any releases. My intent was to keep the spotlight on the issue, to be a part of the collective pressure.

What did give me a queasy stomach sensation was sitting down to talk with a dictator who continually violated human rights, and killed people who disagreed with him. Over several ugly days in 1982 he is said to have massacred 20,000 Syrians in one city alone. I could avoid any suggestion of complicity or compromise by not going. Was my purity, my peace of mind, going to stop me from doing something on behalf of captured and tortured human beings? If I were a hostage I would rather be released so I could then help overthrow the tyrant. Well, if I do see Assad, I can at least admonish him about his reputation on human rights and terrorism. He will tell me "the things they say in the West are untrue," or "the West does not understand our part of the world."

First I talked to Andreas about the idea. He thought it was good but wanted Papoulias, his Minister of Foreign Affairs, to give the go ahead. Papoulias liked the idea. Or he didn't want to say "no" to me. Next I telephoned my stalwart and spunky Arab friend, Chaiza Mandani, the wife of the Syrian Ambassador, and told her as briefly as possible what I wanted to do. I wanted the details of the arrangement to be kept secret for the time being. I would announce the trip just prior to my departure and employ the media during my trip and after, which was the key aim of the initiative. This secrecy gave an intriguing flavor to the operation; one would think I was planning a surprise rescue and would turn the hostages over to their countries on the way back. "Maggie Mitty" would have loved that!

I left Athens in a plane sent by Assad and flown by his personal pilot (a courtesy to me); (excuse me, a courtesy to Andreas). Mrs. Mandani had left a few days earlier to prepare the itinerary for my days in Damascus. She was at the airport with flowers. My secretary Julia accompanied me, and we were whisked off to the Damascus Sheraton Hotel where I was given the presidential suite (a map of the place was needed as a guide), and Julia was given a large double room across the hall.

My appointment with Assad was the next morning. I was ushered into a large room, almost empty of furniture except for chairs on either side of a table next to a wall. I had seen this scene many times on television when Assad held discussions with heads of state, ministers, couriers, whatever they might be. I don't remember having seen a woman ever occupying one of the seats. Perhaps I was the first? A little distance to my right was an armchair for the translator. The conversation started out with a general analysis on his part of the political situation in the Middle East. The only thing new in it was a description of his contacts with Reagan, especially, and perhaps only, when terrorist activities occurred. He felt

Reagan had gone back on his word in instances where negotiations on the situation were underway.

Assad told me his army had recently tried to move into the area in Lebanon where they had information hostages were being held, but would have been faced with a battle against the Hezbollah, a religious sect the Syrian government did not support, but did not want to fight either. I knew that it was considered an Iranian-backed group and Syria had concern that any action would affect the strategic Syria-Iranian Alliance. The sect called itself the "Party of God." "If that's the Party of God, then where do the rest of us belong?" he declared. "Do they have a monopoly on God?" I wondered about his sincerity, but I had no real facts to challenge his description. I sensed that he wanted the issue closed – maybe to earn points with the U.S.? International relations are complicated.

After an hour and a half we concluded our discussion. He was intelligent and open – as much as a head of state can be on foreign policy and security problems. He gave me the distinct impression he wanted to get rid of the hostage issue, also that he wanted good relations with the U.S. He suggested I remain in touch with his Minister of Foreign Affairs. From this austere room I was led downstairs to a highly upholstered gold-fringed room where Mrs. Assad and "ladies of the court" were waiting for me for lunch. Mrs. Assad was an unknown to me. Wives of leaders in Arab countries are neither seen nor heard. She was of ample size, perhaps double the size of her ascetic looking husband. Outgoing and knowledgeable, she produced a feast of food and words.

In the afternoon I spent several hours with the Syrian Women's Union, describing the new international attempt by women to halt the nuclear race, and got their agreement to circulate a resolution to that effect among their members to be sent to the WMS International Assembly meeting in Athens in November.

Opposition newspapers in Athens were ferocious. There was an onslaught of criticism and attacks on me, including my dress. *Eleftheros Typos* wrote "after her international peace initiatives and similar boastful fanfares, Mrs. Papandreou admitted she had gone to Damascus as a mediator – like a good American – for the five American hostages in Lebanon. The amazing thing is there are 17 foreign hostages in Lebanon, but the 'internationalist' Margaret was interested only in her compatriots!" Nowhere had I "admitted" nor said I was going only for the Americans. My first public statement about the trip was made in a short press release the day I left for Syria and did not define what nationality I was interested in, just "on behalf of the hostages."

The publication *Pontiki* called attention to the incorrectness of my having discussions with foreign heads of government and commented on photos in a women's magazine which showed me at public functions over a period of many months. "Is she a model?" *Pontiki* asked. The magazine had located the designer of my clothes (a young Greek new to the fashion world) and obtained the sketches of the outfits. It was a clever way to diminish and ridicule my trip to Syria.

Other newspapers focused on a statement I made about Assad's willingness to do whatever he could toward the hostages' release, and his promise to work closely with the Greek government toward this goal. This was considered an unacceptable intervention in the business of the Ministry of Foreign Affairs. Who was I to speak on behalf of the Greek government, or relay another government's commitments and promises to our government here in Greece? Then they attacked my new role for WMS, saying sarcastically I had undertaken initiatives on behalf of the women of the world to force Reagan and Gorbachev to agree to a solution on the problem of nuclear proliferation. A film I brought back with me from Syria's television station, showing me talking with Assad, was played on Greek TV ("did Margaret take a film crew with her and have her interview accompanied by classical music in the background!") I don't know why this latter seemed to be an affront. Are the Syrians not supposed to be cultured enough to use classical music in their presentations of news?

I felt comfortable with what I was doing; there was nothing unethical about such initiatives. I went in my role as president of the Women's Union of Greece, and I was careful to speak as its spokesperson, and not take on any enlarged mission which could be misconstrued as interference in the government's prerogatives.

Of course, it is unlikely Assad would have agreed to see just any president of a women's organization. This is where being "the wife of" has its advantages. This is what Eleanor Roosevelt did, and other wives after her. I never could figure out what was wrong with a woman using this derived power for good in the world. A wife of a leader should be well-informed and speak out on matters important to her and to her country. This is the heart of my ethical dilemma – just exactly what I can legitimately do and how much I can stretch the limits. Who am I to say what is "good for the world?" What is my definition of "good?" For example, some might say a strong western military establishment is good for the world. Or in the recent case of hostages, that hostages need to be taken because they represent liberation forces fighting for an independent Palestine, and this is against Israel. One can find many definitions for what is "good for the world."

I do believe that in any action involving a foreign power, I must get an okay from the proper authorities in the Greek government. In conversations I might have with foreign officials in my role as an advocate of women's rights, I must make it clear I am not speaking on behalf of the government. My own particular situation is further complicated by the fact I was born American, and how can an American speak on behalf of Greeks, or the Greek government? I have been trying ever since I got in this job to develop a job description for a First Lady. And the big question. Is it ethical for me, as a First Lady, to use my title for my own political agenda? Isn't this disingenuous?

So I struggle with the issue and am aware of its complexities. I was proud of my role as First Lady – especially First Lady of Greece! I yearned to be a representative of Greece for whom the people could feel proud. I wanted Greece, in fact, to be the moral and ethical voice of the world, the strong proponent of world peace, and an intellectual and cultural center. Actually I had a more practical vision for the future of Greece to be the center of Health for the World. I wanted its women to rise on the international scene, to be supporters of human rights, of people's rights, of anti-violent solutions to conflict among nations. I was, apparently, making no dent among my detractors.

Upon my return to Athens I called a press conference and began the process of widespread publicity to draw the attention of the public, in Greece and abroad, to the fate of the hostages. I telephoned Peggy Say, the sister of the hostage Terry Anderson, who had become the spokesperson for all of the American hostages, to tell her about my contact with President Assad. I also reached relatives of non-Americans. Peggy asked if she could see me in Athens, and I agreed immediately. This would help spotlight the situation. Peggy Say arrived in Athens on Tuesday, July 15, and her arrival happened to coincide with a visit by Sister Teresa, who joined her in prayer at the airport for the hostages. At my home in Kastri I filled Peggy in on my meeting with Assad, and she gave me letters of appreciation and encouragement from families of other hostages.

I took to Peggy right away. She was a no-nonsense, level-headed, dignified woman who hardly looked at first glance like the determined fighter she was. Whatever international attention had been brought to the situation, other than the initial news of a kidnapping, was her responsibility. She had been given official "advice" to minimize her efforts on the theory that this gave special importance to the hostages, thus enhancing their value as bargaining chips. It was also implied publicity might increase the likelihood of a hostage being killed. The Reagan government wanted the issue submerged because of past killings in Lebanon which cost the American government dearly. In April of 1983, 63 lives were lost, 17 of them American, in a bombing of the American Embassy. In October of 1983, 214 navy personnel were killed by a suicide crash of a truck loaded with dynamite into the American compound. According to general opinion Carter lost his presidency over botched attempts to free hostages in Iran.

I told her my belief, and I am sure the belief of Amnesty International: the more publicity there is, the safer the hostages would be. As long as they are alive, their ultimate liberation is possible. This had been my practice when Andreas was jailed by the dictators in 1967.

The following day Peggy and I went to ERT, the government television station, for a short, live interview with "Good Morning, America" in New York. I arranged for a meeting with the American Ambassador Robert Keeley and the responsible person in the Ministry of Foreign Affairs in charge of the Middle East desk. He agreed to help her get a visa for a trip to Syria. She wanted to be physically closer to her brother and asked if she could also make arrangements for her visa in Cyprus with the Syrian Embassy there. She left without any assurances, but with high hopes. We had generated tons of newsprint in Greece, often with me as the target. In any case it raised the public awareness of the hostage situation to a high level, both in Greece and internationally.

The next day I had the opportunity to relax and do something I thoroughly enjoyed: watch track and field. The First International Youth Sports Competition was being held in our new and beautiful Olympic Stadium in Athens, and I joined Melina Mercouri and Prince Albert of Monaco for several hours of exciting events. The Prince looks strikingly like my youngest son Andreas. I told him so, and he smiled at me with Andreas's same charm and warmth. When I got in the car to return to Kastri, my driver Panayiotis with a big happy grin told me Peggy Say got her visa to Cyprus and from there would get her visa for Damascus and would be soon on her way.

The whirlwind of activities during this period of time was bringing positive results, but making me extremely visible. In the case of the hostages, I had put myself squarely in the middle, knowing the involvement of the wife of a prime minister in this human tragedy was a natural for publicity- and that this was desirable. But there were other activities. In Athens I visited with Shulamit Aloni, a political activist in Israel who supported the Palestinian rights to a homeland. When a Greek woman was jailed in Egypt I appealed to Jean Mubarak, who helped free the woman. I would have preferred, in these instances, to have remained out of the limelight.

I knew Andreas would not be happy about the attention given to me. The need to dominate, to be Number One, was surely flowering in his Greek soul. And I, as wife of Number One, was not being what had been ordained by God, by all of the gods: a dutiful wife and mother, guardian of the home and family. As a silent and subordinate political wife, I had a poor report card. My ideal had been an equal partnership in our political endeavors, and for many years we functioned in that fashion. I aimed for parallel action in separate areas, mine being questions of equality, the workplace, family code, etc. as they affected women. I promoted the rights of women and children, Andreas stood up for the workers and farmers. We were both committed to work for peace; my work was with an international women's network, Andreas' with governments.

So here I was again, confronting the question of my role. There were no written rules and no Greek models from the past for an activist wife. In addition I had to be careful of cultural values and traditions different from my own. Because I understood and loved Andreas, I was sensitive to his vulnerability, his pride, his ambition and what seemed to be his growing sense I might be upstaging him. He never openly suggested this, but I felt it. For example, when someone said something good about me in front of him, he tried quickly to change the subject. When he read a newspaper and saw a picture of me, he immediately turned the page. There were other cues.

The situation was not improved by our political opponents, who were eager for anything unorthodox, titillating, or damaging about us. *Apogevmatini* stated its "sources" had discovered that during my visit to ERT for the Say-Papandreou TV interview, I looked at clips of the first episode of the new TV series on equality called *Miso-Miso*. This was untrue, but it gave the writer the opportunity to recall that the show had created a storm by its unacceptably low quality. Moreover, the program was scandalous because it had been contracted to an airline stewardess who "coincidentally" was a member of the crew of the Olympic plane which always carried the Prime Minister "The airline hostess, along with her architect husband," the newspaper concluded, "had received approximately $70,000 for eight episodes."

Elliniki Vorras wrote, "When vacation time is over, the Prime Minister will start packing his luggage for a trip to Mexico for the 'Initiative of the Six.' The Papandreou family seldom saw each other this summer. Margarita herself is packing for Denmark, according to informed sources, on behalf of world peace. I report this without comment."

And there was this tiny item in *Eleftheros Typos*. "Because of several rumors that the couple Papandreou is splitting up, the Prime Minister will very soon make one or two public appearances with his wife Margarita."

Although the clouds were forming, I did not take this journalistic gossip seriously. Andreas had asked me to accompany him on his vacation, but I decided to stay in Athens and work. When we were in Athens at the same time we usually had conflicting programs, but were together for breakfast and dinner, or late at night. We were sleeping in the same bed. However, Andreas's appearance on *Miso-Miso* had disturbed me. It was a coup d'état for The Hostess, which she exploited to the fullest by splicing the Andreas interview in parts and inserting them throughout the series. The segments made him the "star" of a very amateurish and unattractive film. He spoke correctly on the "woman's question." He was the Prince standing in a pile of rubbish. My antennae were not yet warning me about the possibility of a fully-fledged affair although the clues were all there. Perhaps I had become desensitized by an excess of experiences.

Toward the end of July, just before our trip to Mexico, headlines changed their tone: "The Seeds Have Sprouted from Margarita's Trip to Damascus," "Important the Trip of M. Papandreou to Syria," "High Politics," "New Efforts for Liberation of Other Hostages." A seeming miracle had happened. One of the hostages, Martin Jenco, an American priest, had been released. The various articles said according to the Minister of Foreign affairs in Syria, Farouk Al-Sharaa, the involvement of the Greek government through the wife of the Prime Minister, and the written request on the part of 260 members of the American Congress had resulted in heightened concern on the part of the Syrian government. The New York Times printed a statement by the Minister saying that the Syrians were making a new effort to locate the place where the hostages were being held, mentioning that areas under the control of Syria were "theoretically" under control, but not always actually under control. Stories appearing sometime later argued that Father Jenco's release was the result of long, secret negotiations which were part of Oliver North's arms-for-hostages dealings. North and me. Politics does make strange and sometimes unsavory bedfellows.

By this time I was getting positive reactions to my trip to the States earlier in June. From Andy Manatos, the public relations representative of the Greek government in Washington, I received the following letter:

"Your trip to the U.S. has had a favorable impact on an enemy I have been fighting in the House and Senate for some time now the 'presumption of Greek guilt' by many Senators, Members of the House, and Americans in general. They are suspicious about nearly anything Greece is involved in. As a result of your extraordinary successes with opinion leaders in the women's and peace movements in the U.S., I am beginning

to see in some quarters the name Greece and the name Papandreou evoke spontaneous reactions which are positive. The negative 'Qaddafi-ist' images that were evoked by a public relations campaign that has been carried out by elements within our Executive branch and the Turkish lobby are beginning to be superseded among a growing number of people.

"The approximately 400 women involved in television and radio that gave your speech a standing ovation in Dallas will carry this positive impression of Greece and Papandreou all over the U.S. and that should have a ripple effect. Also, in terms of having a more immediate impact on Washington's public policy. One of the most crucial swing votes in the U.S. Senate Appropriations Committee – that of Senator Dale Bumpers – should be substantially improved by the positive images of Greece and Papandreou that have been created by your work on peace issues with the Senator's wife, Betty Bumpers."

This was hyperbole, but I needed it. I needed to know there were people who believed I was helping Greece and Andreas. These people understood I sincerely wanted to assist him as much as to forward my own causes. I was hoping people would tell him not just what a great speech I made, or how effective I was in organizing, but that I was a considerable asset to him and to the party. I got few kudos from him directly. I learned he sometimes praised me to others when I was not present. We had made the tough decision to leave a solid academic career at the University of California, to leave my possibilities of a career, either as a journalist or a public health educator, or maybe a politician, when we chose Greece over the States in 1961. I was attracted to this country, I was attracted to politics. And I thought there would be a role for me. I wanted to serve people; I wanted to bring words like "caring," and "understanding" and "mutual respect" and "love" into the political arena. But like every other normal human being, I yearned for appreciation and praise from the person who meant so much to me, knowing it was a mistake to base one's life on one man's approval.

On August 7th we left Mexico City for Ixtapa on the Pacific Ocean. Ixtapa was great, getting away from the city pollution and intensity of the meetings for the Initiative of the Six in Mexico City. Olga Pellicier, my friend and Mexican ambassador to Greece, had contacted feminists, women in women's studies in the University, and a young, charming and popular television talk show hostess for meetings with me. A number of these women, and others whom I couldn't contact in Mexico City, came to Ixtapa to continue our talks. After the second meeting I understood there was a split in the feminist contingent from Mexico City between lesbians and non-lesbians, although their sexuality was not the only basis for the split. It had to do with tactics and philosophy. The lesbians tended to be radical, that is to get rid of the political system hook, line and sinker, and the others social democratic, willing to work for reforms within the system. Most were not in conflict with the lesbian women because of their sexual orientation, but rather because they were too far left on almost all issues. Given what I had seen of the life of women in Mexico City and what I'd been told about the corruption in government, I tended to agree both with the lesbians' rage and their revolutionary thinking.

I had a chance to meet with a woman I had met in New York at a meeting of contributors to Robin Morgan's anthology "Sisterhood is Global," Carmen Lugo. Carmen was an outspoken fighter for women's rights, and founder of a dynamic feminist organization, Revista FEM. Most of the other women were university professors or research workers, none of whom, unfortunately were interested in grass roots work. They had fought to become respected department members in their universities rather than visible forces in the community. I have run into them before. They come to international conferences as scholars rather than as activists for the poor and the disadvantaged. Women, they insisted, were uneducated and too busy trying to survive to be interested in political action. But it was clear that after the big Mexican earthquake earlier in the year, it was the working women, the housewives, the seemingly "uneducated" women who organized the rescue work and the subsequent reconstruction of their communities. They took the opportunity to argue and lobby the politicians for clean water, a better sewage system, decent housing, and more greenery. If that isn't political action I'm in the wrong lane.

I spent most of my time in Ixtapa plugging for reduction in nuclear weapons and looking for someone who could help collect signatures on a resolution to be given to Gorbachev and Reagan for WMS's next trip to a summit meeting. Carmen agreed to translate the resolution into Spanish and to circulate it. Flor Belanguer, the woman who interviewed me on television, was an enormous help in this campaign. She read the resolution during the interview and then faced the camera and asked all women who believed in peace in the world to come to the station to sign the document. Later she announced other places where women could sign. I passed it out to the high-level participants in the conference of the Initiative of the Six.

Meanwhile Flor had gathered thousands of signatures, more were coming, which she would send to me in Athens. This enthusiastic response again belied the assertion that the average Mexican woman is uninterested in, or too busy to take on, social issues. It's a good feeling to know there are people who care, who want to join the struggle, who seem to be passionately committed to help, and that women can make a difference.

Andreas used his time – well, most of it – I think – in discussion first with President De La Madrid in Mexico City, and then in meetings with the other five members of the Initiative, as well as "friends of the Initiative," an impressive assemblage of women and men active on peace issues. This included Alfonso Garcia Robles, a winner of the Nobel Prize, Carl Sagan, Flora Lewis, the Mexican writer Gabriel Garcia Marquez. It included old friends of mine and Andreas's whose names we had placed on the list to be invited: Stanley Sheinbaum, Ken Galbraith and Meg Beresford. And the big and pleasant surprise, it also included my plane acquaintance Pierre.

The next day, just before I was to connect with Pierre for lunch at a small village near Ixtapa, I witnessed a scene from our balcony window. Andreas had gone down for an early morning swim, and I was concerned because the waves looked big, and I know what a strong undertow the ocean, unlike the Aegean, can produce. I wasn't sure he had ever had an experience with undertows, and I told him to be careful. I didn't join him because I was almost wiped out the year before by an allergic reaction to a jelly-fish which stung me while I was swimming in the otherwise benign Aegean. It produced an anaphylactic shock, a life-threatening experience. The quick arrival of a doctor, a speedy ambulance ride and frequent shots of cortisone and adrenaline to bring my blood pressure back to normal, saved my life. But it changed my relationship to the Sea.

There were at least ten figures in a circle around Andreas, prancing and cavorting in the surf near the shore. I recognized the Minister of Foreign Affairs, Carolos Papoulias, and men from the Olympic Airlines crew. There was also an Amazon – like female figure bouncing around Andreas. She would throw herself on her back in the water, her breasts pointing up like mountains of jello, her legs virtually encircling Andreas. I was under the impression Andreas was not encouraging these theatrics. He kept swimming away.

While I was watching this performance with a mixture of curiosity and disgust, Angela walked into the room. I asked her if she had noticed that The Hostess was clinging to "the boss." And I meant in general, not just in the sensuous foam of the Pacific. I told her to take a peek at what was going on down below. She looked at me with a strange expression on her face, studying me, perhaps trying to understand me. "I don't have to look," she answered. "Just now you noticed this?" She was telling me a relationship was developing, or had developed, between my husband and the airline stewardess, giving confirmation to my own suspicions.

At the same time I was tripping around the edges of my own affair. More and more Pierre broke into my consciousness, occupying space in my mind. The excitement was building. These were symptoms of a romantic connection. Maybe I was dropping into the trap of macho mentality; maintain a conventional marital relationship for the eyes of the world and an out-of-bounds relationship for spice. I have not in the past been able to play the game with two men at one time. And yet…I met Pierre at noon, a complicated feat because communication between our hotels was difficult and taxis almost unavailable. The day was hot and muggy, the white wine warm and the flies persistent. Still, I was happy to see him even though my mind was in a swirl from the early morning scene. Pierre had tanned to red-brown color. He was wearing a white short-sleeved four-pocketed captain's shirt, which had become the costume of the conference. All the leaders and most of the invited observers were in something similar, including my husband who had hurriedly sent Mihalis out to purchase the proper top.

"Okay, Mr. Pierre, come on and tell me, why didn't you mention that you would be here in our last telephone conversation?"

"I didn't know at that time."

"I told you I would be with the delegation." I said this like a reproachful child.

"All the more reason for me to agree to come when I was asked."

"Okay, I accept your apology."

"What apology?"

"As to why you didn't tell me."

He laughed. "Well, if that's your idea of an apology, I have obviously apologized."

I asked him about the conference. He said it was clearly going well among the leaders, but the "friends" were isolated in another hotel, and unable to express their ideas, or to have a sense of participating. "We are beginning to feel like window dressing, or cheer leaders."

"Or spouses," I interjected.

"Is that said with personal bitterness, or is it a feminist position?"

"Right now with personal bitterness, or unhappiness, if you like." I wondered if I should tell him anything of my troubles, the early morning scene was still spinning in my mind. That was, however, not the nature of our relationship. Describing my husband's weaknesses seemed cranky, and talking about his indiscretions disloyal. I had done it obliquely and unknowingly when Pierre and I were together at the hotel in Washington. Otherwise Andreas was kept out of our discussions. Was that caution acquired because of political constraints, or was it my own code of behavior?

I changed the subject and Pierre did not return to my cryptic remark. From Mexico he was going to the Costa Rica University. I told him about the plans for the WMS assembly. It was good to see him, and he was wonderful to talk with, and the chemistry was there, but I was distracted and not as attentive as I might have been. If he noticed, he said nothing. We agreed to try to get together again before departure, but our only contact was at the final press conference where we greeted each other circumspectly. We both understood we would meet again, and soon.

The Greek contingent returned to Athens on the evening of August 9th. August is a vacation month for almost everybody in Greece. For me it wasn't. Because people were off to the islands, or to the mountains, the phones stop ringing and the invitations diminish. My home in Kastri is surrounded by pine trees, lush flowers and singing birds. I prefer to spend the month there, organizing my papers, writing, reading, planning, contemplating, and reflecting on the complexity of human affairs.

Foreign friends come through, and the slower pace of August provides leisure time for chats, or a performance at the Erodos Attikou Theater below the Acropolis. I didn't see much of Andreas. He continued to work too. We had a few receptions – the standard one in August honoring the armed forces, and the return of democracy to Greece after the fall of the dictatorship. One weekend we spent in Vouliagmenni, the presidential suite just outside of Athens. The children came by for food and sleep, out for swimming and surfing. Andrikos was on vacation from Oxford University in England. Nikos was doing his service in the Army (I grit my teeth on that one). We were planning the highlight of the summer – our annual family vacation together, at the end of August. We selected the island of Limnos, where Nikos was stationed, so he could join us when he was at liberty.

Chapter Thirteen

Women of Limnos Set an Example

Limnos is a northern Aegean island, remote from Athens, hilly, covered mostly by scrub brush. Few tourists visit and the island remains pristine. There are more sheep and goats than humans. If tourists do discover it, they will find an intact Venetian fortress in the harbor, lovely sand beaches and crystal clear water. Because Limnos has been claimed by Turkey, a sizeable Greek military detail is stationed there. The military is not much in evidence, though, and we were all looking forward to relaxation, sea and beach frivolity, fresh fish and lots of laughter. Laughter had become the most dominant element in our family get-togethers.

I did not confront Andreas with the mermaid vs walrus scene I had witnessed. His subsequent behavior seemed completely normal; no sign of outside attractions. I was ready to forget the whole thing, to dump my suspicions, but during our vacation he was restless and self-absorbed, disappearing to Mihali's cabin apparently for telephone calls though our cabin had a functioning telephone. Then he decided to cut his stay in Limnos by two days. The family stayed on, with a nervous, distressed and preoccupied mother whose summer vacation had been spoiled.

On the last morning, with the children taking their final dip in the enticing waters of the Aegean, I sat brooding on the terrace of my cabin, slumped in a chair like a damp towel. My eyes were fixed on the stone floor, mechanically and indifferently following the movements of ants. When I looked up I stared at the hill with a steep cliff across Moudros bay. My memory was pricked, and I recalled a myth one of our EGE members had told me having to do with that hill. (It is a distortion of the original myth, a feminist version which suits me fine.) The men of the island were sailors and spent months away from home. Once, the "cargo" they brought into port were women they had picked up along the way while their wives were faithfully keeping the home fires burning and preparing to celebrate their return. The wives were furious. They tried to persuade their husbands to ship the women back to their home countries. The husbands were not persuaded. Their spouses decided to organize and proceeded with the preparation of food, music and drink for a glorious feast, a "picnic," to be held on the peak of the hill.

The men were pleased and excited about the event, feeling they had been forgiven and their concubines could stay. The women found the headiest wine on the island and carried copious quantities up the hill. The pleasant aromas of roast pig and lamb rose into the air in curls of smoke, nectar to the nostrils of the men who by now felt like gods, sitting at an eternal dining table, engaged in permanent merry-making. The men became so intoxicated their muscles turned to jelly. The women, fierce, clever, glorious creatures that they were - threw them one by one over the cliff.

This story gave me an immense amount of delight and satisfaction. I got up from my chair with a faintly satanic half-moon curve below my nose and retrieved my camera from the bedroom in order to take photos of the hill. I would enlarge and frame the best one and hang it on my bedroom wall in Kastri to remind me there are ways to deal with philandering husbands.

In early September I held a lawn party for very precious and special people – handicapped children. This was becoming a summer tradition at Kastri. I wanted to lend my name and prestige to focus attention on these kids. It was also fun. One problem: the wife of the Prime Minister has no budget whatsoever to show from time to time the government's concern for various categories of people who are marginalized in our society. The best way, of course, is to provide funds which will train them to help themselves. But activities like the one I organized put pressure on the decision-makers for reform.

The problem of funds is broader. The First Lady, in fact, is not given secretarial help, nor money to pay for stamps to answer the piles of letters that arrive each day, directly to her. And yet it is these actions, more than anything else, she is expected to do. I would like to have campaigned for a change in the pattern of dealing with the wife of a P.M., but I was hardly in a position to do so. It's a little like the U.S. Congress voting for salary raises of its members, something I always found weird and rather obscene. There must be a way this could be done by people with no self-interest. In the end, I paid the expenses of this affair from private contributions, including my own.

September and October were devoted to preparations for the International Assembly of WMS. I turned to it with a vengeance, not only because I was committed to it and excited by it, but also because it provided an escape. Such work for me is cleansing; it washes other thoughts out of my brain, and fatigues me sufficiently so I can fall into a deep and unperturbed sleep. I blocked out any thoughts that Andreas was carrying on an affair, and if a smidgen of suspicion entered my mind, I would just say, "So what – it's not the first time."

Something happened which gave me a different perspective on life, sorting out the important from the trivial. On September 14 I spoke in Kaladonia in Crete at a memorial service for Olaf Palme, the Prime Minister of Sweden assassinated in March. We had become more than political colleagues with the Palmes when we lived in exile in Sweden during the year after Andreas got out of jail, more recently Andreas and Olaf had collaborated on the Initiative of the Six.

Seeing Lisbet, the wife of Olaf, only six months after her tragedy was very moving, and after the ceremony I sat next to her and took her hand. It was cold and clammy. She looked grey from the effort and the emotion. I told her to take a few bites of food. She looked at her plate with despair. "I don't think I can eat, Margarita," she whispered to me.

I was afraid she was going to fall off the bench. "I'm getting someone to take you back to your hotel," I said. "Everyone will understand. Don't worry." She hesitated, not wanting, I was sure, to offend anyone. Yet it was clear that my suggestion brought her a feeling of relief. I told her, "We will be on the same plane back to Athens tomorrow. Let's sit together."

On the plane she told me her concerns. She truly believed Olaf had been assassinated because of his participation in the Initiative. Indira Gandhi had been assassinated not long before, and she was certain all the other participants would be killed. She begged me to tell Andreas to be cautious, and to add to his security guard. Her words unsettled me, and I returned to Kastri shaken by the image of Andreas, the man I loved, crumbled on the ground, with bullets in his body, or hanging from a tree, the same images I had seen the night Andreas was dragged out of the house by armed soldiers

The next morning at breakfast I told Andreas everything Lisbet had said to me. He listened, asked a few questions about her, but didn't say whether or not he would take her advice on increasing his bodyguard. After he left, I decided I wanted to go somewhere where I could walk and breathe. My body ached. Images of assassination and Lisbet's taut face clashed with images of Andreas splashing in the Pacific Ocean and talking on Limnos telephones. I called Panayiotis, my driver, and told him, "Damn it, I've got to get out of here. I need space. I need the sea." Panayiotis' dark eyes crinkled as he smiled happily. A thin, slightly bald fifty year old, he recently had his second baby. It was a girl, because, he said, I had converted him to feminism. He was protective of me and kept me apprised of what he thought were burgeoning conspiracies within the women's organization. Sensitive to my moods, he had undoubtedly observed my sagging spirits during the last few weeks. I was sure he knew why, too, although we had not talked about the gossip spicing the air of Attica.

After taking care of a few household tasks, I climbed into the car, and we were off toward Ana Visso, a village at the tip of the Attica peninsula. September and October are my favorite months. When I was younger, I delighted in the sensuality of spring, and summer allowed me to indulge my love of swimming and expanses of water. Autumn ended this delicious span of time and tended to throw me into melancholy. Now, however, I find it brings me serenity and tranquility. The sun is friendly, not searing the skin or blinding the eyes. The human swarm that clogs the beaches with color and trash and noise is gone. The water is cleaner and cooler, as smooth as oil, not boiling and fretting as it often does in the summertime. The Greek winds of July and August, called the Meltemi, have died down to a whisper and caress the body like the brush of a feather.

I was headed for a favorite cove. The footpath leading to the beach curves in and out through craggy rocks, scrub brush and an occasional tree, dropping a considerable distance at a sharp slant down from the road. Once on the sliver of sand, about forty feet wide, I felt snugly encompassed by the awe-inspiring cliffs at the back and the sea at my feet. I loved walking barefoot in the surf while the many-fingered hand of the sea gently stroked my toes and soothed my soul. I occasionally picked up white stones and tossed them into the sea to a new bed in the morass of seaweed and sand at the bottom. The beach was vacant except for one couple lying in a shaded corner, oblivious – as lovers are – of anything or anybody around them. Panayiotis found a flat rock to sit on under an overhanging ledge and kept an eye on me as I walked along the water's edge. Even though I did not intend to go into the water, he was concerned about jellyfish. One might appear in one of the ripples I was allowing to kiss the sides of my feet.

After about a half an hour walking back and forth from one end of the cove to the other meditating idly about life, violence in the world, egoism, my marriage, fate, power and the abuse of power, and smilingly thinking I was in the right location to "cover the waterfront" in my musings, I joined Panayiotis in his shaded alcove.

"Isn't it great?" I said as I sat down. "There's nowhere on Earth more beautiful than Greece. And this beach – this is my idea of paradise. "

"Except that you wanted to plunge into the water," Panayiotis responded.

"Yes," I agreed, "That would have made it exquisitely perfect."

"Are you okay?" he asked me somewhat timidly, knowing he was getting close to treading on sensitive territory.

"I'm fine," I answered, and I really felt that way. The sea air had helped. I felt good and strong. I counted my toes and they were all there. I don't know whether I was doing a lot of rationalizing in my meditation stroll on the beach, but I felt there was too much good in life to worry about the bad. I was just damn lucky to be in excellent health, to be able to do the things I wanted to do, to have a marvelous bunch of kids, to have a cause that was beyond my personal, mundane needs – in short, I was thinking in a higher level, an area where philosophy takes over. I ventured to bring up "the issue." "You have understood, Panayiotis, how often I have been stressed out these days. I have, well, you know, a meandering husband."

"But he loves you, Mrs. Margarita," was his swift and soft reply.

"Some way to show it," I smiled.

"No, no. I see him. I have watched him. Remember what he said after the jellyfish incident… 'I would have lost the most precious thing I have in life.' He loves you. I know he does."

"Once he loved me. We loved each other, desperately and passionately. Erotic, magical, romantic love. Probably too intense to last. I think I was able to bring remnants of those feelings into the next stage of love, the stage of friendship and companionship, the "comfortable old armchair feeling." I continue to feel an element of excitement in our relationship. Andreas has lost it, or what is left is not enough. He needs something new, he needs to experience the all-consuming feelings of a new romance. It's an addiction. He's hooked on romance."

Panayiotis was a trifle overwhelmed by my analysis, "romantic love, old armchairs, excitement, hooked on romance. "He will come to you, though. You will see. He loves you." Panayiotis was trying to buoy me up. He was so positive and so sincere I almost believed him.

"Panayiotis, do you know the story of Ceyx and Alcyone? I don't know much mythology, but some stories stick in my mind. Ceyx, if I remember correctly, was a king in Thessaly. His wife was the daughter of the King of the Winds. They loved each other devotedly and hardly ever were apart. One day Ceyx decided to take off on a trip by sea, which his wife objected to vigorously, having a premonition of danger."

Panayiotis, simple, wonderfully innocent in many ways, was listening to me with the earnestness of a child.

"He was gone for a long time, and Alcyone would often go down to the docks, looking for a sign of his return. One day she saw something floating in the water. As it drifted closer she felt a grieving sense of horror; she was convinced it was a dead body being carried in by the tide."

I gesticulated out to the sea, and Panayiotis's eyes searched the water as if he expected to see an object floating toward us. "Alcyone cried, 'Dearest, dearest husband,' and jumped into the waves. But instead of sinking, she was flying over them, and feathers sprouted from her body. She had wings. She had been changed into a bird. The gods had looked after her, and when she reached Ceyx, he too had been transformed into a bird He joined her and they flew together, over the waves, their love as strong as ever."

"That's the end of the story?" Panayiotis was more interested in the story than in any significance it might have to me.

"That's all. I am trying to tell you I am a romantic, and I like the idea of everlasting love, of total commitment. The stories one remembers are the ones having special meaning to you. I probably couldn't tell you much about Helen of Troy and the battles fought between the Greeks and the Trojans, because I hate the idea of war."

He returned to his original tune. "Yes, yes, I understand-and that's the way it is; you are together like that. Whatever he's doing, it won't last. He loves you."

Chapter Fourteen

Peace and Troubled Waters

When I was not being mesmerized by the sea, or haunted by the storm clouds forming around my personal life, I was busy with my homework on women and the peace movement. In studying the history of women working for peace, I was amazed and distressed to discover we were using many of the same appeals used by women activists in the early 1900s. Those women asked then: "Have we made no progress in the last half century? Isn't it time that disputes between countries be settled in an international forum, with women playing an equal part?"

In 1915, just before the Women's Peace Congress in Holland, Jane Addams said: "We do not think we can settle the war. We do not think by raising our hands we can make the armies cease slaughter. We do think it is valuable to state a new point of view. We do think it is fitting that women should meet and take counsel to see what may be done."

One paragraph in the initial manifesto of the Women's Peace Party in the early part of that century reads: *"Therefore, as human beings and the mother half of humanity, we demand our rights to be consulted in the settlement of questions concerning not alone the lives of individuals but of nations. We must be recognized and respected. We demand that women be given a share in deciding between war and peace in all courts of high debate – within the home, the school, the church, the industrial order, and the state."*

In Nairobi in 1985, I presented Greece's report to the U.N. Decade of Women Conference in Nairobi, that report actually echoed the early feminists. Our report concluded with the following:

"We women are a rising force in society, and we must find a way out of the circle of fire into which established male-dominated concepts and the exercise of power have led us.

"We must fill the ranks of the worldwide mass Peace Movement, and we must follow our instincts for protecting life, where our concern for human rights can become the dominant force in affecting the future of the planet and the future of humanity."

Happily I got a thunder of applause as I sat down.

Then, as now, women were received with hostility, anger and ridicule by the press. The British press referred to the 1915 American peace delegation sailing to Holland as "This shipload of hysterical women," or "Folly in Petticoats," "Pow-wow with the Fraus," and "This amiable chatter of a bevy of well-meaning ladies."

Someone in the U.S. administration stated before the first summit meeting in Geneva in 1985 that, "Few women understand 'throw-weight' or what is happening in Afghanistan, but would rather read the human interest stuff of what has happened." Meaning we want to know what Ms. Reagan wears, what recipes she and Ms. Gorbachev talk about, how many children or grandchildren they have. In other words, we were still being belittled in the same way our sisters were in the early part of the century.

Meanwhile, the Organizing Committee for the International Assembly meeting of Women for a Meaningful Summit in Athens had been working with a great deal of zeal and energy We were not immune to mistakes. The printed program proved this by writing that the discussion would be a "free-frowing, brain-storming session." Each of the sixty or so delegates would want to have a chance to present something in the general meeting. Most of them coming from the Soviet and Eastern bloc were obliged to do so. The Soviet Union needed to be heard, and wanted to affect international opinion. Besides, women had so few opportunities to be heard that it would have been criminal to deny anyone that opportunity. The Soviet women made it clear they would participate in the conference only on the condition of being equal partners with the United States. All previous women's conferences involving both East and West had been under the aegis of one of the super-powers. The Soviets wanted this one to be neither controlled by the West nor by the East, but a partnership between the two.

We gave five minutes to each delegate for a statement. Five minutes! About war and peace. About nuclear weapons. About the militarization of international relations. Arms trafficking. Peace education. How could anyone cover such topics, or even approach them, in five minutes? We needed to provide the gist of the conference, in a sense its heart. In order to find this focus; we had to ask ourselves what motivated us to organize. People organize when they are angry, dissatisfied, frustrated; in short, when they want to change something. In this case to reduce the continuing multiplication of nuclear weapons, we had to change the existing situation, the exclusion of women from the decision-making bodies. We were planning to be present at summit meetings wherever they were held. So I asked myself, what if Gorbachev, or Reagan, said, okay, ladies, let's sit down and go through this thing together. What do you want to tell us, and what would you like us to do?

This thought became the core of our invitation. Time was already exceedingly little for sending out the invitation. To get things going we sent the invitation out signed by three names: Claudine Schneider, of the U.S. House of Representatives; Silvia Hernandez, a senator in Mexico and incoming president of Women Parliamentarians for Peace; and me, as president, Women's Union of Greece. The gist of the conference is described in a few paragraphs taken from the letter of invitation. With this theme, we hoped much more would come out of the meeting than utopian thoughts.

We wrote: *"If you can come we would like you to prepare remarks that would take five to ten minutes to present at the meeting. The remarks should answer the following question:*

If I, or my organization, or my country, had a chance to sit down and talk with Gorbachev and Reagan about nuclear war and disarmament, what would be our main points?"

These remarks and results of the signature campaign will be packaged for presentation to General Secretary Gorbachev and President Reagan at the time of their next Summit meeting. We will request meetings with the two leaders as soon as a Summit date is announced."

Many days were spent by EGE women on the streets of Athens and other areas of Greece gathering signatures on the declaration Flor and I had inaugurated in Mexico. We began an additional campaign to get letters of support for our initiative from prominent women around the world. It is not possible to list all the women who sent us statements, but here is a highly respectable sample that includes: Maria L.B. de Alfonsin, wife of the president of Argentina, Hazel Hawke, wife of the Prime Minister of Australia, Vilma Espin, president of the Federation of Cuban women, Margot Honecker, Minister of Popular Education in the GDR, Petra Kelly, member of German parliament, Green Party, Sonia Gandhi, wife of the prime minister of India, Agatha Barbara, president of Malta, Vigdis Finnbogadottir, president of Ireland, Ms. Tsakako Doi, president of the Socialist Party of Japan; Barbara Jaruzelska, wife of the chairman of the state council of Poland; Winnie Mandela, South Africa, Lisbet Palme, wife of the late prime minister of Sweden; Sally Mugabe, deputy secretary of ZANU, and wife of the prime minister of Zimbabwe.

The essence of what they said was reflected in Maria Alfonsin's response: "I belong to a country that has returned to democracy and maintains the everlasting struggle for world disarmament and peace. I cannot but applaud the noble purpose of your conference whose clear objective is to propose a suitable framework of coexistence in which all countries can realize their destiny of peace and harmony."

Our organizing committee had billowed. We set up a small "think tank" to search for a strategy, for a plan of action in order to accomplish our key aims. Our emphasis was on the de-militarization of international relations, which meant changing a whole mentality – a huge task, and a long task in terms of time. Our tactics were to get to that by going after something concrete, like nuclear weapons. At about the same time, the Oxford Research Group in England published "How Nuclear Decisions are Made." We invited the head of the Group (fortunately a woman), Scilla McClean, to lead one of the workshops, and also discussed the possibility of using the book as a guide to our actions. The Group had carefully studied the five nuclear powers, thus providing a blueprint for dealing with our confrontations with decision makers, the political policy makers in the two blocs and the military hierarchy in NATO and the Warsaw Pact.

Those who ultimately came were spectacular women, powerful spokespersons. Thirty-two countries were represented, plus three international organizations: the Women's International Democratic Federation, the Women's International League for Peace and Freedom and the International Center for Peace in the Middle East. We had high hopes because the new Soviet president – Gorbachev – had introduced liberalizing reforms of reorganization and openness. This may have come about because the communist state was suffering from economic stagnation.

The "guides" were at the airport along with the official welcoming committee when their guests arrived, they were responsible for making sure the guest's visit was a pleasant and useful one. Flowers and a fruit basket were placed in each room. We had designed a very attractive peace bird pin out of copper, which shone like gold, and was engraved on the back with the title and date of the conference. This bird became internationally popular in the ensuing years. Nowhere, I think, were participants at a conference treated with such personal attention and tender loving care.

I, on the other hand, was not treated with such tender loving care. The opposition press took after me. The more successful I was, the nastier were the attacks, so I took the brickbats as reward rather than punishment. Headings like "Who is Paying for Margarita's Show?", "Improper Meddling," "Someone Must Speak to Her", etc. appeared daily during the conference, and after. A few paragraphs from the "Improper Meddling" of the newspaper *Acropolis* will give the flavor of their objections:

"We beg Mrs. Margaret Papandreou to stop mixing in the political life of the country especially concerning international developments. We say this partly because she is an American, but equally because her role as wife of the Prime Minister gives her no right to express an opinion, certainly not publicly, on international political questions.

"It was unconscionable for her to meddle in the 'Star Wars' program and deride President Reagan, who insists on strengthening this defense system. She has no right to represent Greek women on international issues. Let her turn her attention to humanitarian and philanthropic actions.

"It is irritating to see this foreign lady express opinions affected by the Marxist ideas of her husband and which are the antithesis of the opinions of those people who love the American people and are grateful for help during the civil war that thwarted the communists. But, of course, how could Mrs. Margaret understand this when her husband was absent from Greece during that struggle?"

Although the emphasis in this article was on my "sticking my nose into international affairs," the underlying mentality was Victorian and sexist, demanding a rigid sexual division of roles. These were opinions expressed by the opposition, but probably at least one half of the PASOK males in Parliament believed in the separation of male and female spheres. Silently, or to friends, they were also saying "she should get the hell out of our political nest." I should adhere to my "domestic" role, including humanitarian and charitable works. There was no way I could convince them that I, as head of an independent organization that received no money from the government or any political party, could play a role in the affairs of the country and the world. I am not unaware that an organization asking for contributions whose president is the wife of the P.M. is in a particularly favorable position. This derived power, undefined and elusive, causes many problems. With my behavior I was again trying to make the crucial point that the wife of the chief executive has the right to independent political activity outside her traditional responsibilities as First Lady.

The Assembly was a great success. The proposal that we use the Oxford Research Group's book on nuclear decision making was approved and was the guide for working out a plan of action. The Soviet and American women reached out to each other; the barriers were melting. The workshops came up with solid suggestions for action. I should have been in a happy mood. I was not. Although I kept on with my busy schedule, including the November 17th Polytechnic march commemorating the student uprising in 1973 against the junta dictatorship, I carried a rock in my stomach. My public life was going well, despite criticism; my private life was full of thorns.

On December 4th Andreas was travelling to London for an EEC meeting of heads of government. I wanted to see our son Andrikos in Oxford and suggested I go on ahead, spend a few days with him, then bring him down to London to spend time with his father. At the time I mentioned it, Andreas liked the idea, adding Sophia to the list.

I arrived in London on the third of the month and was met by Andrikos who had come from Oxford University to spend that night where I was staying in the apartment of an EGE friend of mine, Aleka, in order to meet the Prime Minister and Sophia the next day at the Embassy reception. I phoned him the following afternoon when the plane landed, looking forward with great excitement to relaxing with family and friends, something I sorely needed, in order to make arrangements for dinner that night.

My husband stunned me by saying we would not be having dinner together. I thought I hadn't understood correctly. I asked him to say it again. He simply said we had not agreed to that. I argued we had not only agreed to that, but we had agreed that his spare time from the meetings would be spent with the family. He claimed he did not remember any such thing.

I was certainly not in the mood when I arrived at the Embassy to mix with the crowd and carry on smiling small talk. I urged Aleka to make an excuse and ask the wife of the Ambassador if I could lie down in an upstairs bedroom until Andreas came. Aleka left me in the bedroom saying she would survey the situation and inform me when Andreas came. An hour after the reception was scheduled to start, she tripped into my room looking rattled and distressed, and blurted out, "He came – with her!"

"With her!" I shouted. "What do you mean 'with her'?"

"Well, maybe it was with others, perhaps from the airline, but she was walking beside him when he walked in."

"Then he's completely out of his mind."

"The Ambassador's wife looked embarrassed. It's clear she's putting a few pieces together – you're not coming down, for instance."

"My not coming down…no, I won't come down." My mouth felt sandy, and I was perspiring, symptoms of acute distress.

"Margarita, I'm so sorry, and furious, and I hate him for what he's doing. But you have a right to be down there, and everyone is waiting for you."

"They'll have to wait in hell. I won't come down until that creature leaves."

I wasn't sure what I was going to do next. I hesitated, then, "Please tell the children to meet me at Andreas's suite in Grosvenor House after the reception. And Angela if she's free. And Mihalis. And arrange transportation for them. I'm leaving for the hotel. We can take a cab." We left.

After waiting for a while at Grosvenor House to see if "their daddy" would appear for the much anticipated dinner, Sophia and Andrikos, whom I always think of as "the children" although they were in their early 30s, suggested with their usual tact and understanding that we order sandwiches and a bottle of wine, and put on music and watch television. The latter was out, I told them. I needed a bottle of scotch rather than wine, but the suggestion for food was acceptable. Everyone tried to cope with the situation in a way to trivialize it without ever mentioning what "it" was. Humor became the palliative. Andrikos performed burlesque exaggerations of people he had seen at the reception. Sophia moved closer to me in a gesture of compassion and solidarity.

I was storing up my rage for a confrontation as soon as Andreas walked through the door. He never arrived. He came into the suite when I was at breakfast, took a clean shirt from the bedroom and told me to prepare for our departure for Athens. We were to fly on the official Prime Minister's plane, with the Prime Minister's official air staff – including, of course, The Hostess. I was already contemplating the ordeal. Andreas and I did not speak to each other in the car, nor in the V.I.P. lounge at the airport. We took our official seats together on the official plane and the official hostess came over to ask if we would like a goddamn official drink before the plane took off. Champagne? Yes, I thought, so I can use the bottle to beat a heavy tattoo on both your skulls. After we were airborne we were served lunch. This time, in contrast to the trip from China, I did not sleep afterwards.

"For Christ's sake, Andreas, she's young enough to be your daughter."

"Yes, isn't that nice," was his cavalier response. That triggered it. I told him I intended to talk to her like a daughter.

"Don't you dare," was his response.

I waited for her to disappear into the forward cabin of the plane, then stood up to follow her. Andreas tried to hold me back, but there was no holding back.

I used her first name. "I'd like to talk to you," I said.

"About what?" This was said with a touch of sarcasm in her voice.

"It is personal, and this is not the place. I want your phone number so we can make an appointment." She dutifully gave it to me, and then asked again, "Can you tell me what this is about?"

"When we get together," I responded.

I walked back to my seat. This brief encounter was a need to take action, any kind, in order to relieve the stress and anger and hurt. This short interchange hardly reduced my anger. In my mind I was formulating the discussion I would have with her, a sort of mother-daughter discussion, not angry, but explaining to her that she would be one of a series of liaisons, and that my husband always returned to the family. At the time I was serious. After a few days, this plan smelled like a scene in a soap opera. And how could I be a mother to a being like her? The scheme was never actuated.

The rest of December went by in a blur. I was in a terrible state of emotional turmoil. Andreas limited his public appearances so he wouldn't have to appear with me, and I tried to dodge those I thought I could legitimately refuse so I wouldn't have to appear with him. When we did go somewhere together, it became a theatrical performance, my public grinning face a facade for the personal agony. Under the headline "Just Between Us – Sincerely" one perceptive journalist wrote in 'Tahidromos', "Margarita seems very worried of late. What can I say? My friends, she has problems…Anyway, just because she's the wife of the prime minister doesn't make her immune to problems."

My sister Evelyn, realizing I was trying to make a decision about the course of my life, took a plane to be with me at Christmas. The day after Christmas we left for the island of Rhodes with two women friends for a three day holiday. This separate vacation was called "Marriage ala America," by the yellow rag, *Eleftheros Typos*. It asked "Why are the Sultan and Margaret passing the Yuletide season separately?" The paper speculated I was furious because Andreas had not given me the political powers I was asking for, and in his government reshuffle he had dropped ministers I favored, and that he was not giving enough positions to members of EGE, and so forth. They missed the point. Or they were scrupulously avoiding to speculate on the real reason.

Shortly after I came back Pierre phoned, and I could barely talk to him. He told me he could arrange to stop over in Athens the second week in February after a trip to Tunisia. I felt like telling him to forget it; I didn't want any men in my life ever, ever, ever again. I offered him a few excuses, then asked him to call me in a week when I would know my schedule better. My voice was flat, my senses were flat, my life was flat and rudderless. I was especially upset because I liked what I was doing in public life. I loved being inside the mainspring of history; I loved the opportunities to work for causes I believed in; I was exhilarated about bringing women's voices, women's values into the halls of power. I passionately desired an active partnership with my husband: me and you against the world. I wanted to operate in a decent fashion in one of the ugliest games in the world – politics. And I was ashamed to be spending so much time and thought on my personal situation, a common place triangle, sex and politics, marital bickering and shouting, adultery, jealousy-general unproductive nastiness.

I wanted this story I'm telling to be different, to be less focused on my unhappiness, on my pain. I wanted something important to come through – about the magic of life, about power, about justice, above all about love and beauty – not all the warts, the pimples, the shoddiness of life. I am telling it in the only way I can, however, by speaking the truth.

Margaret Chant Papandreou as a young student, 1940

A very young Margaret with her sister Evelyn, 1928

Margaret's mother, Hulda Pfund – year 1930

Margarita and Andreas Papandreou – The Newlyweds –
Nevada, USA 1951

Margarita and Andreas Papandreou – The Newlyweds – 1951

The Papandreou Children, George, Sophia, Nikos – 1957

A family portrait of Margarita with her father in law, George Papandreou and the Papandreou children – 1959

The Papandreou children with the Acropolis in the background – 1960

Andreas arriving back in Greece after a trip abroad 1962

Margarita and Andreas Papandreou at the start of the election campaign, Athens – 1964

One happy family – the Papandreou's at their home in
Psychico, Athens – December 1964

Andreas Papandreou (with his family and mother) returns
home after being in prison – December 1967

Andreas and family – the morning after his release from prison – December 1967

Andreas and Margarita share a special moment with their son, George Papandreou

The Papandreou family – 1967

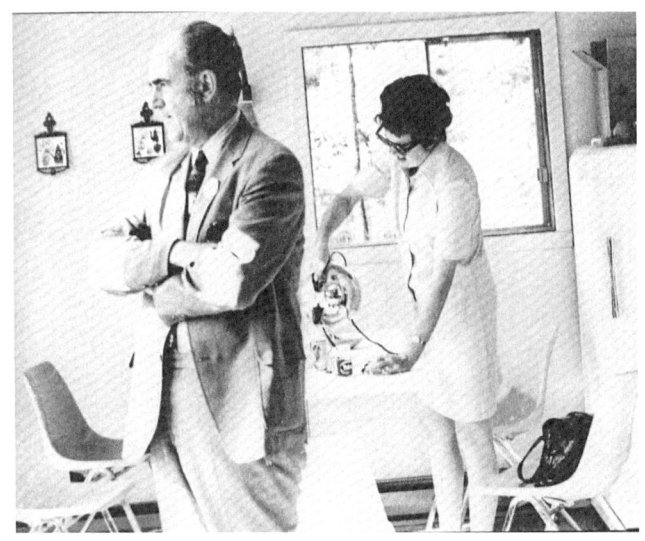

Margarita the housewife – while in exile in Canada, 1972

Margarita and Andreas – Canada, 1973

Margarita attending a demonstration in Greece for EGE – The Women's Organization – 1983

Margarita with members of EGE attending a meeting in 1983

Andreas and Margarita returning back to Athens from a pre-election campaign in Greece in 1981

Andreas and Margarita – Easter celebration – 1982

Margarita at an EGE conference, Greece – December 1982

Standing with Senator Sarbanes and meeting a collegue of his in Washington, USA – 1983

With the EGE committee in Molivos, Mytilini, Greece – July 1983

Papandreou family dinner – Kastri, Athens – 1984

Margarita chairing an EGE meeting, Athens – 1984

Margarita wearing a traditional white dress – 1984

Andreas and Margarita in Toronto, Canada with Prime Minister Trudeau – 1984

Margarita with Ms Marcela Feraz de Cuellar and Nancy Reagan at the First Ladies Conference at the UN in New York on drug abuse – October 1985

Margarita at First Ladies Conference – 1985

Official visit to Egypt with Andreas Papandreou and President Mubarak – 1985

Party for children with special needs hosted by Andreas and Margarita at their home in Kastri, Athens – June 1985

Margarita with Valentina Tereshkova (Russian Astronaut)

Margarita with Stanley Sheinbaum an American Peace & Human Rights Activist and Greek Actress, Melina Mercouri

Margarita in her office at home in Kastri, Athens – 1985

Visit to Brazil – Margarita with children

Margarita with President Alfonsin in Argentina

Margarita with Jules Dassin, American Movie Producer

Margarita with Raúl Alfonsin and Melina Mercouri

Margarita in Athens at a "laiki" (people's) market/ for the 1985 elections

A tender moment between Andreas and Margarita Papandreou
– 1985

Margarita in Sweden with Prime Minister Adolf Palme family

Learning to bake bread the Greek way in Larissa

Official visit to China

Official visit to China

Margarita in her garden, Athens

Margarita attending an art show with Melina Mercouri

Margarita attending a concert at the school for deaf-mute children. Argyroupolis, Athens

Margarita speaking at Harvard University invited by the wife of Governer Dukakis (Madeline Albright in the audience)

Margarita being interviewed by Peggy Say for The NBC Morning Show – Athens

Andreas and Margarita sharing an Easter lunch in the country side

Margarita speaking in Geneva – Peace Talks – January 1986

Group photo with Margarita and John Kenneth Galbraith

Family summer holiday – Limnos, Greece – 1986

A visit to the Greek Embassy in Washington, USA

Enjoying a buffet in Syria

Speaking at an EGE event

Andreas and Margarita Papandreou attending an event in
Salonica – 1986

On an official visit to India 1986 with Prime Minister Rajiv Gandhi and Sonia Gandhi

Christmas card with two grandchildren, Athens – 1987

Margarita at an EGE dinner function

Margarita having tea with Raisa Gorbachev in Moscow – June 1987

Plenary Session with Raisa Gorbachev – June 1987

With Valentna Tereshkova – Soviet astronaut on her visit to Athens – 1987

Attending the South Bend Special Olympics

Andreas Papandreou – the Prime Minister of Greece – 1987

Margarita and Andreas at the Euro Basketball Championships

Margarita playing basketball with her grandchildren

Visit to Brazil – Bank of Women's Association – 1987

A family get together – 1988

Speaking at the United Nations on Peace, New York – 1987

Peace Boat with Coretta Scott King, wife of Martin Luther King

Rescue practice session on the Peace Boat

Speaking at the Carter Centre, Atlanta Georgia

With women of Australia working on anti-nuclear and conflict resolution issues, May 1988

Cutting the New Year's cake with organization AWOG – American Women of Greece 1989

Having a discussion with John Brademas – President of the University of New York

Easter visit to the army barracks in Greece – April 1988

Talking with Shevardnadze (Foreign Minister from the Gorbachev Government) in Moscow – June 1988

Meeting with Shevardnadze (Foreign Minister from the Gorbachev Government) in Moscow – June 1988

Meeting with the Bulgarian President, Mr Zoubkov 1988

Speaking at the Sane-Freeze Congress, Atlanta, Georgia – 1988

Summit – Soviet and American citizens attend a peace concert in Moscow – 1988

USA visit with Jerry Lewis – Republican member of Congress

Hosting a dinner for women diplomats in Athens

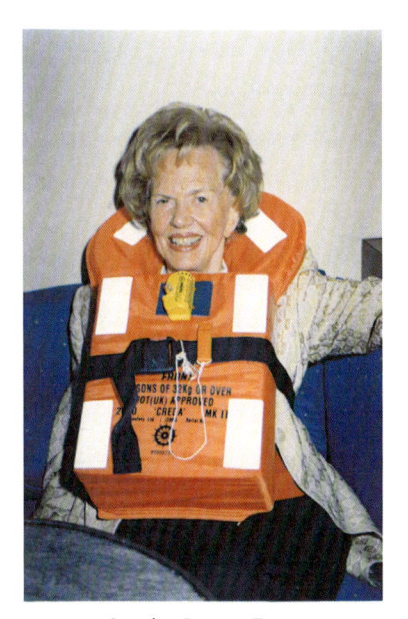

On the Peace Boat

Margarita's sisters and mother, Hulda Pfund, USA

Margarita Papandreou attending a meeting in Salonica, Greece

Chapter Fifteen

Beginning of a New Year

(Diary entry) – *January 4th, 1987, Kastri*
I have graduated from diary writing to diary dictating. I received a small, hand size tape recorder as a gift for Christmas. My thoughts and feelings will now be transmitted into a machine. Now I hear my voice, analyzing events from a variety of perspectives. These fragments will help me someday understand better who I am and what meaning these events had in my life.

Yesterday Andreas and I had our first discussion after the incident in London. We didn't talk about London. We talked of a way of making it possible to come back together. But the way Andreas wanted was avoidance, not of confronting the situation. Is there something wrong with me? I continue to make compromises, to excuse him, to try to adjust, to try to forget, overlook, to be indifferent, to be cold. The shock and the pain from his first philandering which goes back many years was so overwhelming and devastating that I trembled and my legs wouldn't hold me up. I don't have these symptoms anymore. I am more sanguine. Isn't that a sad commentary on what happens to your soul so you no longer feel so devastated with subsequent affairs? Maybe it's age. Or a hardening. In the process you lose respect for yourself, and for the perpetrator.

In any case, we agreed to get together soon with Kostas to discuss a "transition period" – that was Andreas's expression

– to create the atmosphere which would keep us from making decisions in the midst of emotional turmoil. As best as I could understand it, we might find ourselves on the road to divorce because we were not seeing each other, or because public speculation might force a decision before either of us was ready. I wonder, after this calming- down period, would we then make a cold and rational decision about a divorce instead of an emotional one? Maybe a slow unraveling might be better and easier. Most probably a slow unraveling started a long time ago.

Three weeks later the meeting took place with the two of us and Kostas. When I entered his office space, Andreas looked uneasy, as did Kostas. The two were eyeing me as if I were an extraterrestrial, unsure if I would bite or produce unfamiliar noises. We blubbered for a while with small talk. Kostas, as moderator or counselor, didn't seem to know in what direction to go. I wondered what was going on in Andreas's mind. Is he saying to himself "I wish I could get rid of this whole issue – whatever I do will be difficult? I would like to live in a different fashion and not have to confront Margarita with this problem?" Perhaps he was internally repeating the words of the country song "please release me, let me go, for I don't love you anymore." One of the reasons I like country music so much is because the words are always expressive and wise on the problems in life.

He started talking about our life together. I said I wasn't interested in getting into the past. I may have made a strategic error here, because talking about the past could have been positive. Memories were not something to be divided between us if we separated, and, in any case, I was eager to get to the present.

Finally we came around to this big balloon idea of a "transition period," and agreed to set up the rules. In the course of the transition period I wanted sessions with the three of us together about our relationship. In responding to my proposal about sessions together, Andreas indicated that he didn't like putting our emotional, intimate world on the table and examining it. We would both become defense attorneys for ourselves. True to a certain degree, but in doing so we might gain knowledge and understanding of each other, or of ourselves as a couple. I told him, "I am interested in learning how you see your private life now that you are a powerful public figure." He gave me a bewildered look.

Then he told me it was difficult for him to sleep in the ranch house – noises, field mice. He hinted he wanted to come back to the Big House, that was, I thought, a positive statement. A hairline of hope streaked through the center of my body. His face appeared to have mellowed. I was doing it again, searching for pinpoints of light. During all of this discussion, I said nothing about The Hostess, only that I was embarrassed by his behavior in London, and by my behavior in the airplane on the return trip, thinking all the time that the two behaviors, or misbehaviors, were hardly equal. This was the only reference to the "event," although the "transition period" began to appear to mean a shedding of the problem, the extra-marital affair, and a slow return to B.H. (Before Hostess) era.

In the end, there were no rules, and no sessions, simply a slow warming up of the relationship. We started seeing each other more and attended an occasional function together. He hinted he wanted to come back to the Big House, or at least he wanted to get away from his ranch house.

One day, during this time, I had lunch with Karolos Papoulias, the Minister of Foreign Affairs. After all the public attacks, I wanted to make sure I was not overreaching my rights as an NGO head, or at least not doing anything in conflict with my role as First Lady of Greece. I complained that every move I make, whether it is going to Syria, holding a peace conference, helping Peggy Say get a visa, or whatever, was criticized as improper behavior. I remember reading once about a British man who had the perspicacity to comment that, "There is no right way for a woman with power to act. People don't take her seriously and many women overcompensate by being more blokey than the blokes." Despite my brusque rejection of the criticism thrown at me, I was sensitive to Greek attitudes and standards, if not the political opposition's standards. I deliberately overstepped the margins of tradition as the only way women can effect change, but I don't want to go over the cliff. That will limit my own effectiveness. Karolos assured me I was acting properly. But then I was the wife of the prime minister, and also a strong supporter of Karolos, therefore a factor in his maintaining his post. I don't think he would risk being honest with me (am I becoming cynical?). When one is in political power, one has to divide friends into two files, the true friend and the flattery self-interested friend.

We also discussed the missing Greek Cypriots in Turkey, the "unknowns" who disappeared with the Turkish invasion of Cyprus. I suggested we either work with the M.I.A. (Missing in Action Committee) in the United States which is concerned about the missing soldiers of the Vietnam War, or we call them "hostages," to bring more attention to a situation which was being neglected by the diplomatic community and the international press. Greece and Turkey are historical enemies, but my anger was not based on the four hundred years of Turkish occupation, although I understand Greek feelings. It sprang from the blatant violation of human rights.

Karolos was contemplating a trip to African countries and felt I could be part of the delegation. I might also visit Cuba, since we were opening up an Embassy there. Vilma Espen, president of the Cuban Women's Union, had urged me to come. The trip would include Nicaragua where in the early stages of the Nicaraguan revolution, women participated actively in political organizing and decision-making. This participatory process was being eroded because of the increased involvement by the people in defense preparations in anticipation of a U.S. attack. The U.S. was defeating the development of democratic institutions by its support of the contras, by its desire to keep the country under control and within the capitalist camp. My native country since the Second World War had become an empire. And that required what in the past would have been called colonial control, or more recently economic control. Whatever you want to call it – it was control.

WMS received a response to our request for an appointment with Reagan from Roxanne Ridgeway, right hand woman to Schultz at the State Department on NATO and East-West issues. Politely she told us Reagan was very involved and could not see us now. She proposed Kenneth Adelman, the head of the Arms Control and Disarmament Agency. Scilla McClean, our expert on nuclear weapons and nuclear decision making felt this belittled our efforts, since the Arms Control Agency was low on the totem pole. Mae Britt Theorin, Sweden's Ambassador of Disarmament, told me we were being directed to the most reactionary and uncooperative member of the agency. The next best to Reagan would be Schultz. Others were more approachable, but given the power our network represents, she said, we should seek higher decision-making officials.

(Diary entry) – *January 5, 1987, Kastri*

So many interesting possibilities opening up! Strangely enough, I seem not to care what Andreas does. I don't care if he has one, ten or a hundred girlfriends! I don't care whether he wants to risk his political career by making an ass of himself. I want to move ahead and do the things I think are important. I need a love relationship in my life, but a positive one, not one that poisons my soul. Right now I have an overwhelming urge to move on – to be creative, to enjoy the work I do in the days I have, the years I have, to realize the dreams I have in life.

My mood has improved. The talk with Andreas and Kostas made me feel better, even though we came to no significant conclusion. It has cleared my brain to a degree, and I am better able to listen to my feelings and to my intellect. I am thinking more deeply about my life, about my relationship with Andreas. I am examining alternatives.

Yesterday when my son George walked into my study to say hello, a part of me walked in. He will continue when I no longer can. And so will the other children. I hugged the future, and I felt my body exploding with maternal warmth and pride.

This afternoon I talked with Scilla and then with Karen. We decided that our organization should pressure for a congressional resolution – a nuclear test ban. The U.S.S. R., which had unilaterally declared a test ban, would be obliged to start testing again if the U.S. did not respond in kind. They suggested I phone Claudine Schneider and Pat Schroeder to request such a resolution. I agreed to do this. We would ask our members all over the world to pressure the U.S. Congress and President Reagan.

On January 12th, I received a telegram from our embassy in Brazil. "The Banco de Brazil Women Worker's Association which comprises 50,000 women workers invites you for the Association's First Directory on January 29, 1987, and also for a dinner in celebration of the event. If you are unable to come for economic reasons" (Yes, I don't have that kind of money) – "there is a chance airline tickets and lodging can be arranged. A formal invitation has already been sent." This was signed by FoFo Zakarda, our press attaché in Brazilia. Jacqueline Pitanguy, who is president of the National Council for Women's Rights, also wrote: "Brazil's National Council for Women's Rights is pleased you may be coming to Brazil and will be honored to have you give a lecture to us on the work of the Women's Union of Greece." These invitations were a godsend. The trip would be fatiguing but it was a chance to leave my stress behind. I know, of course, that anxieties travel as companions on a trip but I also felt that a little time apart would give both Andreas and me the opportunity to remember how much we both need each other.

That night was EGE's annual cake cutting, a tradition to bring in the new year with praise for the work of the past and high hopes for success in the future. Slices of cake are cut in honor of women of the world, for peace, the president of the organization, the board, heads of committees, etc. I made a brief political statement. Afterwards I met Melina and her devoted friend Zika for a theatrical performance at Athens

College and dinner. Melina and I had become good friends. I liked her passion for life, and even her theatrical, often melodramatic, ways. She liked my calm and direct approach to life. I reminded her, she said, of Jules, her husband, and she called us the "two Amerikani" in her life.

(Diary Entry) – *January 22nd 1987, Kastri*

Andreas told Kostas he would move over soon to the Big House. We readied the room, even re-painted it, bought a new bed, new rug. It has become a pleasant room. Not terribly roomy, but adequate. Clean. I learned he went up to look at it. We keep fresh flowers in there. Everyone is trying to lure him back with concern and kindness. Everyone from my daughter to the domestic help, to the gardener! They live the situation, and yearn for a normalization of family life. Aliki said, "why don't you put a card in there 'Welcome to your room!'" "Does that mend a marital rift?" I asked. I wonder if it is the superficial things that are in the end significant. I have done those things in the past, and I would do them again if there was the slightest reciprocal tenderness to my gestures of affection.

When I did these things – actually buying six roses to put in his room – and he doesn't react positively in some way, it is demeaning to me. I lose my sense of dignity, of self. I had doubts about having him back in the house, rejection, desire, despair, anger, then hope. These scrambled emotions made me feel like a schizophrenic. I knew it was impossible for Andreas to maintain a long relationship with a woman, any woman. He is a "serial man." He wants to be continually falling in love, to experience the erotic, romantic stage. For men who have idealized women, or have doubts about their sexual capacities, who connect their masculinity with sexual progress, new women are apparently important. Once the affair burns out, the search will begin for the next one.

The next day I met with the EGE chapter on the island of Evia. In my meetings with them and with other chapters of EGE, I concluded that our problems stem largely from the problems of PASOK. Our close ties with PASOK members, as girlfriends, wives, aunts, sisters, what have you, has created a tight link which can't easily be broken. When PASOK had internal problems, we had internal problems. When there was a split in PASOK, there was a split in EGE. Much as we have tried to keep our organization non-partisan, to cut across party lines, focusing on the commonalities among women, we have found it difficult in practice. Here is a lesson for women's organizations, to stay away from party affiliations. I tried to put matters in the proper context, to help the members from Evia see they were focusing on men and not on women. I was a hell of a person to do this.

A few days after trying to sort out EGE problems I was on my way to Rio and a full program of speeches and contacts. From the time of my acceptance of the "transition period" until I left for Rio not much had transitioned I had seen Andreas twice, once for lunch in his ranch house with a mutual friend, Leon Karapaniotis, the editor of a newspaper; and second, a quick short lunch on the day of my departure to Brazil, January 26th. In the meantime I conducted business for WMS, organized events with local EGE chapters all over Greece, went to the theater, receptions, movies, participated in several demonstrations, invited women for "issue-lunches" in Kastri. I read to my grandchildren. I read to them many times the book *The Dancing Granny*, about a frenetic grandmother who loved to dance during her activities – washing dishes, hanging up clothes, visiting sick relatives, attending meetings, dressing, shopping. She never stopped. She looked and felt like me. She was all over the place. I was sure people were asking the question, "What makes Maggie run?"

After my return from Brazil I confronted many invitations that had piled up on my desk, and I decided to accept one to Amsterdam for International Women's Day and others from the States which would necessitate a month of travel. Prior to my departure for this extended journey on March 5th, Andreas and I had lunch together once, this time at "my" house. Andreas had returned from Davos, the high-level economic club for European leaders, the same meeting he disappeared from a year ago. He wanted to tell me about his discussions, and his presentation there. He argued for a more rapidly growing Eastern Mediterranean to benefit not only the member countries, but as a thriving region between the Atlantic and Pacific which would facilitate those areas as well. It would constitute, he said, an enlightened investment in the future; the major threat to inhibit the full flowering of this potential was what plagued Europe at the end of the Second World War – lack of capital for investment.

It sounded like he was conjuring up a picture of profit for businessmen. Investment for these birds means profit. I don't deny that capital is needed, in democratic socialist regimes too, but the purpose is to build a humane society for the benefit of its people, not just for a few money-bags. He could have said that partnership and cooperation within and between regions would help reduce the dramatic gaps in income, reduce pressures for migration, stem the rising tide of unemployment and poverty. Fairness must be a natural concomitant of development.

I confronted him with some of my own thinking, and with a certain amount of concern that something may have happened to his progressive philosophy. He smiled at me and then said, "You think Davos is the place to advance socialist views?"

"Well, at least it would be unique, so why not?"

"Don't worry; I'm the same person you always knew." I was warmed by this statement and felt it had some additional meaning beyond a defense of his progressive views. The few meetings between the two of us over these months, however, were low-key, the conversation tip-toeing through an atmosphere clouded with tension, hostility, resentment and guilt (his, not mine). We were like two war-weary, battle-scarred soldiers, POWs, chained together, making our way through a jungle where mines threatened our lives with each step, moving gingerly toward an unknown destination.

At the airport in Athens departing for New York, I ran into the Soviet Ambassador to Greece seeing off a high Soviet official. The Ambassador greeted me warmly and introduced me to members of his entourage. Before I had a chance to ask, he said he had looked into the issue of WMS's request for a meeting with Gorbachev and expected to get an answer "within the next few days." I had spoken to him earlier in the week by phone.

My other request to the Ambassador had to do with two refuseniks. One was Alex Lerner, a Russian scientist supported by the Jewish and scientific community of the States; the other the son of a Russian woman and Greek man now living in the U.S. He said to me, "Yes, yes. I'm looking into the question of the right to emigrate for the two names you gave me. "If it were me," he said, almost out of the corner of his mouth, "I would give exit permission to all of them." I couldn't tell whether he meant "good riddance," or "they shouldn't have been mistreated in the first place."

Also in the VIP lounge was Christos Maheritsos, diplomatic advisor to Andreas and a member of the secretariat of the Initiative of the Six. I didn't know if he knew about my situation with Andreas. The occasional innuendos in the press, including the notion that the government may fall as a result of the rose scandal, were not taken seriously by the political world. Melina once told me that if the government does fall from power "you will see how the new government and international officials will ignore you, and how many people will turn their backs on you." I wondered at the time if this was simply sage advice from a woman who had grown up in Greek politics, or whether it had meaning in our personal relationship, whether she was talking about my falling from power and her own reaction. I banished the thought from my mind.

Maharitsos had recently been in Argentina and told me many people asked about me and sent their regards, including Rolf Alfonsin. This soothed my sore soul. It reminded me of a special trip in the past with our Minister of Foreign Affairs to attend the inauguration of Alfonsin as a gesture of support by the Greek people for the return of democracy in that country. That was one of my duties as First Lady of Greece. At that time I met Vice-president George Bush. All of the delegations were in the Parliament building, waiting to be taken to their seats for the ceremony. Most of us had introduced ourselves to the people standing near us. Suddenly Bush walked in and promptly proceeded to move around and introduce himself. It was an impressive performance. I heard the Star Spangled Banner in the background.

When he came to me, I reminded him that that he had met Andreas in Moscow at the funeral of Brezhnev. He was very cordial and asked if I had met his wife Barbara. I told him no, and he responded by telling me that she would be at several of the functions, and he hoped I would have a chance to talk to her.

After the inauguration in parliament, we were all sent to another building where everyone had the chance to shake hands with Alfonsin and several cabinet members. Drinks were supplied, the waiting was long, and more drinks were supplied. At some point I saw the back of George Bush standing a few yards away talking to a cluster of men. Having by then a heightened inebriated courage, I walked over, tapped him on the back and asked "Where is your wife?" The tapped man turned around in bewilderment and said, "She is in Norway." I had the wrong guy! I struggled to find a speedy reply to undo this faux pas, excluding saying he looked like Mr. Bush, which might have been offensive to him. Instead I said, "Oh, fine, yes, I see, well, my husband isn't here either." This befuddled the Norwegian even further, and I decided not to stuff my foot deeper into my mouth by uttering more nonsense. I did the best I could by fading away mumbling soft, incomprehensible sounds. I often wondered how many chuckles this fellow got out of the incident, you know, "this woman comes up to me, and she starts this proposition…" After recovering from my blunder, I managed to rasp out a chuckle myself.

For the record, I did meet Barbara Bush the next day at a women's reception in the old Peron mansion. She was in good humor, and I almost told her about my gaffe. Then I thought,

Maggie, let well enough alone. I can't say I was a sensation on this mission. With my Greek colleagues, however, after my blunder, I was a hit. I became the comedian, the court jester. Everything I did after that was a source of great revelry, the comic relief in an often tiresome celebration. I could see the headlines: "First Lady Morphs into Clown." It gave me assurance I would not be bereft of a career.

Maheritsas and I talked about my recent trip to Brazil at the invitation of the Banco de Brazil Women's Worker's Association. I told him we could develop a flourishing tourist trade with the Brazilian people. Not the vast impoverished population, of course, although I wished these desperate souls could come. I had a scheme. Wealthy Brazilians could be induced to spend vacations in Greece by luring them with an exciting program which would meet their tastes. Then we would put a tariff on their trips to pay for disadvantaged Brazilians to visit Greece. Christos looked at me as if I had lost my marbles.

I put on my feminist hat and told him Women Parliamentarians for Peace were meeting in Mexico the summer of 1987, and a woman parliamentary deputy and EGE member, wanted to go but our president of parliament, told her he had no funds to support her trip. "How," I asked, "can we carry on a foreign policy and not support activities like this, which in turn support the Initiative of the Six?" He agreed with me and said he would arrange it. Good boy!

The airport auditory system announced the departure of my plane. I said good-bye to Maheritsas and boarded the plane. I changed planes in Rome.

"Are you alone?" The Alitalia agent asked.

"Yes, quite alone."

I watched him to see if he caught the underlying message, which was quite silly since he knew nothing about my personal life, or what was going on in my head. What did probably surprise him was that the wife of a prime minister was travelling alone. I am an "economical" First Lady- no security, no secretaries, no hairdressers. The advantage for me was no limitation on my freedom, nor on my right to act and breathe like an ordinary human being. Some would say this was foolish, for two different reasons. I make myself an easy target for kidnapping, harassment, even an assassination – although I think the latter would serve no major political purpose. The second reason is a more cynical one. Since I have this position, why not take advantage of the perks? It's simple. I don't regard strong-bodied, gun-toting men, shouting and pushing the public out of the way, as a perk. The "perk" that I accepted and which I felt was not wrong was to be able to use whatever derived power I had for the human good.

The Alitalia agent settled me into a VIP room where the Greek Ambassador was waiting to keep me company during my two hours between planes. He was Christos Stremmenos, professor in an Italian university, resistance fighter in the Pan-Hellenic Liberation Movement, the organization Andreas founded during the dictatorship to fight for the overthrow of the junta and the restoration of democracy. We reminisced a bit on that period of time in our lives. PAK solidified friendships as we fought for a common cause. A liberation movement is the most idealistic of struggles. The cause is clear and just, and opportunists are virtually non-existent since there is no real power to divide and no certainty of goals being achieved. Christos was "our man in Rome" during the dictatorship and had helped set up a radio station – Radio Free Greece – in order to broadcast to the Greek people. Such an installation on Italian soil was illegal. When the station was discovered by the authorities shortly after its first broadcast, Christos disassembled the transmitter and mounted it on a boat to get closer to the shores of Greece, out of reach of the Italian polizia. The only ones who heard Andreas's messages, analyses and exhortations were, I'm afraid, those of us present when he recorded them in Canada, while we were living in exile. It was a valiant effort, defeated primarily by lack of technical expertise and money.

Christos reviewed quickly the current political crisis in Italy. He knew I would be interested to hear Bernard Craxi had resigned as head of the Socialist Party in Italy, the analogous party to PASOK. Christos believed Craxi was jealous of Andreas, perhaps because Andreas led one of the largest socialist parties in Europe (43 percent in the 1985 elections compared to the Italian Socialist Party's 10 percent). Frankly, I think feelings between leaders are a question of chemistry, as in any personal relationship. People can actually develop a rapport with those whose political philosophy they do not agree with. This was the case with Andreas and Margaret Thatcher, which astounded me and displeased me as well, not because of her known flirtations with male leaders, but because of her political beliefs and stands.

We discussed the efforts being made in Evretennia, an area in northwestern Greece, to increase winter tourism, which has been a dream of Christos's for years for his boyhood region. He told me Tasia Cannelopoulos was the best nomarch (a regional administrative officer appointed by the government) in Greece. Tasia was a member of the Women's Union of Greece, and we had proposed her for the position. It made me feel good to hear about successful women who are members of EGE. She had moved ahead on the infra-structure for cross-country skiing and other winter sports in the most fabulously beautiful mountain region in Greece. I campaigned there when PASOK was in the opposition, around 1979. I remember that we kept warm with the many glasses of tsipoura (Greek vodka) offered by the villagers. We became red-cheeked from the frigid mountain air and red-nosed from the tsipouro.

(Diary Entry) *March 12th, 1987, Rome flight to New York – writing in my notebook*

I am 30,000 miles up, going back home, back to my native land, for a speaking tour on disarmament and peace, on women's role in the international arena, on the connection of economic development with the arms race, and as an ambassador of goodwill for my adopted country. This latter role is self-assigned but is nonetheless the most expected of all first ladies.

Although it hasn't been too long since I visited the states, I have the need to touch base again. It's a yearning that overwhelms me at times, now probably more than ever, to smell popcorn, the sweet odor of chewing gum, to eat a hotdog, to hear my language, the sound of country music, to throw a baseball, to walk into my sister's kitchen. Somewhere on the trip I will walk past my childhood home in Elmhurst, trying to heal the wound still open from the loss of my mother.

I will see her there relaxing on our white painted wooden front porch, talking quietly with a neighbor on a heat-hushed summer evening, the monotonous hum of cicadas joining the lazy calm. Generally she was doing something with her hands: knitting, embroidering, sewing patches on our clothes, peeling potatoes. The last rays of the sun would be streaking through the generous branches of an old oak tree at the corner of the house. Birds would be skirting around making their final noises before it got too dark. I recall a young Margaret in her early teens sitting on the steps, blue-jeaned legs hunched up against a skinny body, looking at the stars, and asking to be given a sign that there was a god.

I never got the signal. Instead I ended up with a missionary zeal to take humanity in my hands and reshape it, to shake it from its lethargy and indifference to injustice, and to insist on its responsibility to protect the abused and the helpless. Those evenings, on the porch, I felt a diffuse love – was it for people? For the earth? For nature? At the same time I felt an indignation toward all forms of injustice committed against anyone anywhere in the world.

My values were Christian, without the metaphysical, without the structure of the church to interpret them. They could just as well have been Muslim, or Hebrew, or Buddhist, or Druze because I believe all religions teach love, understanding, caring, respect for life. The world was my church, my temple, my mosque. The forest, the plains, the sea, the landscape. This is what is sacred to me, nature herself. The life force. My spirituality has more to do with generosity, kindness, the joy of helping.

My mission now was to contribute to the gigantic effort to disassemble the war system. To work for peace you have to have faith; you have to believe that miracles can happen, that you can rise above the pessimism, the cynicism, the mass of historical crud that has kept people at each other's throats. I just cannot not act. I owe it to myself and what I believe in. I owe it to my children.

I will close my eyes for a while and think a bit about Pierre, whom I have seen two times since Washington, once in Amsterdam, and once for three hours at the Hellinikon airport at a stopover on his way to Tunisia. That's another perk I like, to be allowed into the international V.I.P. lounge to see a transit guest. Particularly a special transit guest.

A movie is on now as we continue our trek across the Atlantic. I am working under the spot lamp overhead while the rest of the cabin is in darkness. My thoughts go to my family. George, my oldest, is in Australia for a week invited by the Greek community there. He is more idealistic than the average politician, and I wonder if he will survive the dirt, guff and underhandedness of political life. Does one have to be willing to stain one's character in order to serve others – to bamboozle, to be cunning, to be hypocritical? In that case he is out. Andrikos continues his PhD studies at Oxford, working with Amartya Sen, a sensational economist and wonderful human being. Sophia is eager to have a second child while doing research at the Mediterranean Research Center, and trying also to assist her father politically. She will give a speech to the Women's Union of Greece chapter in Nemea, in the Peloponnesus, this Saturday. That helps her mother, but indirectly her father, because women's votes are critical. This is her maiden public speech, and I am eager to hear how it came out. Nikos is in the Greek army after getting his PhD in economics at Princeton. This coming Monday he will also be helping his mother by speaking at an EGE rally commemorating International Women's Day. Topic: "Has Economic Development helped Equality between Men and Women?" He is an accomplished speaker, so I have no worries there.

Then there are the grandchildren, daughters-in-law and pater familias. About the latter I have no comment. My cares are floating somewhere down below under the bed of clouds which is covering our approach to New York. Any lumps in my throat or rocks in my stomach were dissolved during the cinema, a movie called "Just Between Friends," a corny, sweetish, mawkish story of a friendship between two women, Mary Tyler Moore and Christine Lahti. Because I am an inveterate sentimentalist, I liked it. And it was a chance for me to allow tears to fall in the opaque darkness of the cabin. Now is time to tuck my notebook of cross-Atlantic thoughts into my carry-on bag and get ready for the landing.

The plane settled down in Kennedy airport in the middle of a gloomy, cold and windy afternoon. My taxi driver was an Egyptian so we had much to talk about as Mediterranean neighbors. He was surprised I spoke English so well. I made it a practice not to mention that I was the wife of the Prime Minister. If the question came up as to why I, an American, was living in Greece, I simply said, "married to a Greek."

This time I escaped having members of the Greek Consulate in New York meeting me at the airport. That night I wanted only to see my friend Marjorie for dinner to clue her in on my private despair, and to unwind before jet-lag hit. I picked up a New York Times to begin the re-Americanization of Maggie, a process I went through on each trip to the States.

The news was full of the suicide deaths of four teenagers who had taken their lives in an apparent suicide pact, using the carbon monoxide gas from a car exhaust in a closed garage. Four children: two girls, sisters, and two boys. I can't imagine what could have caused such despair, such a sense of desperation, such depression- at that glorious age! Youth is an exciting adventure; it is a huge canvas to paint on in peppermint colors in sweeping, wild, broad brush swashes. It is the age where one challenges religion, where one begins to disbelieve, and death is a mysterious, frightening event to contemplate, but it is a distant fear. How four kids, at the same time, take their lives, adds a new element to an act of suicide.

I can't believe each death resulted from the same cause and with the same degree of conviction. The paper had many other stories of violence in it, with women frequently the victims. Amidst the familiar smells and sounds of the city, I sensed an aura of danger. I was "home."

Chapter Sixteen

A Rendezvous in New York

The next day I met Pierre in the hotel lobby where I was staying. We had planned to go to a movie. When I came down to the lobby he grabbed my arm and said "Hurry, the movie 'Salvador' starts at 4:20. "We dashed to the movie house nearby, only to see the title on the marquee was "Kangaroo." The film had moved. We returned to the lobby of the hotel and fingered down the list of movies. "Room with a View"? "No, I've seen it," he replied. "Crocodile Dundee?" he asked. "Great film but I've seen it," I replied. "Marlene," a film about her life that neither of us had seen, had already started but was only six blocks away. The icy wind spiking my face like slivers of glass and the air burning my tongue reminded me of early mornings when I plied my way across the University of Minnesota campus for my job of opening up the cafeteria cash register at the Student Union. Now, after two blocks I was shivering from the cold. Obviously, my blood had been thinned by years of living in a Mediterranean climate. We came upon parked horse carriages.

"Shall we take a carriage?" Pierre asked.

"That's crazy," I said. "One takes carriages not for transportation but for romance or for leisurely gawking."

"But it will get us there."

"I can run faster than the horse," was my response. Then I spotted blankets in the carriage and decided the need for warmth was more urgent than speed. The carriage started off at a reasonable trot. After a block, the horse seemed to sag, and the driver didn't push him on. Soon we were trailing the pedestrians. In relative comfort, however.

Marlene Dietrich came through as a pragmatic, unsentimental, unromantic, down-to-earth kind of woman. In her very German way she was a hard worker and a superb technician. She didn't think about the past; she never visited her childhood homes on her trips back to Germany after the war. (Take note, Maggie – don't let sentiment drag you down...) When some of her compatriots booed her because she fled Nazi Germany and helped the Americans, she took it in stride and said simply, "That's the way a few people feel." I had all this image in my mind while watching the movie. I was watching the real Marlene, not the scripted Marlene. Toward the end, in reciting a poem with Maximillian Schell, a poem apparently her mother liked, she broke down and cried. I was glad for that. Although I liked her no-nonsense approach to life, I couldn't relate to her until that moment.

Pierre held my hand at times during the movie. Once he leaned over and kissed me on the temple. Then he said, "More popcorn?" These things warmed me up much more than the blankets in the carriage. We had become close. I admired what he was doing; he seemed genuinely interested in my activities. I gave few details about Andreas's and my relationship. Despite my growing belief that Andreas was not the same as the man I married, I couldn't pull him down nor destroy his positive public image.

We chose a simple restaurant after the movie to catch up on each other. Since our hotel meeting in Washington, Pierre had made no advances, just hand holding and affectionate kisses. I was sure he considered my response in the hotel a rebuff, and he was waiting for a clearer signal from me. Tonight the question hung in the air, "will he, will she, will this be the night?" Sitting there drinking a choice red wine – I felt that question mark dangling between us like fine blown glass, yellow, lavender, soft blue, sending off sparks of light as the candle flickered on our table. Does Pierre see those delicate colors; does he smell the fragrant anticipation of bodies curled around each other, fingers of love touching the flesh? Or are his colors bold red, black, screeching green, penetrating colors that represent the top of the mountain of sexual release? Whatever the colors, the conversation was straight – forward, somewhat mundane, but nevertheless both of us knew it was foreplay.

Pierre didn't like Marlene, not for what she had done, but for the kind of woman she was.

"Who is your favorite actress?" I asked.

"Hmmm. I don't go to movies much, except when I am in the States. If you're talking about American actresses, I guess I would say Meryl Streep."

"She's a good actress, but I find her rather cold. What about Marilyn Monroe?"

Pierre smiled in his winning way. "I thought you were talking about live actresses. Isn't she the idol of every red-blooded man?"

"That means you, then. You are red-blooded, I presume."

"I am a swash-buckling, dashing, exciting, gorgeous hunk of manhood."

"And I am a retiring, hesitant, skinny, dull-eyed gin-and-tonic fragment of womanhood. "

I better be careful, I thought, or the statement might turn into an exclamation point, shatter into pieces and smash me in the face.

Pierre wanted to see if he could know my program so we could agree on our next rendezvous. I told him I had a full two page typed agenda in my hotel room and would get it to him somehow. Then he wanted to know what I would talk about on my speaking tour.

"I know about your feminism," he said, "but what about your socialism?"

I laughed. I told him about a friend of mine in the States who called me in Athens with a piece of advice for my tour:

"Don't use the word socialism in your speeches." I told her that presented me immediately with a serious problem. The name of the party in power, my husband's party, and the party I supported, was called the Pan-Hellenic Socialist Movement. Should I change the name of the party for American consumption? Then I asked her which word was worse, socialism or feminism? "Maybe you could avoid both," was her dispirited reply. She felt torn because she was a staunch supporter of what we were trying to do in Greece but she was also a loyal friend, and wanted to protect me from attacks. She had forgotten I had grown up in the States and was thoroughly aware of the knee-jerk reactions to these words. Also, Andreas and I had lived the first years of our marriage during the McCarthy period and experienced the fear progressive people had that they would be charged with being communists – and socialists were considered in the same camp. Also, I had enough connections with the women's movement to know about the antagonism to feminism.

"Let me say first, that I think there are a lot of common elements in feminism and socialism. I think you are probably asking me whether I think socialism has a future. I honestly don't know. I did not like what I saw in the eastern European countries I visited, nor in the Soviet Union."

"Yet you consider yourself a socialist."

"Not a socialist in the way it has been practiced in the Eastern European world. I do not support the restrictions on their freedoms, their centralized, controlled economies, and their violation of human rights. I am interested in the fundamental principles of socialism, the organization of society, cooperation and mutual help, partnership of man and woman, equality of opportunity among persons, no subordination of the worker by management. And, very important, I do not accept a free-market economy. Well, "I smiled, "that's quite a list. Isn't it?"

"Is that it?"

"You want to hear more?"

"I'm a good listener."

"Not always." I was teasing him. "Anyway, what I consider is at the heart of true socialism is a democratic government with maximum participation of the citizen in decisions concerning society, and, of course, freedom of expression."

"In my opinion," Pierre said, "socialism never even got started in those countries. In order to build a socialist society you have to overcome the power of capital and the social division of labor. And you don't regulate the lives of people through a party state."

"We seem to be describing the same type of society. What is the answer? And most important, what is the way?" I asked. "Capitalism has taken over the world."

"I tell you, Maggie, I like the socialist ideal – the way you describe it. I perhaps have less faith in the individual than you do. If everything in the economic sector is to be owned and run by the state, and if income is distributed more equitably, where is the incentive for people to work their hardest and their best? Socialism is a managed society, and who will be the managers? What skills and what motivations will they have to develop a profitable enterprise?"

"I believe there are ways of allowing private enterprise into a system without having a totally free market economy. I don't see myself as a reformer of capitalism but rather as someone who wants to replace it with a different system. Then I could work on reforms within that system. You see, I don't like the debris of capitalism: unemployment, homelessness, corruption, destruction of the environment, subordination of women, crime, alienation, huge income differences. Not to mention war."

"I would agree," Pierre said thoughtfully, "that there is a growing failure of capitalism to solve the basic requirements of most people now living in capitalist regimes. About war, well, I believe socialist and communist countries go to war too."

"Now that opens up a new chapter, whether these are aggressive wars or defensive wars." (I was using my experience from our NATO and Schervernaze discussions.) My partner in this discussion was in a good mood and did most of the talking. We talked about the vitality of New York, about whether Cuomo would run for president; I said "no," Pierre said "yes." He described an article he wanted to write for "The Bulletin of Atomic Scientists." I suggested he consider submitting it to Stanley Sheinbaum's "New Perspectives Quarterly" which I considered the best journal on international affairs. I told him also how Stanley had helped get Andreas released from jail under the dictatorship. If Pierre was going to write a good article, I wanted Stanley to have it.

Three hours passed without it ever dawning on me that I was supposed to be jet-lagged. Ten 'o clock in New York was five o'clock the next morning in Athens. Finally, feeling my energy dipping, I suggested we call a halt to the tet-a-tet and head for the hotel. We walked the few blocks in silence, largely because we were concentrating on battling the wind and the cold. I realized also that in my feminine need to dress up for the evening, I had not chosen warm enough clothes, and my heels and sheer stockings did nothing to enhance my sense of well-being. What did enhance my sense of well-being was Pierre and the red wine, in that order. We blew into the lobby of my hotel, and I headed for my key at the reception desk. A message was waiting from my daughter: "Nothing urgent. Just wanted to talk to you." I would have preferred no reminder of family – no reminder of Andreas- at that moment. Pierre stood waiting. Clearly, I was to make the move.

"I have my itinerary upstairs. I'd like to give it to you. Maybe we can look at it together and see where we might collide again." We had already discussed a possibility in San Francisco. Pierre was speaking on NATO and the nuclear threat at a foreign policy meeting in Denver around the time I expected to be in San Francisco, and he thought he could fly over for an evening together.

In the elevator going up he took my hand and squeezed it. For him it was a fait accompli; we would sleep together. Through my head went two lines from Byron:

"A little still she strove, and much repented and whispering, I will ne'er consent – consented."

Less poetically, I was seeing that glass question mark and at the same time wondering what he would look like without clothes. I tried to remember if I had ever made love with a big-boned, heavy-set, tall man. The elevator door opened, and we headed for my room. An older friend of mine, passing her wisdom on to me when I was young, declared that "men are sex machines. Absolutely men are interested in just that one thing." I hadn't made love for so long that I thought I was interested in "just that one thing." The longer I was away from it, however, the more it appeared to me as indecorous, a curiously animal activity causing two ordinary, decent beings to claw and scratch, legs apart, undulating, humping, squealing and groaning.

Despite this image we made love. It was good love, but not sensational. The problem was me. The negative image disappeared, everything felt natural, but apparently I had buried my sexual desires. Abstinence in this case did not make the body more hungry; it had put those instincts on ice-they were in deep freeze. I consoled myself by saying that my body was out of whack from the long plane flight, that I had drunk too much wine, that, well, yes, age might be a factor. Before I had a chance to grieve, or dwell on this development, I fell asleep.

I opened up my eyes the next morning and remained motionless trying to sort out where I was and who was next to me. My first thought was Andreas. When I became aware that the side of my leg was lined up alongside Pierre's body, flesh to flesh, the whole hip to foot caught fire and a pleasant tingling swept over me. Soon his arms came round me, and in the dim, pale early morning light we made love again. My head inside was singing. One thought came to my mind. "God, it's great to feel young again."

Chapter Seventeen

"A Spectacular Woman"

My U.S. speaking tour was a kaleidoscope of airports, suitcases, auditoriums, Pierre, microphones, hotels, radio interviews, discussions with Greek-Americans, press releases, old friends, sore feet, headaches, laughter and Pierre. Several events stand out. In San Francisco, making love again. In Detroit, speaking on Greek National Day in the State House. I was overwhelmed by the welcome of the audience. At New York University I was honored to be on the podium with John Brademas, former congressman and present university president, George Schultz, Secretary of State, and Michal Dukakis, Democratic candidate for president. At the Kennedy School of Government, I was excited by the many women who turned out for my speech and the introduction by Kitty Dukakis.

In Oregon, a young woman student, Sharon Bosserman, who was responsible for inviting me, asked if I would like to meet the president of the University during my visit. I hesitated, having met many unexciting university presidents during Andreas's academic career. I was about to inquire if it was really necessary when she said, "You know, he's a peace advocate. You'll like him."

How could I say no? Sharon scheduled us tentatively for 10:30 to 11:00 in the morning squeezing it between two other of my appointments.

"Do you think we could reschedule this for 3:30 in the afternoon?" I asked. "It's important for me to get a university president connected with the WMS network, so let's allow enough time."

"He usually schedules half-hour appointments."

"Alright, but I don't want to feel pressed by rushing to the interview between appointments." At 3:30 I was there. I walked out of his office at 4:50 and then only reluctantly. It turned out to be a banquet, a feast of ideas and talk. Part of my enjoyment was simply that he listened; he was genuinely interested and supportive of what I was doing. It wasn't all one way, though; I also learned about him.

Paul Olum was his name. His office was simple, almost like a living room with a desk. This was Andreas's style. He liked his office to feel like a home, the desk an integral part of it. Olum sat in a chair in front of the desk which brought an air of informality to the meeting. He had an open, friendly face, neatly trimmed white hair, and the bluest blue eyes I had seen in a long time. Behind the desk was a large window opening to the tree-laden campus. It felt and smelled like the thirteen years of academic life I had as the wife of a professor.

I was comfortable and nostalgic.

"I understand," I said, "that we are brethren that you are working on peace issues also. How did you get into peace work?"

"Well, my concerns about peace go back to the Second World War. I was a graduate student in theoretical physics at Princeton when I was asked to join the Manhattan Project. My role in the Project was to work on a scheme for the separation of uranium. I joined the other theoretical physicist, who ultimately became well known – Dick Feynman. This led both of us to Los Alamos which, as you know, is where we developed the atom bomb."

I gulped on that one. Feeling as I did about atomic and nuclear weapons, those who dropped these bombs were criminals, as were those who conceived and built them.

To catch my breath, I said, "Someday I'd like to understand how a tiny atom can give off that kind of destructive power."

"You know," he smiled, "it isn't just one atom but billions and billions together. I would be glad to give you a simple explanation, the one I give in my speeches to lay persons. Right now I'd rather hear about your efforts in the peace movement."

"My concern about peace goes back also to World War II. It was enhanced by my involvement in the women's movement. I recognized the consequences that militarization has on women's rights. If we don't de-militarize relations among nations, if we don't get rid of the military mentality, the mentality that says conflict can be resolved by power and violence, then we women can never achieve our goals of equality and of a non-violent world. Actually we are out to scuttle the war system, and our organization has made nuclear disarmament our first priority."

"A good goal," was his reply. At least, I thought, he's not protecting his "offspring." He added, "I have seen the determination and dedication women have demonstrated toward this goal. The nuclear threat has mobilized a great number of women in this country."

He talked a bit about his work in the peace movement. He was so easy to talk to, and so accessible that I plunged in with a question dangling in my mind.

"Could I ask you perhaps a somewhat sensitive question?"

"Go ahead."

"Do you feel any guilt in having been a part of the Manhattan Project? I mean, do you think it was wrong to have developed such a powerful instrument of destruction?"

"How do I feel about making the bomb? The bomb itself is an awful thing, but we had no choice as far as I was concerned. The Germans were already working on it. The thought that this would be in the hands of Hitler, for an evil purpose; well, we had to do it first. We couldn't sit by quietly."

"Did you know the magnitude of the explosion before it was dropped on Hiroshima?"

"Sure. The testing of the bomb took place just a few days before the actual bomb was dropped in Japan. I was there in Alamogordo, New Mexico. I saw it at a distance, as a theorist. That is, I was not an experimenter who had worked on the assembly of the bomb. It was unbelievable. I thought everything must have been incinerated in the area, because the light splashed all over the horizon. One newspaper said it looked like the sun had come up twice."

"And you knew that this was going to be dropped on a city?" I was still trying to tweak his conscience.

"Many of us did not want the bomb to be dropped on a city, but in an unpopulated area as a demonstration to the Japanese of what destructive force the U.S. had at its disposal. We would tell them the power of this bomb, where we would drop it, and their scientists could measure impact and results. There was a big debate about this. Oppenheimer was there, General Eisenhower, other military higher-ups…all kinds of people. Oppenheimer wanted to drop the bomb on the town of Hiroshima. He was afraid of what might happen if we did a demonstration and produced a dud. We would get all their military brass and scientists out to watch and then…I think the prevailing feeling was that the bomb was so powerful that it would end the war. General Eisenhower was the one person who didn't want to drop the bomb because he believed the war was over anyway. It was finished. The Japanese were really defeated."

I told him, "I always believe this kind of decision should be a political decision, not to involve the military. Their role is to take orders from the civilian administration. And yet here was a General taking my point of view." Olum did not comment on my observation.

He continued, "Most decisions then were political-military. One thing I can say, though. The second bomb on

Nagasaki was a crime. The Japanese were not given time to admit defeat and to surrender, which would have happened. Absolutely inexcusable; never should have been done. It shows what people do once they have power."

"Your great concern, as I understood it, was to keep Hitler from getting the bomb, and I presume, also to use it against Hitler if considered necessary. But it was actually used against the Japanese."

"That's true. By then it probably was to show the world our power. And particularly to scare the Russians who were interested in occupying territory in Asia. But I'd like to hear more about your work. I've talked enough."

I told him the whole story about how WMS got started with trips to the Geneva Summit and to Reykjavik I explained the strategy we had developed at the International Assembly in Athens, trying to affect the nuclear decision-makers directly, especially Reagan and Gorbachev. "At this moment we are intending to send delegations to both Washington and Moscow in an attempt to get negotiations resumed. Since the meeting at Reykjavik no definite dates or plans have been announced. That will be our first pressure as an international lobby. If dates are announced before we send these delegations, then we will organize to be on the spot when the meetings take place."

"And what will you do while there?" This was the usual question I was asked. I was quite sure Paul Olum knew well the techniques of political pressure and lobbying. Although he had the prestige, the booming voice, the silver-haired elegance and dignity of a university president, there was something boyish, even child-like in his questioning.

"In Washington, making contacts with members of Congress, with the State Department, with embassies of countries that might support our cause, with other peace organizations. No doubt we will try to organize a rally in Lafayette Square. In Moscow, we shall see. We want to see both Reagan and Gorbachev personally, of course, and we are working on that now. In Moscow we will ask to see the

Foreign Minister, some of his staff, people like Petrovsky who has written about new approaches to the problem. But don't forget, journalists from all over the world appear at the summit events. We try to gain access to them, give them press releases, interviews, incorporate them in our endeavors. This is the voice of women in the corridors of power."

"This is really great work you are doing. Let me ask one question, though. Do you believe that containing militarism and building a secure world is going to be initiated by Reagan, or Gorbachev, or by our people here in Congress? Isn't it more of a 'trickle-up' process, that is, from the people to the top?"

"Let me say first of all that of the two, Reagan and Gorbachev, I think Gorbachev is more likely to try." I saw a sparkle in the president's eye when I said this, which signaled agreement. I had not asked anyone his political orientation, but, naturally, I assumed as a peace advocate he could hardly be a Republican. "Anyway, we are fully aware of the need to have grass roots support for whatever we do. We know that we have an organization of politically powerful women, who are in a good position to be heard by the people at the top. While we do that, however, we also try a broader education process, using the mass media, giving speeches, getting peace studies started in schools, and so forth. We have to utilize best what we have, and what we are most effective at. We cannot spread ourselves too thin."

"That I understand," this extraordinarily kind man said. "Scoring touchdowns isn't going to be easy."

"That sounds like you are a football fan."

"Very much so."

"What about baseball?" This was becoming the litmus test in my evaluation of men.

"That too," he smiled. "And you?"

"Also. Mostly baseball. But I attended all the University of Minnesota football games when I was a student and a faculty wife, despite the cold."

"And your husband?"

"Andreas? Well, he grew up in Greece and wasn't introduced to these games until he came to the States. Like most Europeans, his game was soccer. He liked football. I took him to a few baseball games, but he was so ignorant of the rules, and asked incredibly stupid questions, that the fans sitting around us thought he was a comedian."

Olum laughed. I thought it was a trifle strange for him to ask about my husband, but then Andreas was a known public figure and maybe he was just curious.

"How are you going to take on NATO and the Warsaw Pact?" He asked me. If it had been anyone else, I might have thought this was a sardonic remark. After all this was big league stuff and who were we, the gals in petticoats, to confront the power structure? I realized at moments like this how much of the patriarchal mentality is injected into our own female consciousness.

"We start with NATO. What chances we have for a meeting with the Warsaw Pact I can't say at this moment. We certainly intend to try."

"That would be a first, I presume."

"Right. At present we are organizing a meeting in Brussels at NATO headquarters at the end of May for talks with the permanent NATO representatives of each country. There will be WMS women from each NATO country. We've been disturbed by the negative NATO reaction to the almost-agreed upon decision at Reykjavik to reduce nuclear weapons in Europe. Right now we have a study group in Athens, and we suggested to all the other women attending our 'NATO Dialogue' to do the same, studying the mentality, attitudes and assumptions of NATO so we can speak with authority."

"Does that mean you are involved in military thinking and strategy? I would imagine that is a full semester course in itself."

"Yes," I replied, "and frankly, I never expected to be studying the language of defense and war. Of course, we are really more interested in the political and moral implications of their decisions. I brought a list of questions we will be asking and can leave it with you." I handed him the paper.

"I will certainly be interested in these," he said cordially.

"If we are to confront them with cogent arguments, we must be able to debunk the myths such as Weinberger's that the U.S. has a weak security system. And Reagan's that the Soviet Union surpasses the United States in practically all indexes of military power. Even apart from the madness of overkill as a concept, there is no logical reason for increasing arms, and many good reasons for decreasing."

"What you are trying to do, if I understand you correctly," said the president, "is to challenge in every way whatever assertions are made by the defense professionals. Not a small undertaking. In fact, I admire you for what you are doing." There was a pause and Olum seemed to be somewhat distracted, so I assumed this was a signal that our talk was over. Then I saw he was reading the questions on the paper on the table in front of him. He started reading. "What work has NATO done on the possible effectiveness of the diversion of a portion of weapons expenditures to the solution of global problems of ecology or hunger, as a means toward greater international security?"

"How do you like that one?" I asked.

"Good one. I'd like to be there to hear the answer." He continued reading the questions. Each one brought up a new topic for discussion. At some point he took out a piece of paper and helped me understand the workings of the atom, neutrons, uranium, plutonium. When he got into deeper aspects of physics and told me that "quantum mechanics and relativity changed everything in physics," he lost me. He saw my comprehension slipping.

"Excuse me. That's another lecture, and for another time." I thought how nice it would be to have another time with him.

"Mr. President," I said, "I hope you will help us in our work. "

"In any way I can."

By now we had emptied our coffee cups, eaten our cookies, and it was getting late for the reception before my public speech. I had brought with me a necklace of over-sized green glass worry beads. Hanging on it was a brass medallion with the head of the goddess Persephone, the goddess of spring on one side and on the other the insignia – EGE – of the Women's Union of Greece.

"I would like to leave this with you as a small token of our visit together. I truly appreciate your taking the time and the interest in what I am doing. Green is the color of hope – and hope as you know is the last thing to die – and the beads can be used to soothe you in time of stress. We Greeks carry smaller versions of this and take them out on buses, in cafes, during political discussions as an antidote to stress. You simply play with them in your hands, and they heal your soul and vanquish your worries," I explained.

"Well, as president of a university I do have occasions when such assistance may be needed." He stood up with a wide grin on his face and said, "I want to thank you, Margarita." I liked to hear him use my first name. It was so American to go to first names on an initial acquaintance.

"Let me know if there is anything I can do. I wish you luck in all of your endeavors, and I hope we have a chance in the future to exchange ideas, and, especially, for me to hear how your efforts to confront the decision-makers worked out."

An hour and twenty minutes had passed by without my realizing it. When I met Susan, who was waiting patiently in the hall, I said to her, "You've got a great president. We had a marvelous conversation. Do you think I could call him a feminist?"

"That's what he calls himself," was her answer.

I learned that after our meeting Paul Olum had dialed his brother-in-law at Stanford. He said, "I just met a spectacular woman, one I could really go for, and wished I could ask her 'how are you getting along with your husband?' – Guess what, she's the wife of the Prime Minister of Greece!" Both men laughed.

Chapter Eighteen

Swiss Roots

While I was in the States, the anti-Andreas forces back home lashed out at me as a means of eroding Andreas' popularity, and also against The Hostess, for the same reason. Against me because I was too politically active and unable to maintain the decorum and passivity of a political wife; against her because she was the cause of the Prime Minister's rumored infidelity and bad personal behavior. They were less interested in the two of us than in the political dimensions of the battle. It was a power struggle. Some of those criticizing me felt they might have a better chance of joining Andreas's inner circle if I were not around. Lines were being drawn.

I enjoyed a momentary satisfaction from an article in the periodical *Tahidromos*, that exposed the machinations of The Hostess. A photograph at the top showed her sleeping on a seat in an airplane. The thoughts in the balloon above her head read, "Let them say what they want. The best schemes are worked out in the air." This was meant to be her reaction to the bad reviews of *Miso-Miso*" whose weekly episodes were being telecast. There was a second meaning, of course, that her schemes were grander than just getting a contract for more episodes.

The accompanying article stated that a new law would be passed soon changing the administrative structure of the two government-controlled TV stations, and several high level officials would be discharged. One of them was considered a successful director of the TV station called ERT-1. What was his mistake? He had refused to give an extension to The Hostess's serial.

It was a program publicized as a feminist show and had created a lot of interest even before its first episode because the Prime Minister, for the first time, had lent his prestige to a TV serial by giving an interview. This led many people to believe that the program was under the protection of EGE. This really pissed me off.

When the program was aired, all of the mythology about its ambitious aims were deflated because of its low quality, which reviews described from "mediocre" to "deplorable." The presence of the Prime Minister received harsh criticism and condemnation by the opposition press, but also from the politically friendly press. Everyone believed that it would run its course of twelve episodes, and that would be the end of it.

That was a mistake. The air stewardess appeared in the offices of the television station and demanded a contract for fifty-two episodes! Ultimately the director put his foot down and said "either me, or this program as it is." The director was replaced, and although it was dished up as a result of the changes in the law, many understood that his departure was not for this reason. His firing implied that he had displeased the Prime Minister. It was an example of misuse of power – the man in power knocks off an employee because he failed to acquiesce to the requests of whom? His mistress. I couldn't help but be pleased with the comments on the quality of the show. But I was angry because EGE would have loved to produce a top quality feminist program. *Miso-Miso* destroyed that possibility for some time. In addition, The Hostess's audacity in appearing in the offices of the TV channel, ERT-1, displayed her growing sense of power and how she would use it. Not a good sign for me.

I returned to Athens on April 12th. Andreas and I had dinner together on the 13th, and this time he listened with interest to my tales about my doings in the States. I had seen a considerable number of friends from our academic days, and he was pleased that they all sent greetings. We had not been entirely out of touch during that time. I had several phone calls with him, all of which were amiable. Reading him or the situation was just about impossible. Warm one day, cold the next. Interested on some occasions, indifferent on others. He said nothing about Easter when we always "did the rounds" of the army centers together. I told him I was planning a lamb roast at Kastri in the yard with the family, and I presumed he would come. His answer was, "I'll try to come by for a while."

That's what he did. He arrived at 3 p. m, took a glass of wine and a small piece of meat, permitted himself to be photographed with the family by a reporter and left. As he walked out I told him I would be in Switzerland the next weekend for a speech, but I wanted to have a meeting with him upon my return, to sit down and really talk about what was going on between us. He nodded and said "fine." I had reached the point where I had to raise seriously the question of divorce.

As I was flying to Zurich I remembered what my journalism professor Herbert Kubly, whose ancestry was also Swiss, told me once. "We Swiss have the inability to accept defeat." Perhaps I wasn't fighting hard enough to keep my marriage alive. Maybe I was too soft. By running away was I leaving the door open for rivals to enter? At the same time I found it unbecoming and un-feminist for two women to be battling over a man. My Greek friends told me "he is yours, scratch her eyes out!" To be honest, I often felt like doing that. I know I am a good fighter, and can be tough. I like a difficult challenge, and the more difficult it gets, the stronger I become. It must, however, be something I believe in, worth fighting for.

Was this the catch? That I had doubts about the value of the battle, of the prize? Yes and no. Was I just hanging on to a romantic Ladies Home Journal concept of eternal love? Yes. And even if I would always love him, was that sufficient reason to put on my boxing gloves, to stay in the ring?

Probably yes. If he was no longer emotionally connected, could I put a rope around his neck and lead him back home? Come along little doggie, come along. No.

I never had faith in wedding vows or the legalization of a human bond. The concept that he was "mine" because I was married to him was alien to me. The concept of two people experiencing together that they are one and willing to sacrifice not to each other, but to the unity of the relationship is more compatible to me. Such a relationship hangs together through its own centripetal force. Andreas liked to repeat what his father told him as a young boy – major decisions in life are made emotionally. Emotions have a longer history and deeper roots. This meant he would listen to his emotions and I to mine. Emotionally, I wanted to stay in the ring. It was my mind posing these questions.

My thoughts were interrupted by the seat belt sign. The landscape down below didn't look like home, but I was returning to territory of my ancestors. Would I find here who I was? Would I locate my center, that deep sense of being, that life within me, the human spirit? I yearned for an ancestral hand to take hold of my soul, take me out of this morass and show me which way to go.

The scenery on the drive from Zurich to Basel was spectacular. I understood why my ancestors had chosen Elmhurst, lush with trees, when they settled in America. One might have asked why they chose Illinois with its flat terrain. I think they were just following their country folk. Germans and German-Swiss who had settled in Chicago and the surrounding area. Elmhurst was almost totally a German town.

Because of my Swiss roots, I called the participants in the conference "sisters," in more than just the feminist sense of the word, as compatriots. I dedicated the speech to my grandmother Bertha Loehrer Pfund of Zofingen, who would have been delighted that a granddaughter was in her native land speaking about peace. Switzerland is a country where women played an important role for a long time in the Peace

Movement. The activist women who refused to accept war as inevitable were inspired by the book of a young woman published in 1802 and entitled 'A Vision Concerning Peace and War.' All-women peace societies began to develop. In 1854 Frederika Bremer of Finland formed the first women's peace league in Europe, and in 1900 the International Peace Bureau was established in Switzerland, in Berne, coordinating the activities of 200 different peace societies, many of them made up of women only. I ended my speech by saying "our countrywomen have been well represented in all actions, and those of us who are newer to the peace movement call on Swiss women to take leadership globally for a continuation of the efforts for a world beyond war."

After the speech I discussed with the conference organizers the possibility of visiting Zofingren. I wanted very much to have time to explore the area where my grandparents had spent their childhood and early youth. Time was not on my side for doing genealogical detective work, nor to step on paths my grandparents may have trod. As we passed the road sign pointing to Zofingren on the drive to the airport, I asked to stop for a moment. I stood silently in awe at nature's bountifulness. I believe fervently that there is an ecological dimension to the human personality, a connectedness with nature rooted in the psyche. The first time I stretched out on a beach on the island of Spetsis I experienced a feeling that the ancient world still existed, just beyond a nearby clump of olive trees. I was lying in a sand bed of mythology and poetry. I get those feelings when I visit Delphi. Or when I go to Knossos on Crete. And now here alongside a vast forest in Switzerland. So where are my roots? Everywhere?

I did feel a special rapport with my Swiss sisters; a sense of "family," and we gave what my Swiss friend Madeleine, who now lives in Canada, calls "Swiss kisses" all around. They are no different from Greek kisses, just given by people who are Swiss. The trip was a healthy diversion, a magic disengagement from all worries. I was starting to sort things out. My mind, when it did plunge into the ocean of the subconscious, dug up Greece, Kastri, and dwelled on the conversation Andreas and I had agreed to have.

Before that, however, was the Pan-Hellenic council meeting of EGE, a meeting we held twice a year with the presidents and one representative of each local chapter's executive board. This one was in Elefsina, a polluted industrial town outside Athens, on the road to Corinth. Environment was, appropriately, a high priority on our agenda. Outside the agenda, we debated a familiar issue: our relationship to the party of PASOK. I intervened, quietly angry, and asked if I could have the floor to respond. I indicated that we had to set the framework in which we would do our work, and my answer would be an attempt to do so.

"I ask you to try to understand again, the difference between an independent women's organization, whose general philosophy is feminist and socialist, and a party." I had tried on other occasions to address this question, but it hung around like a hungry mosquito on a hot summer night. "I want to remind you that the word 'socialism' refers to a specific ideology and not a specific party." Here was part of the problem. Because we called ourselves a socialist-feminist organization, because PASOK was called the Pan-Hellenic Socialist Movement, women and men interpreted this to mean we were closely connected to the socialist party.

"There are many parties," I continued, "calling themselves socialist which are not consistent with our description of socialism. Our organization has, I would say, a green hue because the vast majority of our members support the party of PASOK. This is entirely different from being an organ of the party, under party discipline and control, as are the women of the party of New Democracy, and of the Communist party. Their organizations are party organizations, and they declare this openly."

Here one of the women in the council broke in. "Perhaps we should do that too." It was unfortunately true that quite a few women members of PASOK had joined EGE intending to capture the organization from within.

"You know," I explained, "when we started the Women's Union of Greece, we had many debates, and arguments, as to whether we should push to become a women's caucus within the party, a party organization outside the party, or an independent women's organization. I believe we have gone over this history before. In any case, our constitution declares our organization independent. When you became a member you accepted that condition."

Another woman said, "Yes, but it is hypocritical. We all work for the party, and for some of us the party comes first. If we do not achieve a socialist society, we will not achieve equality. It's as simple as that."

These PASOK party women were testing the water. The male-dominated party wanted EGE to be under its control, and these women were doing the work of the men.

"The thinking women of EGE see us as a healthy mass organization which agrees with a portion of the platform of PASOK, that portion having to do with equality, using our own methods to achieve that goal. Indirectly and in a parallel fashion, this helps the party. There are some clear differences we should remember. We are not 'Women of PASOK.' Women belonging to the party function like members of a party machine. We are the women of EGE. Some of us wear two hats, EGE and PASOK, but we wear them at different times and never the same together. Those of our critics in the party would do well to examine their own organization and their own motivation. Basically, they are disgruntled because they do not control us. And this they will never succeed to do." By now I was talking with passion and conviction. The women clapped. I had won this skirmish, but would I win the battle?

Before meeting with Andreas on May 4th, I faced two hurdles. One was a sizeable article in an unfriendly newspaper, with an incredible nose for gossip. The title was: "An Official Divorce – Andreas?" It carried an old photo of Andreas and me dancing together. The reporter said he would be accused of yellow journalism, but his sources were good and this was news, whereas the number of eggs Papandreou would click with others in his Easter rounds was not. According to all reports coming from the close ("very close") circles around Andreas, the Prime Minister would sue for divorce. The reporter mentioned the name of the lawyer, Menios Koutsogeorgas, and that the divorce would be by mutual consent. This bit of news, he wrote, was not a sudden bolt of lightning. The separation was an open "secret" for months. And Margarita spent two months in America, returned for Easter, which the two celebrated in separate places. "Family friends say that the pressure for an official step was made by Margarita who can no longer stand the unruliness of her husband." This latter remark was the journalist's own interpretation, unless he had been prompted to say so. My taking the initiative would have been more acceptable to PASOK as a way out.

The other event was my speech of at the Propellor Club, a prestigious and visible American organization formed to promote business, cultural and social relations between the U.S. and Greece. My appearance was given much publicity, before, during and after, and the hall was overcrowded. I sensed a lot of curiosity about this "scorned" and much talked about woman. Who knows, she might blow her top in public. The talk on effective peace actions was well received, and the question and answer period was lively and successful. The most lively question was not asked. All of this certainly served to add to Andreas' growing concern that I was hogging the limelight.

Between the time Andreas had agreed to a meeting and the time of the meeting itself, I had tried to sort out my feelings, confront the situation, think about all the ramifications of a split, and reach a decision. As I walked the stone pathway to the ranch house, I knew I had not reached a decision to divorce, but I was ready to discuss it. I decided to react to what he said in the framework of my own thinking and feelings. My breathing was quick; my heart pounding.

When I opened the door of his house, I was surprised to see both Menios, the lawyer, and Kostas, the psychiatrist. I asked Andreas to have them leave. He said it was important for them to be there. He looked at me for a few seconds. "You called this meeting. What do you want of me?" His look was stern.

"I wanted a meeting with the two of us. What we talk about is very personal."

"Both Menios and Kostas know our problems. We can talk freely. You told me when we had a chance to talk earlier that you had a suggestion. What is that?"

Suddenly, to say coldly that I wanted a divorce didn't sit right in this environment. Also I hadn't expected such a straight-on, direct confrontation. I tried another tack. "I propose we try to re-establish our relationship and keep up some form of public appearances to shut up the publicity."

"I have another idea," Andreas said slowly, and then. "We could announce that we are separated."

I tried not to show any reaction, no surprise, and no emotion. This was the first time he had uttered these words, words which sounded like the beginning of the end. My stomach tightened, but I kept calm.

"Yes, "I said. "We could do that, but that keeps the issue on the fence – will we or will we not get back together again – like a TV serial. Why don't we just announce we are getting a divorce?"

"I don't want a divorce," was his answer. "I don't intend to get a divorce. I'm never going to get married again. It's just not in my plans."

"You don't want a divorce, but your behavior forces me, at least, to consider a divorce."

"Do you want a divorce?"

"I don't see how I can continue to live this way. You are a visitor here. In any case, what does it mean to be 'separated'?"

"Well, it means legally we have separated. It doesn't mean we can't see each other, or be seen with each other. But the relationship has ceased to be a marital relationship. Maybe in a period of time, we might work out a reconciliation."

The latter remark, I felt, was holding out a carrot. I didn't ask him how you could be legally separated without that being a divorce. I said, "If we do announce it, we have to give an explanation. What would we say: we simply stopped loving each other? The least hypocritical would be to say you have fallen in love with another woman."

Andreas didn't like that. "Well, the relationship is known by everybody."

"You've seen to that. But that isn't entirely true. Political circles and Athenian social circles are speculating about it, but the villagers consider it mostly political propaganda as a means of undermining you. Anyway, now that we are talking about this, do you think those who know approve?" He said he supposed not.

"Tell me one person who supports you in this adventure, apart from those who want to placate you for their own personal interests. And it is not a question of taking my side, of being pro-Margarita, but because they are fearful for the damage to your career to the party, which again is in their own self interest. I am telling you this, Andreas, because I want you to continue to be Prime Minister of this country, because I love you, and because I believe your political career is more important to you than any woman. Nobody in your political circle tells you these things that you are in danger of upsetting the apple cart, that this new relationship will ultimately be your political Swan song. They are cowardly little creatures, scared shitless that by offending you they may be out on their ears in no time. In any case, I myself am ready to be thrown out, so let's go back to the problem."

He listened but didn't respond. He knew what I was saying was true.

"Look, Andreas, this 'separation solution'- it's not clean. It puts the whole situation in limbo. This is the worst political choice you could make. Why don't you simply announce your intention of taking a divorce? There will be an initial flurry, but it will be done with."

I asked him why after I returned from the States he decided to live elsewhere. He argued that he was not living elsewhere, that he was living in Kastri.

"What kind of honesty do we have between us since you argue that you are living here? I don't even know how to find you. If something comes up, how do I reach you? Do you know, for example, that Sophia lost her baby?"

He was taken aback. He didn't know what to say. "When was that?"

"She started having problems on Friday, but she wasn't sure. On Sunday she had a miscarriage."

He looked embarrassed and saddened.

"It's not only that. What if something happened to me? Do you feel so distanced from me, so alienated, that you wouldn't even care to know? Or any of the children? The grandchildren? These disappearances without letting me know how to reach you are hardly friendly acts."

He said nothing.

"What about your security? Sometimes I get information important to your personal security. When you are here at least I can tell you, and the house in Kastri is fairly well guarded. When you travel you have bodyguards. Are they part of your trysts? How would you like to be snatched from the arms of your mistress in an unguarded house? Can you see the headlines the next day?" I was trying to point to the danger, and also the potential political damage. Indirectly I was arguing for him to stop the nonsense and steer himself back to a port of calm and security.

We had been talking for about half an hour, in the presence of an audience, and interrupted occasionally by those ever-present political phone calls. There were none of a personal nature. I can spot those by the change in his voice.

Menios proposed we continue this conversation at another time, saying it was a "big subject" and needed much thought.

"No," I said. "I don't get to see Andreas often, and I would like to come to a decision, to finish this." My words were now part of a strategy. In my heart I was not ready to officially tear apart our marriage.

"What is it you want?" was Andreas' question for the second time.

I hesitated for several seconds, then said slowly tiredly, "Well, if you like, okay, I'm willing to hear more arguments for the idea of a separation."

Kostas stepped in and said he thought it was not the right decision. Menios also started to withdraw. My arguments about an ambivalent, open-ended decision had penetrated.

Andreas was thoughtful. Then he changed the subject. "You said something about information about my security?"

"Yes." We got into a discussion of the information I had received the day before concerning activity within the army. I was not in a position to judge its seriousness, but when I gave him the information, with names, both Menios and Andreas took it seriously. They agreed to talk to the Minister of Public Order first and if he thought it was worth pursuing, they would give me the go ahead to arrange a meeting between the informant and Menios.

Things seemed to be breaking up with no response to my request that we study the proposal. Kostas, who had agreed to have dinner with me, suddenly remembered he had a prior engagement, which I read as saying he didn't want to talk to me at this moment. Or he didn't want Andreas to think he discussed these things separately with me.

Before we left, I turned to Andreas and said, "We've been going around in circles. I regret we had to talk about these things in front of Menios and Kostas. Couldn't we just find time for ourselves, the two of us, like old times, and as friends? Do we have to be enemies?" By now he was more relaxed, looser. He came over and kissed me on my forehead just before I turned toward the door.

I walked back to the big house with Kostas and Menios, who said, "Look, Margarita, we all know Andreas. These things don't last very long." Andreas himself had said the same thing: "You know me, and I know myself; these things are temporary." (Like malaria, I thought, which has recurring attacks).

The two men departed, and I was left with my own thoughts. My body ached from the tension, but it was less tension than at the beginning because I was given the chance to unload, to react to a specific proposal, to warn him of the consequences. He no doubt considered my arguments were given in my own interest, a not unlikely assumption. My feminism kept me from naming or attacking The Hostess directly; the woman in me wanted to rip her apart.

That kiss at the end. Was he saying "maybe we can still find a way to stay together, just give me time"? Or was it to say "I am sorry I have to hurt you, but that's the way things are"? I certainly know how difficult it is to get out of a forty year old relationship. Is that his problem too? The difference is that down deep I am still not sure I want to. Is he? These were the questions I would be agonizing over during my sleepless nights.

Although these thoughts seemed to dominate my life, I continued with my activist role. Our Women's Defense Dialogue was scheduled for May 30th to June 2nd in Brussels. Almost all of May was devoted to preparations for it. We set up seminars on NATO, defense strategy, alternative defense strategies, structure of the two alliances, history of NATO, nuclear arsenals, capacity of each military bloc, and what have you. It was a crash course taught by Thanasis Platias, a Harvard graduate in international relations, and a friend of my son Nikos. The group met several times a week at my home to debate the issues. For all of us it was new territory – a dizzying and exhilarating experience.

Looking through material prepared by the Oxford Research Group (with whom we were collaborating on this project), and in debate with Platias, we decided to stress a nuclear weapons-free zone in the Balkans (to include two NATO countries, Greece and Turkey), the immediate adoption of the INF (Intermediary Nuclear Force) agreement, and a better communication system between the two blocs. As the contingent from Greece, we intended to raise the question of NATO's role in an armed conflict between Turkey and Greece. Greece's undying nightmare was the expansionist aims of its neighbor and former conqueror.

Because we knew NATO would be against abolishing nuclear weapons in our proposed zone, we had to be able to support our argument. We also knew that Greek defense experts opposed the idea, particularly those in the opposition party, because this would give Turkey the opportunity to say that Greece was pro-Soviet whereas Turkey was an authentic supporter of NATO. Turkey, thereby would gain credit with NATO, enabling it to secure material or strategic aid. NATO's strength came primarily from its nuclear power, and given the dogma of flexible defense, it needed to be able to escalate a war from conventional to nuclear if necessary. Its credibility to do so would be seriously damaged by a nuclear weapons free zone in Greece and Turkey. Then there was the question of obligations. The Alliance, it was argued, offered benefits to all and its members had obligations to all. It wasn't fair for some countries to be obliged to have nuclear weapons on their soil, and others not to.

What we wanted was to move away from the doctrine of mutual deterrence, which we saw as the path to suffering and destruction, and move to a doctrine of mutual security and a commitment to joint survival. We were aiming for substantial reduction in weapons. By declaring Turkey and Greece nuclear weapons free, we could build some trust with the other side, ask them to agree on such a zone in their territory, and start a spiral which would continue. Security is not found in more and more weapons but in an international order less armed, working together to use its resources to provide food, shelter, freedom and a better quality of life for all. These are not just pretty words. These are specific actions to be taken. Another would be a test ban treaty.

Throughout our study, we were introduced to military thinking. Military strategists live in a different world, moving pieces on a board to see how they can protect themselves, how they can surprise the "enemy." They are talking about firepower that can wipe out major cities. They look at land based missiles and sea based missiles, matching their destructive capabilities with their opponent's and trying to keep one step ahead. They see numbers, money, soldiers, and weapons. They flex their macho muscles by putting pointers on a war map. They don't see the terrified eyes of a child, or the blown apart bodies, or the weeping relatives of victims. They are distanced from all this. The war is a game played in the swank offices of NATO Headquarters in Brussels, on the computer, or on the television screen, or in the reports prepared by military experts. War loses its horror, and the blood and pain is obliterated.

On May 10th, I was in bed recovering from the flu. Andreas learned I was sick, and suddenly he was at my door, and then in the chair next to my bed. In the past he had always been especially tender to me when I was ill and now, like old times, he seemed genuinely concerned. Feverish, and not in condition to talk about anything emotional, I asked him if we could talk about the Greek defense system and what his government's contribution to peace had been over the last six years. He was happy to do this, but what pleased me most was his interest in my plans for Brussels.

He said PASOK initiated meetings for a Balkan nuclear-free weapons zone, signed a treaty of friendship with neighboring Bulgaria, and proposed to abide by an International Court decision about Greece and Turkey's dispute over the continental shelf. There was, of course, the Initiative of the Six as well as his government's proposals about nuclear weapons, to be withdrawn in stages from Greece, and Pershing and Cruise missile deployment in Europe to be postponed in favor of contacts with the Soviet Union for a program of de-nuclearization. This was before the Gorbachev-Reagan summit meetings. I listened to all this and was excited by what he had done. This is MY Andreas I was thinking. These proposals were clearly opposite to the present NATO agenda.

"That's why you are called 'the bad boy of NATO'" I told him, smiling.

"No doubt. But I have a friend there, Lord Carrington, the General Secretary of NATO. Say hello to him for me when you see him."

We chatted on, mostly about my health. I asked him about his. He said he thought he was in good shape, but a little tired. He indicated that he got out of breath easily. I asked if he had gotten a check-up recently. He answered no, but he was in touch with his doctor.

"I wish you would take care of yourself," I said, like a mother to a child.

"I'll be all right." And with that he left.

The visit bewildered me. It was sweet and was a stumbling block in my growing conviction that I must extricate myself from the marriage.

A few days later George Katsifaras stopped by. George had been exiled to an island during the early part of the dictatorship. When he was released he made his way to the States where I met him in Buffalo, New York, and brought him up to Canada where we were living in exile. He was distantly related to George Papandreou, Andreas' father, and had grown up idolizing his older "cousin" Andreas. He lived with us in Toronto for two and a half years, and returned with us to Greece when the junta fell in 1974. I was like an aunt to him, if not a mother. We were fifteen years apart. He was skinny, darkly attractive, full of flattery and forever optimistic. He had become a part of the family, and this evening he wanted to talk to me about Andreas's behavior.

The Hostess now spoke openly about her affair with the Prime Minister, mostly; he thought to provoke a reaction from me, or perhaps to make the relationship appear to be a *fait accompli.* He was sure the situation could blow up in Andreas's face at any moment and ruin his political career.

George himself was a womanizer, but he was unmarried. He was very much against what Andreas was doing and said he was going to talk to him.

"He won't listen to you," I told him.

After Katsifaras left I had a choice between going to the theater or staying home and watching the Iran-Contra Hearings on CNN, broadcast live from Washington. I called Louise Keeley, the U.S. Ambassador's wife, and asked if she would like to join me in seeing the hearings. She was delighted, and soon we were watching Bob McFarland testifying, and hoping he would blow the whistle on Reagan. Nothing of the sort happened and the cover-up continued.

When Louise left I called my sister in the States. She said I should consider Andreas dead. I should expect a mourning period, depression, melancholy, and a sense of loss. Over a period of time I would adjust to the reality that he was gone and come to terms with it. She does marriage counseling at the YWCA, so she should know. When people are dead, however, you don't expect to see them giving press conferences on television. So I wasn't sure about this solution. Maybe as my love for him diminished this would be possible.

On May 12th, Andreas asked to have lunch with me. I thought this day would be historic in my life because I had decided to tell him I wanted out. I would not be an obstacle to whatever he wanted for himself, not out of nobility or self-sacrifice, but because I had to get on with my life.

What I had to accept was not that Andreas was dead, as my sister put it, but the relationship was dead, and there was no hope of reviving it. Let's say he decides to return, as he always has in the past. Return to me in my present state of mind? What will I do with a recalcitrant husband who will feel like a naughty child returning to mama? We would be two hostile strangers groping for a sign of human connection that wasn't there. Let's say something remained and we gave it a try. Then I would be on tenterhooks waiting for the next infidelity.

I was ready to say all these things. When I went downstairs the table was set for three. "Who's coming?" I asked.

"Nikos."

Once again he had made it difficult to talk. I surely was not going to put Nikos in the position of listening to my decision to divorce. It was too painful and too personal. I contemplated asking Nikos to leave us alone. Then he walked in, the son my mother-in-law called Apollo, jaunty, handsome, full of spirit, and happy to join the two of us at lunch, optimistically hoping that our lunch together meant a better situation had developed. I couldn't throw acid on him at that moment.

The conversation turned to politics, naturally, and to Nikos' research in the army. Anything but personal. Nikos gave it a try.

"Dad, why don't we all find an evening to go out to a taverna together? The whole family?"

Before Andreas could answer, I said, "No. I don't think that's a good idea." Andreas looked at me surprised. Nikos was stunned.

"Well," said Nikos, a bit deflated, "maybe we could go up to the Acropolis together."

Then we all laughed.

When the lunch was over, I stood up and said I would leave. Andreas said, "You are tired from your sickness."

"Yes, a little tired, but that's not the point. I thought we would be alone at this lunch, and I have things I want to say to you – which are very important."

Nikos squirmed in his chair and said he would be glad to leave.

"Fine," said his father, not responding to Nikos' suggestion. "We can set up another time."

"Yes, but I don't want much time to pass. What I have to say will not disturb you; in fact, I think you will be rather happy with the things I am going to say."

I believe Andreas understood I had come to a decision. Did he understand I was trying to look at him as "dead"?

There were a few weeks left before we entered the hallowed halls of NATO Headquarters, and our group was meeting more frequently. Not all of us had the means to make the trip to Brussels, so we pooled our resources to send a delegation of three women active in the Peace Movement: Kaity Lazaris, Eleni Stamaris and me. A member of our women's organization who had been elected to the European Parliament and was living near Brussels would join us. The ten women from the seminar, despite the fact they would not be in the Brussels team, were religious in their attendance at the teaching sessions. We would have a list of knowledgeable women on defense issues for the future, and also as spokespersons – if we could get radio and television programs to turn to women for opinions on nuclear disarmament. This would mean another battle because we would be treading on strictly male territory.

We were ready with our questions, we knew what to ask and the ideas we wanted to advance. We would be dealing with experienced diplomats, knowledgeable, informed. There was a touch of naïveté in what we were doing. Still we would bring a fresh and uncorrupted point of view into the debate on defense. I believe in the power of the people, citizen diplomacy and the right and duty each one of us has to participate in the big decisions of our times, of our lives, of the world.

An old friend who was always involved in causes sent me a letter expressing bitterness. "Many of us work our asses off," he said, "trying to establish a better world. And what is the result? What changes do we see?"

My return question to him was, "What do we expect?" Take our NATO initiative, for example. What would happen after our challenge to them? That they would turn to us and say, "Yes, you are right. The flexible defense strategy should be scrapped, we should stop building our nuclear arsenals, and we have to quit the 'enemy image' propaganda?" The frustration of working in a mass movement like a Peace Movement was exactly that – we could not easily point to a specific accomplishment. We were not measuring number of bombs, although a reduction of bombs could be considered a minor success. Many problems in the world stem from what we believe, from our understanding of who we are and how we are related to each other. Our movement was trying to change a people's way of thinking. So we are educators. And how does one measure the success of education? In school, exams are one form of measurement. In the Peace Movement we had to function to a great extent on faith. Faith that only good could come out of what we did, and that if we didn't act, then nothing would change.

Chapter Nineteen

I'm Movin' Along

(Diary entry) – *May 26th, 1987*

During the whole month of May I had a persistent sense of unreality. The image was a husband and wife sitting and talking together while the man was essentially living with a woman somewhere else. We would discuss politics, the children, occasionally The Hostess. It was nutty, absolutely weird. Think of Ronald Reagan living in the White House with, say, his secretary, and visiting Nancy in the Blair House from time to time. I am digging into my psyche to try to understand not Andreas, but me. Kostas was of no help. He told me, "It's simple, you love him, you don't want him to get hurt." That was true. It was more than that. It goes back to patriarchal mentality, attitudes embedded in me as a child which I still can't shake. You have to have a man. Don't lose him. You are the glue holding the family together. It is your responsibility.

Or does it have something to do with possessiveness, control? I know I am very protective of Andreas, as if he were one of my children. We make men dependent on us, which makes us feel important, powerful. I wonder if that is what I am afraid to lose. Some people think I dislike losing my position in society; I am staying because of ambition. Ambition I have – to do things positive for the country, for the world. Being First Lady has helped, but I established a name for myself and don't need the title anymore. I am still Maggie the waitress who found herself at the top of the ladder, but who would be content to drop the title as long as she could continue to make an impact where it mattered.

I discover I am very much alone in this type of thinking. Most of those who are in politics are trying to hold on to their positions. They don't want to tangle with the Boss. They don't want to point out the cost. They take a short-range view – it is easier, more convenient. True friends, those with whom I can speak openly about my inner feelings and thoughts, advised, "Don't bring the boil to a head. Knowing Andreas's past behavior, why push it? Let him take the step, the initiative. Continue with the many important activities you have originated. Be indifferent, unconcerned."

A new set for my mind. But how will I handle my stomach?

It was getting close to departure time for the NATO Defense Initiative. We called a press conference in Athens to explain the aims of our trip to Brussels, saying we were profoundly dissatisfied with the so-called arms control agreements since the last World War. The agreements, we argued, were mainly mechanisms of communication to manage crises – the Bay of Pigs, incidents on the high seas, etc. They helped institutionalize the arms race, giving a blueprint by which conditions of arms stockpiling could be continued. The agreements were presented as arms control, but in the end were propaganda devices. They simply fooled the public.

I told the journalists, "Arms control negotiations by the U.S. have functioned as a propaganda forum which provided welcome opportunities for denouncing the wickedness of the Soviets. Reagan stated that all the indices of army strength show that the Soviet Union is ahead. Weinberger talked about the weakness of the United States defense force. This kind of language has provided an effective argument for the deployment of new weapons considered necessary for rearmament.

"NATO, instead of operating only militaristically, should address the structural causes of global disorder, co-ordinate Western action to stabilize the international economic and monetary system, to sustain development in co-operation with Third World countries, and to pursue active bilateral and multilateral diplomacy. In the long run this will be more effective in influencing global security than military power."

The reporters listened carefully, and took notes, but asked few questions. When I mentioned this to our women afterwards, they said, "Sure, the newspapers did not send their experts on military and defense matters, even though we told them our mission. They sent reporters on social and women's affairs." There we were again, the ladies in petticoats, not taken seriously. Our mission was Margarita's "caprice." In Greek, "*kapritsio.*" I wondered if we would get the same response in Brussels.

The day prior to our NATO rendezvous, we spent a full day in debate with all the women who had arrived from NATO countries. Many of them were parliamentarians, others were members of peace organizations, and two were university professors. Among them were Madeleine Gilchrist and Kay MacPherson from the Voice of Women of Canada, Randy Forsberg, the head of the Institute for Defense Studies in Boston, and Cora Weiss, on the National Board of SANE. Eva Maria Quistorp represented the Greens of Germany and Zeynep Oral the Turkish newspaper MILLIYET. In addition to the general questions we had agreed upon through correspondence, we proposed a series of questions we could ask of every Ambassador, as well as of Lord Carrington, the General Secretary of NATO. We intended to compile the answers into a profile of views and opinions within NATO Headquarters.

We prepared our basic position paper on defense. How did we women look at this whole picture of international conflict, use of violence, war? We tried to use simple words, simple examples, to make our stand understandable to the average person. Citizens did not enter the debate on defense and security, we believed, because it appeared too complicated. This is the last paragraph written in understandable terms:

"If you are the aggressor and try to capture land outside your borders, this is illegal and warrants international intervention and punishment. This means, first, there must be agreements on borders, as was done in the Helsinki Accords for Europe. Then tough and quick international response to violation of those agreements. The decision to intervene cannot be based on so-called "national interests" but on "world interests." If the rules were stuck to strictly and objectively by every nation and state, and every area, then we would have 'a world peace order."

The next morning we had an appointment with Lord Carrington. We sat around a long table in a room where few women had entered, except perhaps to bring coffee. I was tardy, which I seldom am, because the guide given to us by the Greek Ambassador lost his way in the building and had us moving in circles for a period of time. This aggravated me very much since I know this is often interpreted as pulling rank. It also aggravated Lord Carrington who didn't greet me with much enthusiasm as my colleagues and I took our seats at the table.

I spoke of our concern about the few women making decisions in defense policy. He replied that, "We in Britain have no problem with the idea of more women present at the making of defense policy. After all, we have a woman Prime Minister!" He was saying there are no obstacles, all doors are open – so walk in, if you like. I found him arrogant and patronizing in the beginning. He described his role as that of coordinator and said he had little actual power within the Alliance. What we knew was that parliamentarians at a national assembly cannot get answers to questions on policy on grounds that these are "Alliance decisions." This confirmed our belief that there were other centers of decision-making, key among them the United States.

After responding to our questions, the Lord gave a very eloquent dissertation on the need for peace in the world. He knew we would lap this up, but it sounded genuine. The problem, of course, is not to be for or against peace; everyone is for peace in theory. The difference lies in how you achieve and maintain peace. Our women's strategy would be much more conciliatory, less adversarial – and we would stretch ourselves to the limit to prevent the use of force and violence. We would never equate arms with peace. We would not, however, view human behavior through a rosy, romantic, sentimental screen, but recognize there are times when the use of power may be legitimate.

No channel of communications exists between NATO and the Warsaw Pact. When the Warsaw Pact recently invited NATO to discuss military doctrine, the invitation was conveyed through the media. When we talked about this separately with our ambassadors, we were given many different responses: the Icelandic and Norwegian ambassadors knew nothing of the invitation, while the British said "Ask the French." The French ambassador said it would be improper for NATO to have discussions with the Warsaw Pact because the two alliances were "unequal," while the American ambassador was more straightforward: "We can't talk to them about military doctrine because they would want to talk about tactical nuclear weapons, and we're not prepared to do that." As we saw it, there was great danger in this refusal to discuss military doctrine in that the arms race continued to escalate, regardless of agreements. A new approach was needed.

We generated considerable publicity in the Belgian and French press. Some of this was due to the work of our parliamentary representatives from those countries. Articles appeared in other NATO countries' newspapers and periodicals after the women returned home and could communicate with the mass media more easily. Greek newspapers carried the story, using mostly the press release we had prepared, and a few comments of mine declaring the NATO alliance was an incompetent and obsolete institution. One newspaper asked Andreas if he knew what his wife was doing and whether I had gotten his permission ahead of time. What did I know about international affairs? Imagine, they wrote, this colossal theme – disarmament – is being treated as if it were a matter of house cleaning! Another newspaper said I attacked NATO, Reagan and Ridgeway and the prevailing male mentality, but "despite all that, we have to say, she really tries." I was given, like a third grade pupil, a high grade for effort.

What interested the Greek press primarily and which they printed in bold letters was my response to a woman reporter's question: "What would you do if American bases remain in Greece? Would you continue to take an opposite stand from your prime minister husband?" (Andreas had decided on an extension of their leases.) My answer was, "Come on, now. Don't you sometimes disagree with your spouse?" Of all the things we did and said, with all the work we put in ahead of time, and the carefully planned press information sheets for the reporters, what was ultimately important was that I disagreed with the Prime Minister.

The British periodical *The Bulletin* declared sarcastically that "even though believing NATO is irrelevant and irresponsible, the wife of Prime Minister Papandreou proposes that Warsaw Pact women come to Brussels to carry on the dialogue with that institution and then go on to talk to the Warsaw Pact leaders."

The agenda for WMS had been publicly announced. We had found the key to our next action, opening up the channels of communication between the two blocs. Women from Western and Eastern Europe would meet with both sides. WMS could be the first to turn the handle on the door, opening up a crack.

<u>(Diary entry)</u> *June 4th, 1987, on the Ionian Sea*

I haven't stopped running since the London events, and I occasionally feel out of breath, my left arm aching, and pains in my chest. Psychosomatic signs of stress. Calls from Pierre from time to time alleviate my symptoms and are the only positive moments in my personal life. Although I know I must depend on my own strength, on my own toughness, it is comforting to know my feelings of rejection come from one man, not all.

How many people can run away from a problem by going on a cruise? I am privileged. There is a light side of me, fortunately, that doesn't allow me to feel guilty about everything, and permits me to look at life through a prism of humor, through the eyes of a comedian. Humor comes from knowing that the world is weird and scary, and laughter is the means of dealing with it. I am planning to do a lot of laughing on the trip. My marriage-counselor sister is going to take laughter seminars from a woman in California who uses this technique in her psycho-therapy. I am all for this style of therapy. Ruth, my University of Minnesota roommate, and her husband Phil, who are with me on this trip, are themselves comedians. This assures me of the laughter I seek.

Phil just walked by while I'm here on a deck chair writing. I told him I thought he would find the companions on our trip interesting. He said, "I never find people interesting," in a flat, contemptuous voice, and walked on without giving me a chance for retort.

Chapter Twenty

The Early Days of Perestroika

Upon return from a truly relaxing cruise, and after completing a number of duties, making contact with the Board of EGE, answering letters concerning WMS and our future projects, I went one evening to the Greece – Italy basketball tournament at the Stadium of Peace and Friendship in Piraeus – We won. I saw the next one with Yugoslavia, which we also won. That took us to the finals of the European championship. Our opponent was Russia. The temperature of the nation rose. National fervor had set in.

Tremendous pressure was being put on Andreas to attend. Everybody who was anybody would be present supporting the home team. Mitsotakis, the opposition leader, Christos Sartzetakis, the President of Democracy, and Melina Mercouri, the actress. His first reaction was, "Me? Go to a basketball game? What would I do there?" A friend of his who was terribly distressed by Andreas's private life, came to me Saturday morning when I was eating breakfast to tell me he would try to persuade the Prime Minister to go, that it was absolutely essential he attend.

Andreas reluctantly agreed. He could not ask me not to be there – if anyone was entitled to be present it was I, a high school basketball player and ardent supporter of the Greek team, that is, ME. He could not go to the game and have me sit somewhere else in the stadium while he sat next to Sartzetakis and his wife. He was, shall we say, "trapped." It had been obvious for some time now that he did not want to be seen with me publicly. Despite his display of extra-marital activity in small, friendly circles, he was not ready to flaunt it openly, certainly not at a national event, where the fact that we were no longer together would be photographed, reported upon, commented on, and probably cartooned. What he was doing was "divorce by attrition." Divorce by slow disappearance of wife.

By now, evidently, he had committed himself to The Hostess, and wanted to prove, (or was asked to prove), that he was no longer connected with me. This sports event was the most incredible exposure conceivable – the two of us in the front row in the official section, Sartzetakis and wife on Andreas' right, the Soviet Ambassador and wife to my left. AGP barely spoke to me. He sat stony-faced and icy. There were moments when I jumped up to laud a perfect play, or to encourage the players – something I always did when I am involved, and moments when we were both smiling because of an important point, but nothing passed between us.

A young woman ran over and gave Andreas a rose. He didn't want to hold it so he handed it to me. Cameras flashed. Andreas presenting Margarita with a rose! At another moment we were both enjoying Sartzetakis' excited waving of the Greek flag. Cameras flashed. TV ground away. The mood had been captured for all of Greece to see. I had a moment of puny, insignificant, inner satisfaction. The country would be watching a happy couple on TV. The newspapers were full of our pictures the next day. Joy! Excitement! Margarita and Andreas together again! They say a picture is worth more than a thousand words. This picture was worth a thousand lies.

The annual Onassis award ceremony to honor persons who had given outstanding public service was on Monday, two days after the basketball game. Both Andreas and I were invited. I usually did not attend these awards, but I had promised the chairman of the Onassis Foundation, when I was in New York that I would come this time. John Brademas, the President of the University, also asked me to come. "We are giving an award to President Pertini of Italy. You should be there."

I suspected Andreas would pull out once he learned I was coming. After our appearance together at the Saturday basketball game, I was certain he went back to an angry Hostess. Another such appearance would have toppled the walls of his trysting place.

His excuse was announced at the opening of the ceremonies. "The Prime Minister regrets his absence because of a "slight indisposition." That was the first time I had been referred to by that title. I wondered how many more titles I might gather.

At the lunch afterwards I was seated next to the President of Democracy, Christos Sartzetakis, not an unattractive bloke, slim, tall, and with whitening hair that gave him a dignified look. This did not, however, lessen the fact that he managed always to show a disdain for me, primarily because of my position on the legalization of abortion, but also because I expressed my opinions on most things, openly and with fervor. Women shouldn't do that, and they should especially respect the institutions of a country – that is, the presidency. I do respect the institutions in a democratic society. Under certain circumstances, however, I have a hard time separating the institution from the person heading it.

As we were talking, he told me I did not understand Greek reality. This reminded me of a friend of Sartzetakis', the Greek ambassador in Brazil who had implied that abortion was a foreign import alien to Greek cultural norms. The fact that Greece had the highest rate of abortions in Europe was of little concern to him. I wanted to make them legal was what bothered him. If it is a cultural norm to do things illegally, secretly and hypocritically, then we have a different concept of norms.

According to Sartzetakis, I hadn't understood the power women truly hold in Greece. They control almost everything. The old and familiar song of anti-feminists. I asked him to give me examples of how women were affecting public policy on defense, on health, on education, public works, and I watched his neck slowly turn red. He didn't respond, asking me instead. "How many women are in the U.S. Congress?" I told him about the same percentage as were in Greek parliament.

"But what," I said, "does that have to do with my question?" He was subtly pointing out that I was an American and should concern myself with American women, not Greek women. When he didn't answer my question on women's power, I pushed him more. "Do you mean to say women have power in the home? There I agree with what you say. But they don't have power to help make decisions on the direction of society."

Visibly annoyed, he asked me, "Am I not entitled to my opinion?"

"Yes, and I'm entitled to my opinion." This was the abrupt and unsatisfactory ending to that part of our dialogue.

He then brought up Dukakis, the Democratic candidate for presidency, again veering toward my American connection. I told him I thought he was doing well, having picked up a part of the Gary Hart machinery and method for the campaign. Hart had worked out his organizational scheme for running for president in the next national election.

"What was that business with Gary Hart? That was odd. The Americans are very strange. That would never happen here, that he slept with a woman one night and thus was ruled out of the presidential race."

"It wasn't only that he slept with a woman. He was arrogant and indiscreet. Furthermore, he understood when the photo came out that this was going to open up the book on his many extra-marital affairs."

"I believe it was due to American Puritanism," was his comment.

"That's not true. Of course, there are standards Americans have for their leaders, but Hart made the mistake of philandering before he got into power, when he was being judged on character, reliability, stability, not only his political views. If he had waited until achieving the presidency, he could have done pretty much what he wanted, and the 'old boy's network' would protect him, as was the case with Jack Kennedy, Roosevelt, Johnson. Men in positions of power should probably not be married. This power makes them believe they are outside the norms of accepted human behavior." I could have added that Hart's escapades were just a continuation of what many men do in their everyday lives, but more power increases their opportunities and makes them feel immune.

At some point I said, "You claim here in Greece no one would give much importance to a sexual indiscretion. Do you go out with women other than your wife?" He was flabbergasted at such a direct question. The food on his fork remained at the plate while his face took on a look of vicious pondering. He was in a quandary as to how to respond, apart, I imagine, from thrusting the prongs of his fork into my tongue.

"At least I can say this, Mr. President. If you do, it is with the utmost caution because no one talks about extra-marital affairs in your case."

Then he went into a long story about how he was one of the youngest lawyers in Greece to be selected as a judge, that he had, in other words, power. Furthermore, he had had an active sex life as a bachelor. God, I thought, what importance a man gives to his manliness, defined, naturally, as sexual prowess. I understood I had almost insulted him by suggesting he wasn't having sex on the side. Then he said that after he got married, he considered it a matter of principle to be faithful. "Actually, it is out of respect for my wife."

Bam! This was a backhanded slap at Andreas, but indirectly at me, too, because obviously I was not a respected wife.

"I'm so glad to hear that. The concept of respect is a very feminist demand." This I said purposely to agitate him because he is not, and would never want to be called a feminist.

Implying I had misconstrued what he said, he repeated it. And I repeated, "Feminists believe there should be equal respect between the two spouses – neither one is entitled to do something the other is not entitled to do. The woman is supposed to respect her partner, but according to feminist thinking, the man is also supposed to respect his partner." I kept reminding him he had expressed a feminist point of view.

I believe he still wanted to jab me with his fork or perhaps he wanted to drop through the floor. He did neither. Instead, he dropped out of the conversation by turning suddenly to the person at his right. I turned to President and Ms. Pertini sitting at my left. I knew I would find two persons in harmony with my kind of thinking and could eat the rest of my lunch without being nauseated.

I called Angela when I returned home and asked her to cancel the family lunch for the next day. Andreas was planning to come. I was tired of the pretense. He seemed to be trying to establish that I was his Kastri wife, his partner in his family and home life, and The Hostess was his unofficial semi-public wife, moving around on the margins of power. Then I called Kostas who was upset because he had urged me to "play the game." He thought, he said, I had decided to live my life, not press Andreas for a solution, not put obstacles in the way when he wanted to see me, and let him come to a decision on his own.

"Look," he said, "you don't lose anything. It requires tremendous patience on your part, but you don't lose your reputation or your prestige. In fact, in this culture you probably gain prestige. You are the mistreated one, but you are the understanding one, and you are the person trying to hold the family together while an errant husband makes a fool of himself."

Patience with pain. The gods or the goddesses were giving me tribulations as a harsh method of proving my worth. I would earn my way to reward through suffering. I would be the beloved underdog. This was a very patriarchal, and Christian, point of view. Kostas was interested not only in

Andreas's political career, but in what he perceived as my own self-interest, so l knew that his patriarchal advice was genuine. I was getting similar advice from others. Finally I was persuaded. Not that I must suffer to prove myself. My reasons were more practical. I was accomplishing nothing by pressing for a resolution, and I was too fatigued, tired and confused to make one myself.

Toward the end of June, the Sheinbaums came, Betty and Stanley. With them we often talked of our conspiratorial days trying to get Andreas out of jail, and a somewhat bigger task of trying to overthrow the dictatorship. We had a pleasant outing on a boat. I can't call it a boat. It was a small, mobile hotel -owned by the Konstantidis family. Along with us were Spyros and wife from Brazil, Effie Ziagas, my daughter Sophia and son Andreas. Also the editor, Nathan Gardels, of Sheinbaum's periodical *New Perspectives Quarterly.*

Gardels and Stanley had interviewed Andreas the day before. Stanley was excited by the interview. The question was whether a country by itself could put into effect a socialist program independently of the international economy. Wouldn't it be easier if there were a group of socialist countries working together toward this goal? The result of the interview will be in one of the next issues. It was to be entitled "Papandreou's Prescient Views on the Greek Economy."

Once again I took pride in Andreas's intellect and his actions as Prime Minister. In the six years of being in power, he had increased real minimum wages and pensions, (including pensions for women farmers who had been neglected – a demand that our women's organization EGE had fought for), granted significant raises to public sector employees, passed laws that favored unions in bargaining with employers, established a free National Health System and, in general, gave social protection to a vast number of people. Andreas had invited Stanley to his ranch office-house for an informal "chat." If this were the past, we would have all been together, something which was always a pleasure to me. He told Stanley that he had no intention of divorcing me. He wants to maintain the legality of the marriage. Yeah, while living with another woman!

Stanley asked, "Does Margarita know?"

"I'm not sure. (Of course he had told me that several times.) You can tell her if you like."

When I saw Stanley and Betty later on the boat they told me what he told them. Then they dropped a small bomb on my bird of hope. They had seen this happen often among their friends. The man is attracted to a woman's youth, and at the dangerous age of 70 wants to confirm his masculinity and his immortality. He wants to reassert his male attractiveness, and demonstrate to the world that he can have a sexy gal hanging on his arm. Something new and fresh. It reminded me of what one of Ring Lardner's characters said to his long-time wife in a short story. "Do you expect everything I say will be something you ain't heard me say before?" In other words, a long relationship gets boring. I was distressed with the Sheinbaums' straight talk, but it was the most honest evaluation I had received.

On a more important issue (I say this because I am trying to convince myself of proper priorities on my Importance List), I was prepared for the Soviet Women's Peace Congress. My speech was ready, I wanted it to be a gem, to produce the reaction my Nairobi speech did. It is awesome to be talking to 3,000 women from all over the world. Speeches of this kind, that is, for social change, should convince people, and motivate them to join the struggle, to take action.

The morning of my flight to Moscow, I sat at my desk gathering my papers, giving instructions, answering the critical telephone calls, and doing all the usual last minute tasks. When I finished, I pushed back my chair and took a step to head for my bedroom and a change of clothes. My right leg had gone to sleep and was completely numb. My foot folded under like a piece of bent cardboard, and I sprawled on the floor. The fall itself was not bad, but the pain in my ankle was. I shouted "damn, damn, damn" and pulled myself back to my chair. I had an overwhelming need to cry, and to let go

– not only from the physical pain. I called upon my Stoicism and controlled my emotions.

Members of the household came running with a pail of ice cold water and plunged my foot in, while I sat picturing myself being wheeled to the plane, but worse than that, hobbling on crutches to the microphone at the conference.

We flew on Aeroflot, the Soviet Union's national airlines. The plane was more like a truck than a Cadillac, both in sound and in shape, perhaps an appropriate comparison between East and West. I was given a front seat so I could elevate my leg on a tall canister brought from the cooking quarters of the airplane. It hurt like hell when I walked into the Moscow airport. A woman doctor was waiting for me and examined my ankle carefully to see that no bone was broken, then sprayed a magical mist on it, saying I would feel no more pain. She would come to the hotel in the morning to give me one more treatment. Result: one day after the sprain, I walked sprightly to the podium, an imperceptible bandage around my ankle and no awareness of pain. My foot had been "iced," like an athlete's. Where was the doctor who could use this method on my heart?

I had fifteen minutes of free time that morning, so I used it to talk to the doctor, who was not a member of the Soviet Women's Committee like most of my previous contacts.

"Let me ask you something. Do you get the same pay as male doctors?" "Yes, of course."

"Do women have trouble getting better jobs in the system compared to men?"

"We don't have trouble. Anyway, legally we have the same rights as men. Our biggest complaint is our work – too many hours. As women, we also have the responsibility of the home and the children." She made this last comment as if it were a given, something natural, not something to fret about or to challenge.

I knew the rhetoric about equal rights – they were written in their constitution, but in practice women were second class citizens as in most nations. They did have rights not accorded to us; the right to work, the right to free education and health care.

"Does that mean you would like better pay for the hours you work?"

"That's not possible. No, we would like fewer hours. In fact, many of us would like to stay home and care for our children."

This was certainly a different request from the normal feminist one. "If you stayed home to do that, wouldn't you lose precious time for advancing in your profession?"

"What time? When we came back, we would quickly regain any lost experience."

"How about your income, wouldn't that suffer?"

"We might get less while at home, but when we started again we would be at our proper scale."

"Do you work through the Soviet Women's Committee to fight against the things you don't like and for your rights?"

"No. I am not a member. They do whatever the party tells them to do." It occurred to me that the constraints on autonomous public action held for men as well and probably had a leveling effect on relations between women and men.

"I work 12 hours a day six days a week. And sometimes extra. I have a job, and I know what my advancement will be through the years. I come home and prepare dinner for the family, wash and iron my husband's clothes. Of course, there are things I like about the job."

She said this as an afterthought, as if she suddenly became conscious of saying more than she should, and saying it through an interpreter. Interpreters were assumed to be hard core communists, who reported to the bosses. It was the early days of Perestroika. Throughout my stay in Moscow I sensed a confusion and uncertainty about where the new society would go and what forces in the society would be the winners. Members of the communist party especially were wary of change. People were speaking more freely, but with hesitation.

"How many children do you have?" "Three."

This brief conversation brought me closer to understanding life in a communist society than any of the discussions I had had with members of the Soviet Women's Committee. The system was simply different from ours. Why would she work to advance herself? Those decisions were made by others and advancements were routine, not based on capabilities or excellence. She was overworked, weary of her job and weary at home. Yet she could not organize on her behalf, or on behalf of the other women in the profession. The money she made was adequate for her needs, but there was no way she could make extra money for anything special. She did not, however, have to worry about education for her children or health facilities for her family. She could not speak freely except perhaps in a private conversation as we were having now, with a foreigner.

This woman doctor was ready for a market system, to try a change, any change. I wondered when she lost the security she had, a guaranteed job, free schooling for the kids, free health services, housing, would she feel like wanting it back? I suppose this would depend on how she as an individual thrived under the new system. Would Gorbachev be able to retain the welfare aspects of the society while introducing freedom of speech, freedom of the press, the right to organize, privatization? And how would women's rights fare in the transition to a free market economy? My intuition told me many of these rights would be lost- especially the woman's reproductive rights. While she had many economic, social and political rights substantially equal to men, the mentality was highly patriarchal, and the image of woman as wife-mother was deeply ingrained in the psychology of the Soviet people.

The morning of the opening of the Conference, I was driven in an official car to the Assembly Hall and taken into a room where "special" guests were assembled: those who were to speak in the Plenary, or headed commissions; women such as Freda Brown, president of the Women's International Democratic Federation; representatives of the UN and

UNESCO; national liberation fighters; and other female personalities considered important by the communist regime of the Soviet Union. The conference directed its attention to the role of women in promoting peace and how this could be achieved in all fields where women worked. The commissions were divided into education and peace, health and peace, disarmament and peace, de-nuclearization and peace, etc.

The leaders of the Soviet Women's Committee gave us coffee and were tending to us while waiting for Mr. and Ms. Gorbachev arrived. There was anticipatory electricity in the air, a heady exhilaration. This was one of the first big shows of the new Gorbachev regime. Time passed and the Gorbachevs had not appeared. We were given instructions to head for the dais, find our seats and wait for them there. As we were walking through hallways to reach our destination, the Gorbachevs, breathless, ran into us. Some of us were introduced. I was "Margarita Papandreou, the wife of the Prime Minister of Greece." Not head of Women for Mutual Security or the Women's Union of Greece, or a guest speaker. "The wife of..." In truth, I was proud to be his wife. I had never had a problem with this.

Mr. Gorbachev shook my hand warmly and said, "I hope to meet your husband sometime soon."

I responded, "He sends his warm regards and wishes you success in the conference, and in your challenging new role." Of course, my absentee husband had told me nothing of the kind, but I was so trained in the art of diplomacy by now that these words came reeling off my tongue like oil dripping off a spoon. Ms. Gorbachev shook my hand and said, "I hope to see you later." My interpreter told me most likely I would be invited for tea with Raisa. Vagueness as a method of security was still in vogue. I understood that in this case I was being invited as "the wife of..." Nonetheless, I was thrilled by the idea and didn't tell them that at the moment I was the half-wife of the Prime Minister.

Because the Soviet Union was in the early stages of perestroika and glasnost, which signaled a restructuring of the economy of the country and a liberalization of its laws – both moves toward capitalism and democracy- the conference had taken on international importance. Gorbachev was expected to use this opportunity to describe the problems the country faced and how he intended to confront them.

We settled into our seats. Those of us who were speakers occupied the front row on the dais, and the rest of the honored guests took places in a raised area behind us. When the Gorbachevs walked in there was spontaneous, long applause. I wondered whether women's hands made a different clapping noise than men's. This noise sounded so all-embracing, so warm, so friendly, so womanly.

Gorbachev's speech was inspirational. He is charismatic. He talked about reform, new thinking. He credited women with being in the forefront for peace. He grew lyrical describing women as mothers who contribute unflinchingly and unselfishly to society. Communist ideology both promoted equality between the sexes and extolled this image of woman as the keeper of the hearth – compassionate, strong, the comforter of the flock. An ideology that he thought of as progressive was deeply patriarchal. And puritan. I myself love my role as mother, but when the role is used politically to hold women back, to make them feel guilty if they step away from the household, I rebel.

Chapter Twenty One

Children's Voices for Peace

After his speech, and before the women speakers, an international organization called "Children for Peace" filled the aisles, singing songs of peace in clear, bell-like voices. When the singing stopped momentarily, a child cried out an appeal for peace in her own tongue, then another; then another. It was a most moving experience. We were all standing and applauding. I turned at some point to look at Gorbachev who was in the middle of the speaker's line on the podium. He was trying discreetly to wipe the tears away from his eyes. He appeared overwhelmed and finally turned around, pulled his handkerchief out, wiped his eyes, blew his nose, and turned back with a shake of his shoulders, as if to apologize. It was great to see a leader cry from feelings of tenderness.

The program began. Freda Brown spoke, then I walked sprightly to a microphone to face the 3,000 faces in the auditorium. I know all the methods to reduce nervousness: yawn, take deep breaths, think of the audience sitting in their underwear, pretend you are talking to a field of cabbages, pick out 10 faces around the hall and direct your talk to them. None of them work too well. What does work is getting started, hearing your voice come out strong and receiving that first applause. What also works is a belief in what you say. This is a brief synopsis of how I began:

"I have no explanations for my children, my grandchildren, the youngsters in the neighborhood as to how we human beings could place on this earth thousands and thousands of nuclear weapons I have no way to explain why the two super-powers, with less than 11 percent of the world's population, account for 60% of the world's defense expenditures. I have no way to explain why the Third World is adding at increasing rates to its arsenals of armaments.

"When my grandson asked, "why do people and nations shoot at each other, kill each other?" I just have no explanations. There are no explanations for madness or violence.

"I am reminded of the old Eric Bogel song called 'The Great Fields of France' its words carved on a rock in a French cemetery after the First World War It went like this:

'And I can't help but wonder how, Willie Mac Bride, do all those who lie here know why they died?

'Did you really believe them when they told you the cause? Did you really believe them that this war would end wars?

'Well, the suffering, the sorrow, the glory, the shame, the killing, the dying – it was all done in vain.

'Oh Willie MacBride, it's all happened again, and again, and again, and again, and again.' "

I ended my short speech with a declaration:

"We declare now from this very special women's summit in Moscow that our dreams, our desires, our politics, utopian at first glance, comprise the only real politik. We are asking for a new international order, a program for survival, and the opportunity to help shape the world's future in peace and welfare, in solidarity and dignity. We direct our efforts to fundamental change – in institutions, in ways of thinking. We pledge to use – in practical ways – the feminine element in world culture and our instincts for the preservation of life to contribute to the development of worldwide moral and ethical

values. We insist on dealing with human beings rather than bloodless abstractions or self-serving institutions."

When I returned to my seat on the podium, Raisa Gorbachev, who was sitting next to me, put her hand on my arm, whispered something in my ear which I interpreted as congratulations.

After the first gala opening day, we got down to work and attended various commissions. Each day I asked my interpreter if there was any word from Raisa's office about the tea. "Not yet," was the answer. Wednesday came, the last day of the conference, and I had concluded that the tea party was off. Around 11, while talking to women outside one of the commissions, I was told that Raisa Gorbachev would meet me at the official residence at 5 p.m. that afternoon. I had promised the Greek television crew which had come to cover the twenty Greek women present at the conference to arrange for them to film Raisa and me talking together. This was not for my personal projection. I thought it would give courage to other women in the world to enter the halls of power. When I asked Tatjana, my interpreter, to arrange this, she stood speechless for a moment, and then said she didn't think it was possible, but would check with the authorities.

A few hours later she came back with the answer. One camera would be allowed in, with one cameraman and an assistant. The crew was normally seven people. I objected, and the head of the crew objected. He claimed it was impossible to work that way; he needed all the members of the team. We asked for a reconsideration of these restrictions. The second time around we received the same instructions. We came up with a scheme: the entire entourage would pile into their rented van, follow me to the residence and there we would argue with the guards, the interpreters, with Raisa herself, if necessary. Anyway, we would give it a bold try.

As we drove through Moscow with the van behind us, Tatjana was nervous. I assured her the crew wouldn't invade without permission. Guards at the outside gate waved our car through, but stopped the van. I told Tatjana, "Tell the driver to back up so we can explain who we are." She told me she would go back to the gate as soon as I was deposited in the house on time. I was skeptical. This was an easy way to get rid of the issue.

Raisa was waiting for me in a small reception room and motioned me to a divan. Julia, my secretary and an active member of EGE, was given a seat next to it. I had not taken a good look at Mrs. Gorbachev in the hubbub of the congress. Now I was surprised at how petite she was, with fine features, more French than the wide faced peasant stereotype we are used to see. In newspaper photographs she looked Russian. In person she appeared delicate. Her outfit was perfect in color and style, suiting her complexion and hair. There was an interpreter in the room and one other gentleman from Raisa's office. My interpreter had indeed done what she said-disappeared to handle the television van.

We started the normal introductory chit-chat, when the double door flew open and in walked seven of my Greek compatriots. Bodies, notebooks and equipment filled the room. I wondered how Raisa would deal with these excited Mediterraneans. Public figures who are constantly followed by reporters often pretend they are not there, ignore them, or even worse, consider them obnoxious interferences. I have seen them treated badly, rudely and arrogantly. Perhaps because I was trained as a journalist, I am sensitive to this mistreatment. Their job is to get as much information as they can, which makes them frequently aggressive.

"Welcome to my home," Raisa said, kindly, apparently enjoying the fuss. "Is this your first trip to Moscow?"

There were "yeses" and "no's" as seven voices responded to her question.

"You there, with the big camera, have you been following the Women's Congress?"

"Yes, Mrs. Gorbachev."

"How is it going? What did you think of it?"

The cameraman was taken aback. He had come to film, not to be interviewed. But he was clearly pleased that his opinion had been sought, and he described with eloquence his impressions of the week.

"Then you think it was a success? All of you?"

There was a chorus of affirmative answers.

"Can we turn on the lights now?" the camera man asked.

"Yes, turn them on," replied Raisa. "Now you are going to pick up all my wrinkles and blind me at the same time so I won't be able to see you." Everybody laughed and relaxed.

They took one minute of the two of us chatting, then thanked their gracious hostess. Seven new ardent fans of Raisa walked back out through the double doors.

Raisa and I got down to real talk. "I want to make a complaint, Ms. Papandreou. I want to make a criticism of your speech. Can I do that? You don't mind?"

"Not only do I not mind, I want you to do it." I was really curious about what she would say.

"You didn't mention the reduction of nuclear weapons."

"I thought I did..." I was trying to remember what might have given her that impression. "Well, I put it in the context of breaking down the entire war system; that is, I think arms reduction is extremely important, but arms in themselves are not what cause war."

"Yes, but at this particular juncture, we must emphasize de-nuclearization. We have reached such a dangerous stockpiling of these destructive weapons that the survival of our earth is at stake."

"I couldn't agree more, and our international peace organization has made that a priority." I went into a description of our aims and goals. "We are trying as well to develop new approaches to the question of conflict, to engage in new thinking."

Here Raisa smiled. The term "new thinking" was Mikhail's expression which he used in his public speeches in the international arena.

"I see what you are getting at. Perhaps I didn't understand too well…the translation into earphones is not often clear, or correct. And if the things you are telling me are what your organization stands for, I can sign on as a member, with both hands."

What an opportunity. I turned to Julia. "We don't by any chance have application forms with us?"

Julia looked crestfallen. Neither one of us had thought of bringing a few blanks along. I could have offered to mail her a form, but her offer was sufficient and a clear gesture of approval.

Raisa spoke briefly to her aide, asking him to check on the Central Committee meeting where Mikhail was unveiling his new economic plan. There had been much worldwide speculation about the response, and it was clear that Raisa, like me, kept abreast of her husband's political moves and was eager for his success.

We moved into the dining room. Raisa sat directly across from me, her two staff members on either side. Very quickly the blintzes and caviar came out, along with vodka. The ban on alcohol had not reached the president's table. Wine from the Republic of Georgia was offered. Raisa gave me an eloquent description of Georgia, obviously loving its natural beauty. She said, "You know nothing of our country if you don't move around and explore it."

I wanted to open the door to her emotional and psychological world. I also wanted to hear about the economic package, but I didn't do what I am sure a man would have done, ask her about the economic measures being debated. "I noticed you were eager to hear about the progress being made in the Central Committee. Do you feel anxious at all about your husband's political and economic moves?"

She seemed hesitant at first, as if she hadn't expected that kind of question. "No…no, not really. Well, I just think it is so important that this plan for restructuring the economy pass...I guess you could say I am anxious for the country." Then she quickly put the shoe on the other foot. "And you? Do you have anxieties of the variety you mentioned?"

I thought, not that variety but others. "I naturally want things to work out well. There have been occasions – his speeches in Parliament when I have been present – when I have experienced tension. I want his success for the country's success – the same as you."

This closed the circle, at least for the moment, of my psychological probing.

"The press in Greece wrote about a document Mr. Gorbachev would present with extensive changes in the management of your society."

She smiled. "Yes, changes unthinkable a few years back."

"Are they still not for public knowledge?"

"I see you are interested."

"For one thing, my husband is an economist, and I got involved in thinking about such things early in our marriage. Until then, except for one course at the university, I avoided the subject. It seemed unrelated to my needs. I think there is a gap between what social scientists do and how we understand what goes on in our everyday lives."

"You know, I have studied philosophy and you are raising an interesting question. Perhaps we'll have time to dwell on it. What Mikhail is talking about is no secret – there has been much speculation already, and now that it is in the Central Committee the outlines of his proposal are known. The most important two things are the end of fixed, subsidized prices and centralized control over many enterprises. I guess that tells you what big steps we are taking. I decided not to give her my lecture on the dangers of a free market system. Not, at least, at a moment of apparent success. In several meetings in Soviet Union Satellite countries I had attended after the fall of the Wall, I found a passion for free market "pure" capitalism. I was hoping that the Gorbachevs could find a way to marry the best aspects of each economic system. At about this moment a secretary came in, all smiles, and whispered something to Raisa. She smiled too, then turned to me. "His proposal passed."

We concluded our conversation with a very feminine subject – diet and obesity. We were both intrigued with the fact that forty years after the World War, when starvation was rampant, people now had crossed the line to the other side – gluttony. Apart from the raised standard of living, we both thought there were psychological reasons. The attitude in Greece was to fatten the children so they had nourishment sources available in their own bodies in case of the kind of deprivation experienced in a war.

My meeting with Raisa Gorbachev was delightful and memorable – and I told her so as we were leaving. I told her also that Andreas would be extending an invitation to both of them for an official visit to Greece, and she responded with enthusiasm.

Accompanying me on my drive to the airport to return to Greece was the new president of the Soviet Women's Committee, Gorbachev's choice to replace the dynamic astronaut, Valentini Tereshkova. Her name was Zoya Pukhova, former head of the Union of Women Garment Workers. She was a large woman, cheerful, unfamiliar with international affairs. She asked me how I liked the Congress. I had found it highly disorganized. The commissions consisted of a series of talks – largely a description by each woman speaker of the condition of women in her country, Questions were not permitted from the floor; there was no analysis and no dialogue. Furthermore, the speeches were often inconsistent with the peace subject of the commission. I concluded that this probably was due to lack of political education of women. I could presume as well, that in a communist society this held also for men.

There was no mechanism for a closing declaration stating the conference's positions and commitments. There was no daily bulletin. Conference rooms were located in various buildings and difficult to find. The real merit, as it often is, was in the informal discussions in the hallways, over lunch, or in hotels in the evening, and the networking that went on. I didn't tell her all these things. I said the organization of the conference was weak, but it was a very positive experience for me, and I learned a lot. The latter was true.

She turned to me smiling and satisfied, but with one more question: "Didn't you feel it was a democratic Congress?" In Russia this was the new attractive word, "democratic." I hesitated, remembering for one thing the lack of dialogue.

"I mean, everybody spoke," she continued. "Every woman had a chance to say something. It was absolutely open and free. And the person could speak as long as she wanted."

Again I hesitated. I wondered if I should give a lesson in democratic procedures. Should I tell her that democracy has rules that complete freedom is more like anarchy, that democracy respects the right of others to occupy and share the time given for debate? Or that a democratic Congress usually includes many of the participants in the planning stage? Pukhova was so elated and so eager for my confirmation, my blessing, so to speak, that I decided to congratulate her and wish her organization and country well. I figured it would take quite a while for a centrally-organized communist country, years in power, to learn the techniques of democracy, and then to put them into practice. We in the West often have problems with the latter. Even countries with deep democratic roots, such as Chile or Greece, are prey to military dictatorships and fascism. The road ahead for the Soviet Union was not going to be easy. I could only hope that this husky woman's wonderful smile and animated face would shine through the years ahead.

By the time I returned from Moscow, summer was full blown in Greece. From a political point of view, the Iran/Contra hearings in Washington seemed to define the summer of 1987. I videotaped many of the sessions and Jules Dassin and I spent hours watching the videos in his summer home in Epidavros. Melina tolerated our American fascination with the congressional investigation, but insisted on a break occasionally for a swim, and for food. I worked over my material for a speech at a peace conference in Coventry in England in the early part of July – which I had accepted partially as an excuse to visit Andrikos again in Oxford.

I was getting accustomed to functioning on my own, being able to invite friends to the house without checking to see if a political event would require my participation or the PASOK Executive Board require the dining room. Before I left for Moscow, I had given a series of lunches for women from various walks of life: actresses, writers, factory workers, radio and news reporters, young girls who had scored the highest grades on university entrance exams. With their permission I taped our lunch conversations, thinking I might collect them in a book "Women's Voices," or "Women's Thoughts," or "That's What We Say When We Eat Together." I read a lot, catching up on the latest in feminist thinking as well as peace issues. Sometimes I attended open air theaters, performances at Erodou Attikou under the Acropolis, or visited nearby islands.

(Diary Entry) *July 11th, 1987, Kastri, just before sleep*

Yesterday was Sophia's birthday. We had a party on the veranda with the family and a few close friends. Andreas came by. I looked at him as if he were a familiar, unwanted guest. I was surprised he came. I presume it was because of his deep affection for his daughter. After he and the other guests left, Sophia and I sat down for a chat. She has had two miscarriages. The doctor says there is nothing wrong with her, nor with her husband. And, importantly, they have already produced one child. Chances are it is psychological, and I would understand that at a time of family turmoil. The situation has affected her more than the boys. I asked if she would like to come with me for a thorough check-upon on my next trip to the States. Her answer was "maybe."

She doesn't speak easily about her inner world, at least not to me. Maybe it's the often talked about tension in the mother-daughter relationship. I know what the psychology books say. The daughter competes for the father's affection. If that is true then when the mother is replaced, the daughter should become competitive with the new one. In this case, the woman is Sophia's age, which is certainly a more complex situation. It is as if The Hostess has replaced her not only as a "wife," but as a daughter. The difficulty is further complicated by Sophia's strong need to preserve the family. From the time she became aware of an interloper in the family arena, she has had a mission: get Dad back to the nest. Her strategy was to spend as much time as possible with her father, turning up at his office to help him and to talk to him. I had mixed feelings about her being in there slugging when I have backed off.

I want to spend the summer in a leisurely fashion, partly to regain my tranquility, partly to remove myself from the newspapers. I am tired of seeing my face every day, and I am sure others are too. I am being pressured to accept an invitation to the Special Olympics at Notre Dame University in Indiana. Eunice Kennedy, the oldest daughter in the Kennedy clan originated this great event of sports competition for mentally retarded children, and she felt, rightly so, that I could be instrumental in setting up a Special Olympics team in Greece.

While Greeks are not very receptive to persons with physical handicaps, they are in general very humane toward those affected with mental diseases. The grown-up "lunatic" is treated with gentleness and is thought to bring good fortune. This harks back to ancient times when the soothsayer or sage was not the best-balanced member of the community. He talked to himself, saw visions, heard sounds and voices. Apparently this went along with his great wisdom. I remember one Athenian man who showed up downtown daily in a special colorful uniform blowing a whistle and directing traffic. He seemed to be enjoying himself; he was fun to watch, and I never saw anyone try to remove him, or get angry with him. So it is lucky to have a "nut" around. I wondered why politicians are not better tolerated or loved.

Before I decided on the trip, I called my sister Evelyn and asked if she would join me in South Bend for the games. She replied "yes" with enthusiasm and suggested that after the games we drive back in her car to Illinois together. The notion of disappearing into the serenity of her home for a week or so was very appealing. I accepted the invitation to her home.

Chapter Twenty Two

The Special Olympics

The Special Olympics started on July 31st with a dinner hosted by Secretary of State George Schultz in Washington. My first task was an interview with Eunice on CNN, after that a trip by special plane to South Bend where we would tour the EXO Center, and have a brunch with First Ladies. I was very much in tune with what Eunice was doing and excited about participating, but wondered if it would only engender a lot of new negative publicity.

In the evening at the Schultz dinner party, I was seated next to the journalist Roland Evans. He and his partner Robert Novak were constant critics of Andreas – his personality as well as his policies. It was a critical moment in Greek-U.S. relations because earlier in July U.S. intelligence reports were made public saying that Athens had for several months been conducting negotiations with Abu Nidal. According to the U.S., these negotiations concerned the release of a handful of suspected terrorists in exchange for a pledge that Greece and Greek interests would not be targeted in the future. Nidal was head of the Palestinian splinter group Al Fatah Revolutionary Council, which has been implicated in the 1985 airport bombings in Rome and Vienna. From all I could learn from the Ministry of Foreign Affairs, these allegations were untrue.

The State Department also strongly expressed its unhappiness with Greece's dealings with the Armenian Liberation Army, which had carried out terrorist acts against the Turks. The Greek government angrily denied the charges. A Greek satiric weekly, *Pontiki*, had a photograph of me eating with U.S. Ambassador Bob Keeley. In the lines underneath Keeley says to me: "Tell your husband not to keep company with terrorists." I respond: "We don't keep company. Only once in a while we dine with you." This was a great opportunity to express my feelings about the word "terrorist." It was ill defined, but created fear in the mind of the listener. The media, in conjunction with the government, could easily make a population nervous and fearful enough to accept the use of force against such an enemy.

Strangely enough Evans did not bring up the terrorist accusation. Just a few days earlier the New York Times said Andreas was threatening to shut down all four American bases in Greece unless the U.S. apologized for protesting his alleged negotiations with the Palestinian "terrorist" Abu Nidal. The Times advised the U.S. government to tell Andreas "to go jump in the lake." Newsweek said Western diplomats were accustomed to Andreas Papandreou's "tantrums." Others said he was "beating the anti-U.S. drum again." Andreas had developed quite an image in the States. Actually, as a government, we did have good relations with the Palestinians and with the Armenians who were fighting our traditional enemy – Turkey. Also our women's organization had contacts with the women's sections of their liberation movements.

Neither women's organization nor the government condoned acts of violence and were certainly not involved in them. But whatever acts of violence occurred in such just causes were not much different from U.S. acts of violence in defending what it considered just causes. A cycle of violence is set up that feeds the production and selling of arms that feeds the violence. The Palestinians respond to the oppression and violence in the occupied Palestinian territories through violent acts. The U.S. bombs Libya in retaliation to the airport bombing by the Palestinians. The Armenians respond to the capture and occupation of their land by Turkey. Turkey responds by wiping out villages. Because I am with the underdog and sympathetic to struggles against oppression, I understand them, while not condoning their use of violence. Because also I have a world view of the Big Wolves – the banks, the corporations, the business class – and the large nations – eating up the upstarts, I understand. But when the child becomes a killer, you don't turn around and shoot him. You deal with the parents – those who supplied support and the means. You deal through negotiation and dialogue. You try to find justice for those who are living in an unfair situation. This is somewhat idealistic, but I consider it real politik, and this is how I would have responded if Roland Evans had raised the question.

In person, Evans was less severe than in print and appeared genuinely interested in learning about this creature Papandreou who had become the bête noire to the administration, to NATO, to the European Community; U.S. criticism was avid because many Americans had considered Andreas "one of ours." He had found a haven in the U.S. just before the Nazis invaded Greece. He was educated at Harvard. He ultimately joined the American Navy, became a citizen, and after the war became a distinguished economist at an American university. All the academic economists in the U.S had fought for his release from prison under the junta. That he should be harsh and anti-American was inconceivable to them and "ungrateful."

I defended Andreas, the man who had stomped away from my dining table approximately forty-eight hours earlier. I defended him because his positions were just. And on the domestic front he had carried out a number of reforms long overdue. Civil marriage was introduced, the Family Code was rewritten to meet the rightful demands of women, the dowry system was abolished. He gave more power to local authorities, and aided the cultural programs in the rural areas. The health system had been revamped to make it efficient and to bring health facilities and medical personnel to the countryside. Pensions had been established for women farmers (I am proud to say most of these actions were fomented by EGE). I slipped in to Evans that Andreas loved the American way of life. And this was true. He liked to listen to jazz, to rock and roll and even to country music, which I had imposed on him, he learned the Charleston and danced it perfectly, he loved American football and liked the freedom of speech all Americans took for granted, and he was committed to the academic community. I asserted strongly my belief that anti-Americanism is not against the entire country, but almost always against the foreign policy of the State Department, and its entourage that benefit from war.

I continued my salute to Andreas and told him about Andreas' national reconciliation efforts. Many Greek fighters were ousted by the post-war government to Eastern Europe and the Soviet Union at the end of the Greek Civil War, which had started at the cessation of fighting in World War II. In truth many had been resistance fighters against the Nazis. They were wrongly all labeled as communists because the leadership of the mountain resistance was communist. This was unfair because they have all been fighters against Germany. The Papandreou government gave them "pardons" so they could return to Greece if they so desired. Looking at this from the American point of view made Andreas appear to be pro-communist.

Actually, the State Department should have known that in Western Europe the Communist Party is accepted as part of European politics, and not considered a revolutionary threat to the governments there. While I was talking, I watched Evans' anti-communist horns emerge through his skull ever so slightly. Like many Americans, he still thought of the Communist Party as the engine of revolutionary subversion. Then I remarked casually, "of course, it was Karamanlis, our rightist premier, who recognized the Communist Party after the fall of the dictatorship." This gave it a stamp of approval. If the Right does it, it is right. At the table Evans and I monopolized each other and joined in conversations around us only perfunctorily before returning to our discussion. I left the dinner liking Evans and hoping I had done a service for Andreas, and for Greece.

The Greek Ambassador to the U.S., George Papoulias, was also invited to South Bend, which ensured press releases back to Greece. I regretted keeping quiet about something I wanted to sing to the world about: the wonderful things the Kennedys were doing. The publicity about my personal life had not allowed me the freedom to be politically effective. Without any nudge on my part, a press release went out on July 27 from the Greek Press and Information Office in Washington:

"Mrs. Margaret Papandreou, wife of Andreas Papandreou, prime minister of Greece, and global coordinator for the peace network WMS, is to lead Greece's delegation to the 7th International Summer Special Olympic Games which will open at Notre Dame University on August 2. The Greek delegation of 12 athletes, entered for events in the field and track and basketball competitions, will march at the head of 6,000 competitors during the opening ceremonies at the stadium. The event will be covered in the US by the ABC national TV network and seen by an estimated 40 million viewers."

So much for keeping a low profile!

One item of interest: of the wives of nine foreign leaders appearing at the Games, three of us were American. The other two were Pennsylvania-born Carolina Isakson de Barco of Colombia and Washington-born Lisa Halaby of Jordan. There have been examples like this in the past, including the American wife of Winston Churchill. I asked Lisa if she thought this was a new form of American imperialism or a more subtle way for American women to rule the world. She loved the question.

I donned a Greek-style white toga gown for the opening parade, hurriedly sewn together in Greece when I learned I was expected to lead the parade, a role given to Greece in the traditional Olympic Games. It was a nice blend of politics, too. Ambassador Papoulias, a rightist, and Margarita, a leftist, appeared at the head of the march into the stadium. I was totally thrilled by the event. Though I had dreamed as a child I would be an Olympic swimming competitor one day, this was the closest I had gotten to an Olympics appearance. It had all the folderol and air of an international sports activity. I adored the children. There were thousands of them, mentally handicapped athletes, bearing the flags of 72 nations. As they marched around the stadium waving to the crowd like pros, their cheery ringing laughter filled the air. Last of all, I was symbolizing the country I had come to love, the home of the Olympic Games, the home of democracy and the home of Andreas and my family.

Eunice and I went together to the basketball court to watch the game between Greek and Italian youngsters. At half-time, Eunice challenged me to a basketball competition. I thought it was just a shooting contest. Then I saw the officials setting up two lines of wooden sticks as in downhill skiing competitions, and I realized this was not to be a test of my deadly aim. At the sound of the whistle we were to start dribbling toward the end of the court, weaving back and forth among the obstacles, then turning around and dribbling back to the start. Eunice and I solemnly shook hands before the race began. With my customary confidence in my general basketball prowess, I was prepared to win.

Then we took off! My dribbling skills were impeccable as I moved ahead with a fast, staccato, low bounce. I used my legs, hips, arms in what I thought were lovely, sinewy body movements, appropriate to a well-coordinated athlete. Out of the corner of my eye I saw Eunice keeping up with me. That gave me a bit of a shock. When we turned the corner, at the end of the first run down the court, she was not only with me, but slightly ahead. By now, I thought, I should have pulled in front. I added steam and power to my legs. I swiveled recklessly close to the pegs. My talented hand produced a machine gun rat-a-tat-tat sound as the ball hit the wooden floor. We were approaching the finish. I saw her lunge forward and break out in front with one last bounce of the ball.

It was then that I understood my mistake. Eunice had been taking long strides, bouncing the ball as little as possible. I lost time in hand-to-floor dribbling, a technique designed more for keeping the ball from being stolen than for racing down the court. My first Olympic showing had brought me a miserable second, in this case, last place. Actually I wanted to ask her if she considered her method as "dribbling." I shut up. Gulping down my loss and disappointment, but showing stupendous sportsmanship, I congratulated her heartily. I told her she had intimidated me by being a Kennedy, the family whose reputation for excellence in sports was proverbial. It was great, solid, wonderful fun, and we promised each other a return performance.

At the end of the week, Evelyn and I piled into her red sports car and started toward the town where both of us had grown up. We stocked up with potato chips, nuts, popcorn and cold Coca Cola – everything tasting good and full of calories. We had maps and music. We felt that wonderful sense of freedom the open road can give. Although people say we look alike, we are quite a contrast. Evelyn has dark curly hair; I have light brown straight hair. Evelyn has dark skin, mine is fair, in the summertime dusted with freckles (yes, indeed, like Katherine Hepburn). Evelyn has a rounded shapely body; mine is slim and athletic. Evelyn is bubbly and spontaneous; I am reserved, less open. One thing we have in common is long legs, hence our self-delegated title, "the Barbie dolls." It was hardly an acceptable feminist appellation, but we were blood sisters, foot-loose and fancy-free, and we didn't have to conform to any ideology.

Together we were gigglers, endless talkers, and singers. I brought a Randy Travis cassette because I wanted her to hear "You've been too gone for too long; it's too late to come home now." These words epitomized my mental state and attitude toward Andreas. The song had some other lines like "You're an old rolling stone that's rolled over the hill," which I found appropriate. Country music is popular not only because of its rhythm, but because it bemoans the woes of human relationships in a simple, straightforward, unabashed fashion.

The day we were travelling the Chicago Cubs, my favorite club, were playing Philadelphia in Chicago, and in between music and singing, we followed the baseball game on the car radio. I planned to see a game in Chicago with Pierre, but not the Cubs, since he wouldn't arrive before they went on the road. We would see instead the White Sox versus the Toronto Blue Jays. The game didn't excite me; seeing Pierre did. In the game on the radio Lee Smith, the Cubs pitcher, was the winner after retiring the last two Philadelphia batters at the top of the 10th. Final score 3 to 2. Evelyn and I were screaming!

Although I insisted on taking a cab to see Pierre, Evelyn drove me to his hotel and dropped me off. She liked the idea of a clandestine meeting between her harassed sister and a lover, considered it good for my soul, and cheered me on. Pierre was waiting in the lobby to take me to the bar for a drink before our evening of sport- baseball, that is. He looked beautiful, as always, his muscles tense and full of controlled desire, his strong body oozing hormones – or was it my body full of desire and oozing hormones? Whether it was intrinsic or my own impression, he did emanate a powerful aura of sexuality. I ordered a martini, a drink I order only in America (it doesn't suit the Greek climate), which puts me in high spirits. Pierre was not much of a drinker, claiming that strong liquor made him sleepy. This time he ordered a scotch on the rocks to match my martini, saying he was in a celebratory mood.

We fell into easy conversation. The peace movement in the States was not very effective, he argued, and I said it was difficult to perceive successes, but it had played a role in forcing Johnson to decide not to run for President, and for Nixon to run on the principle of ending the Vietnam War. Once the military draft, obliging all males from 18 years of age and beyond was called off, the movement lost its momentum. It was a clever move on the part of the government because it made it appear that the resistance was more of an individual self-interest protest than a principled response to the use of force and killing as a means of resolving conflict. At least during the years of the anti-Vietnam movement, it had increased public awareness to the dangers of nuclearazation and of radiation from nuclear power plants, etc. Because I believe a key contribution of a peace movement is educating and raising the consciousness of the public, this could be considered a success.

Pierre contended that the true force fighting nuclear weapons and nuclear proliferation was the European Peace Movement. Its members had begun to halt the addition of nuclear missiles on European territory. Public opinion on nuclear weapons had been turned around completely. I agreed with him but added that the struggle was ultimately helped by the economic deterioration of the Soviet Union and Gorbachev's attempt to break down the barriers between the two super-powers.

"I think," he said, "the problem lies in the failure of the peace movement to do an analysis of the nature of the world, the real sources of conflict, the roots, and the power dynamics involved."

"And if they did so, what would be the result?"

"Well, a movement needs a strategy; it needs to be politically astute, and of course, must have a gut of anger."

"It has the latter. This is its motor, its engine. I can speak as a member of the worldwide movement. It is our sensitivities, our emotions, and our disgust that generate the action. We are moved by morally wrong actions, such as war, or stockpiling huge arsenals of destruction."

"Okay, Maggie, but does it have a strategy, is it politically savvy?"

"You tell me. I think the answer is 'no.'"

"One of the problems in developing a strategy, assuming a good analysis of the nature of the world has been done, is the number and variety of organizations in the movement's network. Some are completely pacifist, others noninterventionist, others will argue that there are times when a 'just war' may be necessary."

"Where are you on this spectrum, Mr. Pierre?"

"Oh, I'm all of those things. Okay," he said, "I'll give an answer. I am of the latter."

"Just wars?"

"Yep."

"And who is going to decide what is a just war?"

"Me."

"Oh, come on."

"Look. I'm being partly facetious. But since we don't seem to have a properly functioning mechanism or method to make that decision, I guess my instincts are as good as anyone else's."

"Well, it hardly resolves the question of strategy for the Peace Movement. As for me, I am against the use of violence period."

He ignored my last remark. "Let me put it in another way. I would like the peace movement to be more than protest. It must come up with some positive proposals to enhance and enlarge and empower what are considered peace institutions."

"You mean the United Nations. I'm with you on that."

Pierre was warming up to the subject when I looked at my watch. "Hey, we're going to miss the first inning of the game."

We arrived at Comisky Park right after the second ball was pitched. A sports announcer friend of my sister's had gotten us excellent box seats, exactly where I like to be, behind third base. The world looked good. I was in a state of euphoria because of the following things (not necessarily in this order)... good conversation, feeling attractive, fresh and physically fit – even though I had not beaten Kennedy in our basketball contest – hotdogs, mustard, popcorn, beer- and watching my favorite childhood spectator sport.

I was due in New York on August 10th to give a speech at a U.N. anti-apartheid meeting organized by my friend Sotiris Mousouris. It was a Day of Solidarity for women struggling against apartheid in South Africa. Dear Lisbet Palme, who had recently taken up a post with UNICEF, was also speaking. We sat next to each other in the first row of the auditorium. She looked so frail and yet was so strong. I wondered, is it harder to struggle for the things she and her husband worked together for after he left this world, or after a divorce?

In my speech I emphasized the connection between the anti-apartheid struggle and the struggle for world peace and security. I also argued that the days of the South African government were numbered because women were the unheralded forefront of the anti-apartheid battle, and therefore its success was assured. "But of course," I said, "solidarity and assistance in the struggle is needed from other sources. The U.N., whose resolutions are positive, should see that those resolutions are put into practice."

When I returned to Greece a few days later, Andreas was nowhere to be found. He finally turned up in the newspapers. He was off on a cruise with The Hostess. I, and the public, were able to follow his travels in the company of Miso-Miso, her newspaper nickname, from Lagonissi to Corfu, to Skiathos, to Porto Heli.

Shortly thereafter I turned into an impersonal observer, watching and feeling nothing: no welling of anger, no jealousy, and no wounded pride. My body and feet were not attached to anything at all; I was in suspended animation, numb. I knew in some layer of consciousness there was a far off wail, a wail with the sound of my voice. At times I thought I heard it, but I was indifferent to that too. I was walking through life from practice, not from any inner motivation. Unless someone read my silences, there was no way of knowing what was or wasn't going on inside of me. Nor did I seem to know either. The only thing I knew for sure was that the end of this long, hot summer would have to bring a denouement of one kind or another.

The early part of September I invited handicapped children for a party on the lawn of Kastri, by now a yearly event. I visited a few nearby islands. I had meetings with EGE Board members in preparation for the fall program. I convinced my son Andreas to play a game of golf with me at the Glyfada golf course. Someone informed a newspaper I was out on the course and a photographer and reporter appeared to memorialize this rare event. A series of photographs was published in the newspaper's magazine. My mood was so placid that I was unconcerned about whether there was publicity, or not. One merit of the photographs – they enabled me to see the imperfections in my swing.

Two organizations on the island of Zakinthos – ELKEPA (Greek Productivity and Management Center) and the Prefecture's Committee for People's Education – invited me for the opening ceremonies of a tourism cooperative organized and run by women. I was able to observe how farm women had turned their homes into space for tourists – bed, bathroom facilities, and breakfast. In these homes tourists could enjoy the glorious Ionian Sea inexpensively and live for a while with a Greek family. EGE could make this the blueprint for such a program in other areas of Greece.

We were into the middle of September. My personal life continued to be muddled, and on this trip I got clues that it was to be further muddled. I was going into a hornet's nest of antagonism from an elected deputy in parliament whom I distrusted, his seething hostility toward me was covered up by gratingly sugary pronouncements of affection. Thus I expected unpleasantness. What I found was more complicated than that.

Chapter Twenty Three

A Simple Citizen

When I arrived in Zakinthos I was told the hall reserved for the EGE meeting was not available, but we could meet in a hotel lobby offered by the owner. I found this strange to say the least. The plans had been made several weeks in advance, and no one gave me a sufficient explanation for the change. Early on the first day we had transportation problems. Cars arranged by the Nomarch for me and the women accompanying me arrived extremely late. The attitude of the Nomarch, who was an appointed PASOK official, was unresponsive. Usually because I was the First Lady, PASOK officials were generally very courteous and overly eager to please me.

My schedule on Zakinthos was to join with the local chapter of EGE for a trip to Laganas Bay where Loggerhead Sea Turtles, (Caretta Caretta), were being threatened by the increasing tourist trade and new hotel developments. Laganas Bay, I was told, was distant and would eat up much of my program. We had been scheduled to have lunch on the beach at a small taverna there. My program was free until 6 p.m.! In other words, my trip to the turtles was cancelled with a pseudo explanation.

We survived the two days; our activities were positive and the response of the people of the island enthusiastic. Yet I knew something was in the wind, and suspected machinations by the local deputy, my honey-dripping enemy. He had property on Lagano Bay beach and was fighting every effort to protect the turtles, because they were a barrier for his plans to commercialize his property. I also knew he had the power to foul up my schedule, power which surpassed that of my young friend the executive secretary. I knew something further. He disliked me and worried about any influence I might have on Andreas that might be bad for him. He was salivating surely for my apparent removal from the scene.

(Diary Entry) *September 19th, 1987, late night, Kastri*

I've had several days back home from my sweet-sour experience in Zakinthos. Am trying to get the sour taste out of my mouth and hold on to the sweet. I am also trying to turn my attention to what is going on with the nuclear debate among the super powers. Gorbachev says an agreement to eliminate intermediate-range missiles could be worked out this year. The U.S. Senate is scheduled to vote on a crucial defense spending amendment. This is a measure backed by the Democrats and would limit the funds for Reagan's Star Wars system. If they manage to pass this, I give them a big "bravo!"

CNN reported the details being worked out for a Summit meeting between the two leaders for later this Fall. Discussion revolves around the elimination of two classes of missiles, which the Soviet Foreign Minister calls only a beginning. Secretary of State Schultz says "It is time to bring in the harvest." Right. Good signs. The meeting will be in Washington and WMS will be there! I am watching now an interview with Lord Carrington on CNN. As NATO secretary general, he welcomes the accords being worked out, but cautions the Alliance not to disarm unless verification procedures can be worked out. That I agree is basic. This is a time when the initiative of the Six and Andreas personally could be instrumental in organizing the verification process.

For some time now newspapers mentioned the possibility of my leading a new political party. I ignored these untruths. The day I returned to Athens, the satiric periodical *Pontiki* had a sizeable article about an actual event in an EGE Board meeting the day we learned about the victory of a women's party in elections in Ireland. This is the article:

At the end of the meeting of EGE, a member of the Board expressed her excitement for the success of the women's party in Ireland. In the middle of the general enthusiasm one member shouted out, "Why don't we form a party?"

"Let's do it, let's do it," Maria Kypriotaki responded excitedly.

"You want to make that a signed suggestion?" asked Didi Yiannopoulou. "Well, certainly," Maria answered, believing it was all in the spirit of a joke.

At that point one of the members of the Board produced a white paper napkin and the following was written down: "We must start a party." And Maria signed with broad, sweeping letters.

Kypriotaki forgot the incident, as did the rest of the Executive Board. Days passed and then came a message to her to appear at Kastri. She was wanted by the president of PASOK.

For her it was a relief. She had been asking for her own political purposes to have an appointment with the prime minister for some time. At last it was to be realized. As soon as she was seated in his office, she started to thank him for responding to her request for a meeting, when he stopped her and waved a white paper napkin in her face. The napkin bore her signature.

"What is this? You are taking action to destroy PASOK? I need an immediate explanation."

Kypriotaki, poor soul, rushed to explain it was done in fun and the rest of the Executive Board would substantiate this fact. Later, when she learned the napkin had been discussed also in the Executive Board of the party of PASOK, she realized she had come close to being written off by the party.

Someone from the Board must have given a detailed description of the discussion, and the napkin (!) because the story was true, exactly as written. It was also true that it was all done in a spirit of fun. I again paid no attention to intimations that I, or EGE, might form a party. The next day, September 21st, just to break the tension, I went up to a friend's office in Athens to hear her Pakistani friend's analysis of my astrological chart.

"How about reading the part on Love and Marriage?" I asked.

"Sure." She ran through the pages and found the section. "Relating to the opposite sex may carry a few problems." (A few?) "You are of a faithful disposition. The idea of secret love affairs appeals to you." (How does the last sentence relate to the previous one?) "With your loved one you avoid criticizing and don't dominate. Your romantic attitude to love makes you inclined to idealize the whole question. When a relationship comes to an end, you have some reluctance to face the fact." (correct) "You are very good at expressing your love, in constant need of demonstrations of love yourself, and possessive. " (I am not possessive enough.) "You have a strong sex drive with few inhibitions." (Well, well) "Your partner will find you interested in other things besides sex." (Not really.) "You constantly use sex as a manipulative force to gain something." (Tsk, tsk) "Marriage will be very lively." (An understatement) "There is some probability that your spouse would be a loving person." (He was.)

While she was reading to me and explaining the chart indicating I had a good future and would reach the pinnacle of my success sometime in December, the telephone rang. It was my son-in-law, Sophia's husband, himself in politics. An official statement had come out describing my political activities as private events not of concern to the government. More precisely, the statement, attributed to "circles in the government," read: "The political activities of Ms. Margarita Papandreou concern her and her alone."

"Theodore," I asked, "what the hell does that mean, and what are 'government circles'? Great white males?"

"It was Kouris from *Avriani* (a pro-PASOK newspaper) who called me with this information. He didn't say who told him."

"Well, Roumbatis is the government spokesman, what does he say? Is he the 'circles'?

"He was asked by reporters, and he said he didn't comment on statements made anonymously. That seems to suggest that it didn't come from him."

"What in God's name is this all about? What political activities? My visit to Zakinthos? And if Roumbatis didn't orchestrate this, who did?"

"I'm stunned, too, Margarita."

"What do you think I should do? Ignore it?"

"Let's wait until I can get more information. I'm going to call Karapaniotis of '*TA NEA*'."

"Call me back immediately, okay?"

In about ten minutes Theodore was back on the line. "Karapaniotis can't get any more information than we have. He thinks, however, that you should just let it go by. Don't make any statements."

"Is that your opinion too?"

"Yes, I would agree with him." They were scared of what I might say. This gave me a fleeting moment of satisfaction.

"I've been sitting here ruminating on this strange development, and I think I've found the key," I told Theodore.

"What's that?"

"Almost a week ago *Pontiki* wrote the story of Kypriotaki, EGE and the white napkin. A day or two later *Apogevmatini* wrote that the wife of the prime minister wants to form her own party. Andreas said everyone tells him to watch out for Margarita. Newspaper reporters who have come in contact with me during this week always raise the question of a party. The papers have been full of it since then. You know what? I think Andreas believes it!"

"Ridiculous," Theodore exclaimed.

"Yes, ridiculous, but he's being fed by people around him who want to hurt me."

"Hurt you? They want to cut off your head!"

"Dumb as the whole thing may be, I think I have to take it seriously and make a statement. I don't want to stay silent on this one."

I wrote the following and sent it to eight key newspapers:

"It is not my habit to respond to various conjectures about me from time to time in the newspapers, but the fuss surrounding the 'news' that I am founding my own party compels me to make a statement. In very simple words, all of these hypotheses fall in the realm of fantasy and are sheer nonsense, complete stupidities."

The next morning reporters rushed to the government press room as soon as Roumbatis was available.

Journalist: What do you have to say about Ms. Papandreou's declaration?

Roumbatis: It is a statement from a simple citizen. The government press representative speaks on behalf of the government and will not comment on that declaration.

Journalist: In the recent past, Ms. Papandreou has undertaken missions of an international character, to the United States and elsewhere, and she is the president of EGE. In any case, she has operated as a political personality. Isn't your characterization of her inconsistent with the political activities of Ms. Papandreou?

Roumbatis: No, because she was and remains a simple citizen.

Journalist: The treatment that Ms. Papandreou received from all of the public services and from the Press Office was not that received by all simple citizens.

Roumbatis: I disagree.

Journalist: With what facts?

Roumbatis: (After some thought and with a touch of resignation) I have nothing further to add.

Journalist: Ms. Margarita recently made a trip to the States and brought a message to the Greek-Americans from the Prime Minister. With her was the Minister of Foreign Affairs, Karolos Papoulias. When and for what reason did these acts cease to be of concern to the government?

Roumbatis: The government can assign to anyone the taking of a message. Even to you, who are dignified journalists.

A number of newspapers tried to analyze this bizarre development, my being declared a "simple citizen." Nowhere in their analysis in the days following did they pounce on the extra-marital affair as having something to do with this weird development. *Apogevmatini* said the Prime Minister "shot his wife in cold blood." It continued, "This column will not shed tears for the American wife of the Prime Minister who had taken on the role of teaching Greek women how they should be Greek women. However, the behavior of the prime minister toward Ms. Margaret Papandreou, at the personal and political level, displays a peculiar hardness worth noting. It indicates conflict at both levels. At some stage, perhaps suddenly, he saw in the person of his wife a dynamic opponent."

Others regarded an unexpected announcement of changes in the government as an effort to smother the clamor ensuing from what appeared to be a family battle. Later on Roumbatis gave the names of three members of the government who had been removed: a diplomatic advisor, an economics advisor, and the Deputy Minister of Defense. There were those who connected it with me somehow. Although I had convivial relations with all three, I certainly did not consider them agents or cohorts of mine in any way.

After a few days there was an article entitled "Reorganization of the Government a Cover for a Rose Scandal." One columnist hinted at the hidden scenario saying one would have to be an idiot not to understand what was as clear as day and disquieting. "No one wants to write about it openly," the columnist said, "because it would become third rate copy for a cheap magazine, but Margarita has become a nuisance as a wife." The person who wrote this perceptive and honest article was a woman. A newspaper in northern Greece listed all the headlines in the Athenian newspapers and simply said, "Good night, Margarita." (This was the title of a popular theatrical play of previous years.)

Another article compared Andreas to Alcibiades, the adopted son of Pericles, who became a general in the army. An egotist, he showed contempt for laws, mores, ethics and customs of the society and for most of his fellow men. He was, however, kind and courteous to those under him, the little guys. His adolescent frivolities followed him all his life and led to strong reactions. Sometimes the people loved him and forgave him his dissoluteness because of his charisma and his rhetorical talent. At other times they lost faith in him and rejected him.

(Diary Entry) *September 23rd 1987 – Kastri*

Just finished a lunch to which I invited women resistance fighters against the Nazi occupation during World War II. The Resistance Movement in Greece was one of the least heralded and one of the most courageous and bold of any in Europe. Almost half of them were women. These women are women of strength, strong ethical values and a deep love of country. No one asked me about the screeching headlines in the newspapers. I asked them whether at the time they were in the Resistance Movement they had thought about the question of equality between the sexes, about the general mistreatment of women by society. I anticipated their answer. The problem of sex discrimination was not on their minds at the time. They had gone into the Resistance Movement to throw out the oppressors, to fight to free their country. A free Greece, they argued, would give the opportunity for a new society, an open and democratic society in which issues of equality, development, and world peace would be handled properly! I loved these women; they had stood up to be counted under life-threatening circumstances, and although they were all in their 60s or 70s by now, each had that fresh inner glow which comes from working for something...above and beyond oneself. I wanted to learn all about them.

When the excitement of this meeting slipped away, my mind returned to my personal issues. First my actions were dismissed as of no concern to the government of which my husband is the head. Next, the government spokesman gave me a demotion and a new title, from First Lady to "simple citizen." It was divorce via press room. I was not First Lady, not an activist, not president of EGE. Well, I thought, they can kill me but they can't eat me, as the saying goes. I'll fight my own war to preserve my dignity and self respect.

The EGE Board officers wanted to give me support, to react against the behavior of the P.M. I didn't see any reason to involve EGE; it was not an EGE problem. If Andreas wanted to cut my political wings, my strength, the only thing EGE could do was to give me support by struggling harder for what we believe in. What Andreas had done was separation as fait accompli, a separation without a formal announcement. I was trying to handle it gingerly, as a private matter, trying not to throw oil on the fire with incendiary statements or to become a subject of debate by a women's organization. Was I forgetting my role as understanding wife? Was I neglecting my duties, my responsibility, as president of a feminist organization? Don't women's organizations take up cases of wife-battering? Again that continuing dilemma between the feminist and the woman...

The children, the three of them who were in Greece (Andrikos was in Oxford) were angry. They considered the "situation" a public humiliation for the family. Nikos talked to his father and had a difficult discussion. The only person with whom Andreas was reasonable was Sophia, who came home happy after a meeting with her father. He said to her, "You know, all this will pass." He tried to give the impression to those who have contact with me that he was somewhat involved, but it would not last, hoping this would get back to me and neutralize my reactions. There was another explanation – he could have been in his own dilemma. On the one hand he liked the feeling of freedom, a delight in a new and young relationship and the rather unorthodox way of handling it – or maybe there is no orthodox way; and on the other hand, a sense of guilt and commitment to a long – though somewhat rocky – relationship.

Kostas, the psychiatrist, still insisted that it was temporary. He told me Andreas was angry because "there were six pages of Margarita playing golf...I don't get six pages in a magazine." I told Yannis to remind him he never plays golf. Kostas said also that Andreas believed I had serious plans to form a party. So, I was right! Kostas was sure his antagonisms and suspicions were fed by The Hostess. That was hardly news to me. Isn't it typical, though, to blame the woman?

Strangely enough, I thought he might want to hold open the possibility of returning home, but returning home with all the rights to an independent emotional life apart from me in order to be able to go on to the next one. He continued to say he didn't want a divorce. His father never got a divorce from his second wife Kyveli. They ceased being a couple, she moved out, and he carried on with other women. But – and this is macabre – it was Kyveli who handled his funeral arrangements and who appeared on the scene as his legal wife many years later.

Several weeks earlier I had accepted an invitation to attend festivities opening up a five year program to celebrate Christopher Columbus's achievement in discovering America in 1492. I was confused about the connection between Columbus and Greece. A joint committee had been set up under the sponsorship of Francesco Cossiga, president of Italy, Ronald Reagan, president of the U.S. and Juan Carlos, King of Spain, for a series of international events entitled "Columbus 1992." Apparently, Columbus had spent time on the island of Chios on several occasions during his boat travels. This was the justification for having festivities take place on the island under the auspices of the Greek Ministry of Culture and the Ministry of the Aegean. This celebration was called "The International Cultural Conference Chios-Geneva." Much pressure was put on me by the Ministry of Culture, Melina, to attend the event. The American Ambassador would be there along with dignitaries from Italy, and since Andreas could not go, I should take his place. This was a moment when I had to struggle with my conscience because of my support for Native American rights – and Christopher Columbus' name is anathema. I said "yes" but was seriously considering withdrawing.

Now the picture had changed. Invited to appear as an honored guest, I had in the meantime become a "simple citizen." Where would a "simple citizen" be seated according to protocol? I was both curious and intrigued. But more than that, I was determined not to be hog-tied and flung in the slop-bin by a mafia of male chauvinists. If it had been the eighteenth century, I would have lost my head like Maria Antoinette. This was a different era and modern methods of cutting me to pieces were being used. I wanted the world to see I was not in tiny pieces; my carcass was together and carrying out its responsibilities as usual. I reconciled myself on the question of principle by arguing that the progressive Americans and the Native American Movement would slaughter Christopher Columbus by the time 1992 came about. Therefore, on the morning of September 24th, I flew to Chios.

As a result of my new title the journalists showed increased interest, following me everywhere, photographing me everywhere, reporting my activities, my dress, my walk, coughs, tilt of my head, nail polish and other significant observations. The press was awed with the many honors I was given, hardly consistent with my status as "simple citizen." One newspaper said, "This is the way we treat simple citizens in our country – with honors." The image was of the top "lady" performing her role, performing it naturally, and receiving affection and support. From the welcome at the airport- the prefects, the mayors, the receptions, the seating arrangements – everything, but everything, belied my new title. One newspaper said I was more "prime ministerish" than the prime minister himself. This didn't help my situation.

Moreover, the attention is usually greatest at the beginning, upon arrival at the airport with officialdom present in all its glory. Leaving, I am usually escorted to the airport by a smaller contingent. But this time the troupe came out again to see me off after three days of honors! I was certain they wanted to show their reaction to the government's treatment of me, and they did not truly believe that Andreas's escapades with a chorus girl – that's the way they perceived her – could possibly be serious. Otherwise they would have been scared or cautious. It is the power game. Whoever is losing becomes Typhoid Mary to those scrambling to gain power. Especially in a small country where power is intimate; it is woven into the fabric of society, it is near you, around you, receding from you. You smell it. You feel it.

From Chios I called the children to arrange a get-together the night of my return. That night their father was scheduled to give a speech to the youth of the party- and neither George nor Nikos wanted to attend, so they arranged to be out of town. I learned by phone that Sophia had left with her father to be present at the Youth Festival. That upset me, I must admit. She had joined him in the car driving to the Festival. She loved him, of course, but I felt certain that he was exploiting that love to show to the public that one of the children was "on his side." I slammed down the phone, started shouting obscenities, pounded the wall in the hotel until I saw my roommate, Didi Yannopoulos, a co-board member – coming toward me with a bottle of tranquilizers in her outstretched arm – and then I stopped. I was damn determined not to take tranquilizers.

When I arrived in Athens, the airport was swarming with journalists. I told them I would not give an interview or a press conference, but I did want to say one thing: "I am honored to be a simple citizen of this country."

Apparently I was in for a series of hits. The next one came from Melina. She invited me to come to her home for a drink and a chat before we attended a performance at the ancient theater below the Acropolis. She phoned in the afternoon to tell me something had come up and she couldn't see me at the house. I suggested we meet below the Acropolis and walk into the Erodou Attikou Theater together. She said she didn't know what time she would finish. The ministers would all be present at the performance, and most likely she would have to walk in with them and sit with them. Perhaps I was unduly suspicious, but I didn't have to be a genius to guess she was trying to untangle herself from her arrangement with me. This was unexpected. We were close friends, and she had supported me a few days earlier when someone asked her how was it that she, as Minister of Culture, had invited me as a V.I.P. to the Columbus ceremonies on Chios. Her answer was she had not invited me as a simple citizen, but as an outstanding personality.

I asked her directly, as I am prone to do: "You don't want to be seen with me? You don't want to walk with me? What the hell is going on?"

She shouted at me, "Now, wait, we can't have this in our relationship. You cannot doubt my commitment to you, and my love for you."

It was a good scene, but I did indeed doubt. I remembered she had told me when you lose power you find out who your real friends are. I didn't want to doubt her; I valued our friendship too much. Yet her behavior seemed like proof of her statement.

I went to the theater with Sophia and received ample applause as I walked in. The Acropolis Theater is a magnificent outdoor ancient structure made of stone and marble and holding 5,000 people. I am sure the strongest applause came from the women in the audience in a display of solidarity. Most of them either were going through similar "other woman" experiences, or had in the past. In any case, I felt very grateful. Melina arrived a few seconds after me, took a seat next to Sophia, told me she heard the applause and thought it was wonderful. We exchanged no other words until the end of the performance when she said simply, "I'll call you tomorrow."

The end result of all this was a renewed invitation to her home. This was typical Melina. That big heart in her chest must have told her "Margarita needs you," and she immediately tried to make amends for what I at least perceived as abandonment and a betrayal of our friendship. I accepted the invitation without comment. After a few words about the music of Vangelli Papathanasiou at the concert and with glasses of ouzo in our hands, she started the conversation.

"Margarita, do you think all of this public exposure irritates Andreas?"

"Of course it does; I'm sure it does, and I'm sorry."

"I see him agitated about your activities." I was positive that she had talked to him. I didn't know if she was coming as his agent, or if she had taken the initiative to "advise me."

"What can I do? My schedule has been planned long in advance."

"Yes, but he is bothered."

"The only thing I can do is lie down and die, or lie down and hibernate. And the newspapers will still write stories. They like the topic – for circulation, for political purposes. Why the hell did he give them this opportunity with his open romance? And why my new title? I am surely not engendering this publicity by my actions on behalf of women and peace. Andreas has created the fuss – for other reasons. It's his responsibility, not mine."

"Those things, well, yes, you are right, but I'm talking about your personal relationship."

"My personal relationship," I told her, "is related to all those things. And it steadily gets worse."

"Well, you know, I think if you were to play it with more emotion, with passion – like screaming your commitment to him, your need for him and like falling back and fainting. I think there would be more concern on his part for you, more tenderness, and maybe even more desire."

I laughed a little. "You like passion, Melina. Greeks like passion and stories that have to do with sex and life and power and torture…"

"And that's one reason the newspapers won't let go of the story – until it comes to a conclusion. You still love him, Margarita?"

I looked at her to see if she was mocking me. Her expression was serious and sympathetic. My answer was "Yes, deeply."

"Then show your passion. Do what I say."

"My god, Melina, you're the actress, not me…"

"And maybe a few steps back, a little less projection."

"Play the little woman? The understanding, forgiving woman? That reminds me of poor Ortega in Nicaragua. Everybody told him if he would only take certain steps toward democratization, give a little, the U.S. administration would forget its plans to overturn his government. And every time Ortega took a step, the Reagan administration said 'we just don't believe it…he's doing it for public relations purposes, and he will recall all of these measures at a future date… yes, good, but it's not enough.' Don't you see, whatever I do it's a no-win situation."

"Maybe you can't do much at the public level," Melina said, not quite convincingly. "I would advise you to play it better in your personal contacts with him. I'm sure the other one is weeping and wailing, playing the helpless, awestruck femme."

"I can hardly be helpless or awestruck, Melina. I am a mature individual. I have been politically active all my life. I cannot pretend or put on a theatrical act. I have to be true to myself."

"You told me once you would have loved to be an actress. Try it now."

"Can you picture me swooning and swaying, moaning and sobbing? I'd probably break into laughter in the middle of it. Look, my adoration for the guy is monumental. And his for me. We've lived too long together to have that kind of response now. If he doesn't know how much I love him, and how I have fought alongside him during very difficult periods, then he is insensitive. And ungrateful."

"Men are never grateful, Margarita."

"I trust your knowledge about men. You are probably right. But I would feel like a clown doing what you suggest. And if I didn't break out laughing, Andreas would."

"It's your marriage I'm thinking about. And this is Greece, and you are married to a Greek man. You should act more like a Greek woman."

"Is that what Greek women do?"

"Yes. Even attempt to commit suicide."

"That I know from previous affairs Andreas had. None of them succeeded, unfortunately."

"You are very much a woman, Margarita. You should be able to do this."

I thought about what she said all evening. What was most revealing was the fact Andreas was envious of my success. He saw me as a competitor. I had sensed this for some time now. But to such a degree? I couldn't believe he was that insecure. If it meant so much to him, I thought, I ought to try more studiously to keep a low profile.

On the following day I sent him a handwritten note with Mihalis. It was written in large black letters. "ANDREAS, I LOVE YOU. I AM NOT YOUR RIVAL."

The next few days through my birthday on the 30th of September, the press continued to be enchanted with the love story, with the triangle of sex, power, and politics – all the ingredients for a Molotov cocktail. I wondered when the bomb would explode as something serious, not just gossip, in the international press. That was an inevitable next step.

Chapter Twenty Four

True Love Travels on a Gravel Road

On Monday after I returned from Chios, *Eleftheros Typos* published a piece entitled "With Frankness," directed to Andreas as straight-talking friendly advice. The writer claimed he would not have written the article if the circle of Andreas had not made a statement calling Mrs. Margarita a "simple citizen."

The article began by saying: "It seems about time we call a spade a spade. Half-truths and half-lies do not help when it is already a public secret."

Mentioned was the cruise at the time of the anniversary of the Kalamata earthquake, his insensitivity to public reaction and his duty to the office of prime minister. It concluded by saying, "Finish with the story, however you wish, but with irreproachable means. The people who have faith in you to govern this country do not excuse back fence methods. Do it quickly before people repeat what is being written every day, that PASOK will not fall because of its economic policy, but because of a personal story."

Having started the hullabaloo, Andreas was now truly concerned about its consequences and that it was bringing me more positive publicity than ever before. In the meeting of the Central Committee of PASOK he argued that the idea for damaging him with stories of his personal life came from the United States. (!) Quite a few newspapers satirized this by saying, "Yes, the CIA came and told us they had placed an air stewardess next to him, and we were ordered to write about it." Evidently, some people agreed with Andreas. One day, two men came to my driver Panayiotis to ask permission from me to beat The Hostess up. They explained she was part of a circle with connections to the CIA, which plotted her moves and her strategy. I told Panayiotis I would give them permission on one condition – they also beat up my husband. This shocked these connivers sufficiently to cause them to scotch the idea.

Another newspaper said Andreas had finally lived up to his pre-election promise of "change." He is changing Margarita for The Hostess. Meanwhile, he was throwing out of his entourage anybody who he considered pro-Margarita. Cartoons flourished. Tons of newsprint were devoted to this hot issue. *Kalami*' a weekly periodical, offered a heartening paragraph:

"The past week Margarita was just one of the "personalities of the week". "This week she has risen: she is THE personality of the week." Why? Because although many tried to vilify her, she, with dignity, stood up to the mud throwing on her personal and family life. She accepted with forbearance the desertion of old friends. With character and with an irreproachable stance, she bore all the slings and arrows of the rightist press which were nourished by the pronouncements of Roumbatis. For us, Margarita, you are truly a lady and the first citizen of the country."

Well, something to salve the bruises. Newspapers were also writing about the attempts of the children to forge a bridge between the two of us. Sophia was the most determined and managed to turn up at many of her father's activities, just to remind him she had one request, "make up with our mother."

There were indications again in the midst of all this that he was coming to his senses. He told Sophia he had never proposed the name "simple citizen" It was a concoction of Roumbatis. He also asked her how I was surviving the attacks, as if they came from an alien source, and he was concerned about my health. This must have been a strange moment when he thought he was on my side. I felt a touch of optimism streak through the fog.

While all of this was happening to me, I was dealing with another problem in the American section of W.M.S. Although the regions we divided into at the founding Assembly meeting were considered equal one to the other, in reality some were more equal than others. The importance of the U.S. contingent in nuclear disarmament goes without saying. The other superpower was important too, but it was already on a path – by necessity or design – committed to reducing nuclear weapons. Gorbachev had declared his intention to fight for a nuclear-free world. Unless the U.S. responded positively to this initiative – and I was fearful that Reagan would not – the world would lose a precious opportunity to turn an important life-preserving page in the history of mankind.

Our U.S. women's contingent was not satisfied to be a regional office, but wanted to set up a more formal organization with a board, president, general secretary, etc. In other words, the Americans wanted a leadership role. They were not willing to accept the agreement made in Athens. I was on the spot because I had promised the Soviet women they would be on par with the American women. In addition, I had accepted the role of international coordinator on condition that I would abide by decisions taken in the founding meeting. The U.S. – Canada region was extremely important to our success. I hesitated to make an issue of this change in organizational structure not consistent with decisions of the Assembly. I had assumed we would still work in the spirit of equality. That was my mistake.

I discussed the situation with other members of the International Assembly who all agreed we needed the continued amicable participation of the U.S. women and the problem should be handled as tactfully as possible. My strategy was to try to negotiate for a good president of their board who would have considerable prestige and with whom I would be able to function well. In other words, the U.S. would have a president vis-à-vis the Soviet Union's president, and I would become the coordinator. The name Randy Forsberg, head of the Institute for Defense and Disarmament Studies in Cambridge, Massachusetts, came to my mind. I spoke to the women in the United States who were delegates at the Assembly, and they urged me to make the first contact with her. Randy indicated she was interested in heading up WMS-USA, although she didn't want to get involved in organizational and administrative details. I told her we saw her more as a spokesperson with power to guide strategy and to deal with substantive issues, rather than being responsible for the daily running of the organization. She wanted a good staff-line director, which I also believed was important, and she agreed to attend the next regional meeting in Washington.

That seemed to be going well. Beyond this, everything was in the hands of the women in Washington. There had been two meetings to discuss the shape and goals of the new WMS structure. Randy did not attend the first because it was strictly organizational, and she missed the second because of her acceptance of an invitation from the Dukakis campaign staff to brief them on disarmament. A third had been scheduled, and while all the members had been alerted, Randy had not. That was the game then. They would call her at the last minute, she would be unable to attend, and they could argue she was not really interested. I could not intervene anymore. For me, Randy was the ideal choice. I was worried about interpersonal rivalries and jealousies in competition for the title, but I was walking through my own personal human relations nightmare. I felt relieved I was 5,000 miles away from this one.

A total of approximately twenty peace activists would be chosen from the various regions. What we needed in the delegation to Moscow were women of political clout and stature, particularly in the American delegation, to make the chances for meetings with both sides more likely. The regions would find local funds to support their delegates. This meant what it always meant, women from the developed countries would find the financial means; women from the developing countries would be left out. I offered to find funds for a few of them. What we had not determined, and what everybody was asking, was if we met with Reagan or Gorbachev, who from the twenty women who were coming would be in this probably smaller delegation?

Meanwhile, I accepted an invitation to speak in Antwerp prior to the Washington summit in order to meet with Paula Rose, head of the NATO Alerts Network, and Scilla McClean, my guru on nuclear disarmament, director of the Oxford Research Group. These meetings were ten days away. A nearer meeting was one with my errant husband Andreas.

(Diary entry) – *4th October, 1987, Kastri*

Later in the day I am supposed to have a meeting with Andreas. I have not seen him for five weeks. It is a critical meeting. It comes after a crescendo of publicity – and after my "demotion" from First Lady to simple citizen. I don't know what's in his mind. I have hope. Kostas has arranged it and may participate in the discussion, or come in later. That was Andreas's idea. He also asked Sophia to be present – why I'm not sure. Possibly to comfort me after the unpleasantness, or to be here to support him in his moves. Maybe there will be no moves at all. I told Kostas I didn't think it was wise to include Sophia. What I know is something definitive must happen soon or I will lose my sanity.

The meeting took place and was both positive and negative. Just the two of us at the beginning. Kostos came in later. Andreas started the discussion, saying he wanted to give his viewpoint. For one thing, he wanted to explain the two government statements: the one from "government circles" that whatever I did "was my business and my business alone," and the second from Roumbatis that I was a "simple citizen." The first announcement he admitted he gave to Koutsogeorgas, a minister and his personal lawyer, to give to the newspaper *Avriani*. This also cleared up that "government circles" was Andreas himself. With a little help from his friends.

The second announcement? Why had Roumbatis continued the barrage the next day by calling me a "simple citizen" when I had made a statement in the press denying I was forming a party. Andreas claimed that the second statement was not his. It was a concoction of Roubatis in order to explain the first statement! In any case, he – Andreas – wanted to "calm down the atmosphere" and give less importance to the estrangement. I was not clear what he was trying to say…that he wanted to be less hypocritical, to be more honest about the situation? Not to get out of the extra-marital relationship, but to present it in a more acceptable way to the public?

He said he was getting a lot of information that was unsettling. Maroudas, the Zakinthos deputy, claimed that when I was on the island I asked for the Coast Guard to take me to the turtle beach in order to see the environmental conditions for the turtles. In addition I had insisted on time off for public servants so they could listen to my speech at the inauguration of the women's cooperative, and that I had demanded special traffic arrangements in order to move around more quickly. The way it was described, I behaved like Queen Frederika, who at the height of her power before the monarchy was abolished, wielded a nasty whip.

I sat there with my mouth open. "Really, Andreas, do you understand who I am? And what I am doing, and how I function? Because you are cut off from contact with me, you believe whatever anybody tells you about me! Don't you know me? All of this is utterly and completely untrue! Let me tell you something else. That turtle shelter is in an area where Maroudas has property with his sister, and they have been fighting right along to stop the Ministry of Planning and Environment from making a reserve out of the area. I was right when I understood the obstacles put in my way when I was on his island. Orders came from him."

I took a deep breath and continued. "I heard you were upset because of a battery of photographs of me playing golf at Glyfada – a photo spread I had arranged. But I hadn't arranged anything – and if you want to find out how it happened, call Phillipopolis at *Ethnos*. He, through his own network, found out I was at the golf course and sent a photographer. Maroudas has connections with the newspaper *Ethnos*. This was evidently a scheme devised by him to increase your hostility toward me. That's the way your so-called friends operate."

He seemed ready to accept my version. What he was also ready to do, and this I guess was the gist of the meeting, was not to be seen in public anymore with the "creature." This was not new; Sophia had reported the conversation with her father. Now it was I who was on the side of the angels. Not long ago, he had accepted the condition from her not be seen in public with me!

What disturbed me was his attempt to turn the affair from public to clandestine. I asked him how he could make it a discreet relationship after it had been blasted all over the mass media. "Everybody is watching everything you do, and as long as you do not clarify our marital relationship, the public will guess that the affair goes on. There will continue to be new or old publicity about it."

I reminded him of the cover picture on the periodical *Eikones* showing the two of them shaking hands at a reception in the Greek Embassy in Moscow. A wealth of such photos existed because the crew of Olympics' official plane was generally included at Embassy functions on foreign visits. He said yes, that was true. I told him that the tremendous publicity I got on my trip to Chios was a gift from Roumbatis. Everyone was curious to see what a "simple citizen" does when she is in fact the First Lady of Greece.

"Well, that didn't hurt you," he replied.

"You're right. It didn't hurt my prestige. The hurt was the stab in the back from you as a means of telling me I was through. Finished."

He looked at me like a boy caught with his hand in the cookie jar. The two of us were sitting in comfortable chairs around the fireplace, drinks, cheese and crackers on the table.

The room was full of books and dark wooden panels, its ceiling high and cross-beamed, reminding me of better days in Canada during our exile when Andreas was professor of economics at York University. Now I was struggling with this familiar stranger to regain a lost relationship. I wanted to touch him, but I didn't dare. The advice of Melina to concoct some passionate demonstrations of love didn't even enter my mind.

He claimed the opposition press was building me up as a person of high standards and ethics, which made him look by comparison like a heel – all done purposely to reduce his image. The applause I got in Chios had been orchestrated by the opposition for the same reason, as was the applause in the theater at the Acropolis to add to my popularity, thus diminishing his. I stared at him. I honestly didn't know what I was dealing with. All of these events were a conspiracy against him? Was he unable to see himself, his own behavior? Did he consider himself entirely blameless for whatever happened? I had to conclude power had affected Andreas – the heady spell of power, that fascination, that intoxication which distorts reason, values, and relationships.

"Thanks a lot," I said, "you certainly give me little credit for being who I am."

Now Andreas stared at me. He didn't comprehend. While the press was building me up publicly as a woman of class, he said, it was implicitly making the comparison with The Hostess as a woman of the streets, a prostitute.

"I don't think they are manufacturing that story. Her past reputation is known."

"She never did it for money."

"Oh," I said. "She just likes it." I could have said "I like it too," but it seemed inappropriate at the time.

"She never takes money, nor gifts. That's not her style."

I decided it would not be fruitful to attack her at the time he was being protective of her, and of himself.

We talked about the "new party" I was presumably organizing. I told him initially I had taken it as a joke and therefore didn't respond immediately. However, it would have been easy for PASOK, since I am a member, to have asked me directly to deny it. Why all this round-a-bout stuff? As soon as I understood he had taken it seriously and peculiarly enough was looking at me as a rival, I made a public statement, and sent him a note as well.

"That was good," he said. "Anyway, I think this whole thing will die out."

"You mean about the party?"

"Yes, and the interest in my personal life."

"You must be kidding. The party, yes. The personal life, no. No, it will not die out. It will spread even more. It will become an international scandal. A debate is going on now as to how much a politician's personal behavior can be a barometer of his political behavior and decision-making. The personal being debated does not concern financial shenanigans because in our family there have never been such shenanigans. It concerns sexual behavior, marital relations, etc., such as the cases of Gary Hart, Brandt, Peurifoy, and others. The columnists would love to get a handle on your case to raise such a question. Andreas, there has to be a change, and a change the public will understand and accept, a clarification one way or the other"

"If I do it suddenly, it would look like I bowed to public pressure...I didn't know what I was doing...I finally woke up and came crawling back. This, I think, is belittling of me, and would not make a good impression."

Concern about not acting like a man. Why is everything looked at by men as a test of their masculinity? Women do not question their femininity. The statement had given me, however, an indication he had been thinking of a "change of heart."

"What does Kostas think about this?" I asked, assuming they had discussed this possibility.

"You'll have to ask Kostas."

"You want my opinion?"

"Go ahead."

"I don't believe for a minute such a decision would demean you. Up until now you have been known as a "womanizer," but you also have a strong image as a family man, with a great bunch of kids. The side affairs have not been significant, have not destroyed your family – and that's the image the public wants to preserve."

He admitted that. Of course, I was being my own defendant and inwardly wondering if I was over doing it.

"This period in my life, Andreas, has been very harsh on me. I have suffered greatly. It has been probably the most difficult period I have experienced – and I have experienced quite a few, as you know. I truly miss you – terribly."

"What do you want?"

"I want you back. I want you to stop looking at me as if I were competing with you. This has never been my aim. I have withdrawn from the activities where you were most involved – PASOK, the government, not sitting in on conversations nor participating in decision - making. I decided it was better to use my political energies elsewhere. I never considered I was a rival; I thought my activities were an adjunct to yours, an addition, which helped your political career. Remarkably, there is little hostility in me toward you. I have always loved you, from the very first time we met. That has never been shaken. Sometimes I am puzzled by this lack of anger in me. I seem incapable of feeling deep despair or rage. Just pain. I asked Kostas if maybe I was emotionally sick."

Andreas, uncomfortable by my open declaration of love, called Kostas in. He told him we decided we needed to have a direct means of communication, and if something disturbing came up, he or someone will reach me immediately. "We both hear too much from other people. I believe the things Margarita has told me; I have no reason to doubt her. There has been an attempt by people I considered friends, not enemies, to undermine Margarita and to undermine our relationship which has agitated both of us."

Kostas said the emotional relationship between the two of us had to be repaired – with no hostility – so he was very glad we would have an "open channels" policy. Andreas said he would return to the habit of family lunches and other activities with us. Then he injected the question of a sudden announcement, and asked Kostas if that wouldn't be demeaning.

Kostas hedged, much to my dismay. He said some would look at it one way, some another. There would be headlines. He couldn't support totally a "sudden decision." Perhaps he didn't want to appear to be on my side. Perhaps he felt Andreas needed more time. Kostas felt The Hostess could not be really disturbed by a clandestine relationship – she would still see Andreas. Kostas, a Greek and a man, had not seen through her designs. I was dumbfounded.

"No, you're not right," Andreas replied. "She likes to have social activities, not to feel holed up. This will be a continued source of friction."

This meant he felt comfortable with the decision to dump her, but he wanted us to know it was not going to be easy. He foresaw the need for conditions so the break would be inevitable over a period of time. That was up to now how he was playing the game with me. Now it looked like it was her turn to get the treatment. She will suffer. I didn't feel any feminist solidarity.

After I talked to Kostas alone, I came to a few conclusions. The lack of direct contact between us was catastrophic. Our rather long relationship – almost forty years – had changed both of us, and the political platform we performed on, something we worked so hard for, had undone the glue that held us together. On the positive side was his promise to Sophia there would be no more public appearances. He said this as if he swore on her life. He indicated there would be problems between him and the Hostess that might turn out to be positive for the family. Thus we were back to the term "transition period," which meant a space of time before we resumed our usual roles.

The following morning I woke up with a mini-migraine, stress induced, pain radiating from the base of the skull downwards through my shoulders and upwards to my temples and eyes. It looked like crimpy weather outside. This room, I thought, my private sanctuary of bliss and coziness, was also my torture chamber of pain, anguish, uncertainty, wrath. It was a simple room, not big, beige painted walls, a double bed facing a large French shuttered window. White nubby curtains with a crocheted band near the bottom covered the shutters. I kept the curtains open so I could awaken to the early morning spill of sunlight across the tops of pine trees in the yard. Many times I laid on the bed, thinking, like Dorothy Parker's short story "The Telephone Call ," *"Please, dear God, let me hear his footsteps in the hall, let him come home now, let him come into this bedroom with a smile on his face, and a soft 'are you sleeping'? It isn't much to ask. Such a little thing. Please, please."*

This kind of thinking did not diminish my headache. I had been fighting back with dignity, and, yes, with occasional humor. The cost was this rat-a-tat drumming in my head and an occasional irregularity in my heartbeat. I thrust my legs out of the bed and ushered myself into the bathroom for aspirins to dull the pain and a cold shower to get my blood pumping, to clean up the accrued anxiety-produced pollution of my body.

Late in the morning before my departure to Antwerp, Andreas called on the phone and hemming and hawing suggested I might do an interview for a newspaper which would put the situation in its "proper light," and hinted we would be re-establishing our relationship. This took me by surprise. I didn't expect much of a result from our last talk. Apparently he had made up his mind and wanted to get started on the long journey home. I told him I would arrange it so he could read the interview before publication. I wanted this to be a cooperative venture; otherwise whatever happened afterwards would be my responsibility. He agreed.

All of this required a friendly reporter who would let me write the interview ahead of time, then work on it with me for presentation. I knew there would be no problem in finding a newspaper to publish my interview, the first one since the rumors of an extra-marital affair burst onto the front page. I chose *Messimvrini*, the conservative paper that had treated me fairly. I chose the journalist Barbara Tsimbouli, and she jumped at it. We agreed on the method, and I committed myself to having it ready as soon as possible. She would give me a list of questions and I could choose the ones I wanted to answer, or develop my own questions. This was a difficult challenge – to find the best way to talk about a messy situation, convincing the public, satisfying Andreas and not making me sound like a pleading wife or a compromised feminist.

When I arrived in London, I went to stay with Aleka for a few days to refine my Antwerp speech. And to relax. Now I had a new assignment, one which could be the basis for a fresh start of a troubled marriage or another axe blow to a tottering tree. I set up my writing space in Aleka's apartment: a comfortable old armchair, a yellow legal pad, a pen and a hot pot of coffee. Aleka did not put much importance on the interview I was writing, arguing I could do it when I returned to Athens. For me it was a last chance to turn my life around, to bring it back in harmony, to put the pieces together, to resume a partnership which had nourished my soul, but, god help me, rocked it at the same time. After two and a half days of writing, reading and re-reading, I phoned it to my secretary, and asked her to have it ready for my final review upon my arrival back home.

On the 12th of October Aleka and I took off for Brussels in time for a lunch with women members of WMS working with me in preparation for the summit meeting in Washington. We consulted with Paula Rose, head of the NATO Alerts Network, with whom we were collaborating for our various discussions and confrontations with the military alliance. In addition to Paula was Scilla McLean of the Oxford Research Group, Leona Dietege, Belgian socialist party parliamentarian, and the Austrian wife of the Greek Ambassador in Brussels, Eidi Vandalis.

In early evening we left for the Political Debate Club of Antwerp where the meeting organized by the Remish Socialist Party was being held. Representatives of the Greek press were waiting for me at the press conference set up by the Socialist Party. I held my breath waiting for the hot questions. Before it started I asked the president of the party, Mr. Marcel Kallo, to introduce me simply as the head of the Women's Union of Greece and coordinator of WMS. I said I didn't think he needed to mention that I was "the wife of..." He did as I asked, and then said, "She does not accept to be announced as the wife of the prime minister of Greece, although we all know who she is." I nearly drowned in embarrassment, and distress. It sounded like I was publicly shedding my role as First Lady of Greece, which of course was not the point. I wanted it understood I was not there representing Greece. I was trying to establish a political identity of my own, and had been trying ever since we returned to Greece in 1974. At the moment when I was searching for the glue which would act as the adhesive agent in our shattered relationship it seemed I was announcing defiantly that I was no longer Mrs. Papandreou!

A few questions, carefully worded, were asked concerning my personal life. I danced around them. After the press conference was over, the Greek reporters bombarded me with additional questions, huddling near me like chickens pecking at a plate of corn. The stories in the press claimed I remained "mum" as usual, refused to answer questions about my being a "simple citizen," but had struck down my title of "wife of..." They observed and commented on my having been met at the airport by the Greek Ambassador who proceeded to "shepherd me around the entire day." That was true of the Ambassador, bless him. The only thing they reported from my talk on de-nuclearization and de-militarization of international relations, was the response I gave to the question "do you believe the American government is sincere in negotiating with the Soviet Union?" My answer was "I am not in a position to judge the sincerity of a government. The women's movement starts with the basic position that all governments are sincere. Then we judge them on their actions."

I wondered if they would make something of the opening lines of my speech: "It was Freud who said, 'What do women want?' And it is women who say sometimes 'Who are we? Where do we fit in?" At that point I realized no Greek reporters had stayed for my speech. They had all scooted out after the press conference, obviously burning phone lines back to Athens.

The stories in the press the next day about my trip to Antwerp were nestled in amongst bigger and juicier stories about Andreas's love life. My predictions had come true: the affair had become international news. *Headlines such as "Worldwide Commotion for Half and Half," "Prime Minister's Air Hostess Tryst Rocks Politics in Greece," "International Show, The Love Life of Papandreou."* The articles in the foreign press were translated and printed in our newspapers, with or without comment. It was a field day for the opposition, and the friendly press was obliged to report the news. It was probably the greatest international attention Greece had ever been given. The children wanted to hide under a barrel. I wanted to join them myself.

Immediately upon my return I made final adjustments on the Kathimernini interview, sent a copy to Andreas and called Barbara to arrange for the oral part of the interview for October 20th, at EGE Headquarters in downtown Athens. Andreas responded quickly: "It's good." No changes. All during the past week the press was steaming with the private life of the PM; one could almost see the vapor curling in hot smoke from the piles of paper delivered to the kiosks around town. "Never," said one newspaper, "has a European leader experienced such publicity and comment on his personal life."

Many articles concluded, "This is bound to have political repercussions."

I wondered, given his attitude toward me, if he suspected I had orchestrated this recent publicity campaign. He had been granting me surreal powers – building a political party of my own and getting magazine photo spreads, among others. It made sense he might be ready to accuse me of vast control over the international mass media. If he did, I never heard it expressed. The gear had been pulled to "reverse," and he needed me to help hold the wheel moving back down the road.

(Diary Entry) *Friday, October 16th, 1987, Kastri*

My appointment with Barbara went well. We added a few items, but mostly we chatted while a photographer took pictures. I wanted the interview to appear on Sunday so it could be read by the women of the regional EGE meeting we were holding on the island of Aegina. Barbara said she thought it would be published on Monday. I understood the paper preferred Monday in order to do advance publicity for sales purposes. Perhaps I should have charged a fee!

I am looking forward to the trip to the island, everything from the forty minute Flying Dolphin boat ride to the sweetness of the island breezes to the contact and work with EGE women. And I am eager to see my interview in print. I am hopeful about its impact, and to the thought of once again hearing Andreas's footsteps in the hall approaching our bedroom door. Despite the problems in our relationship, I still need to be near him.

Sleep time. I am reminded of the book "Good-night, Moon," which I used to read to the children. So, "Good-night, CNN. Good-night newspapers. Good-night, Kastri. Good-night, pine trees outside my window. Good-night, Andreas. See you soon."

Officially there are 1,425 islands in Greece. Together they comprise about one-fifth of Greece. Most are uninhabited and of the 170 or so inhabited islands, goats and sheep far outnumber human beings. The image of scattered jewels lying on the Aegean Sea has been invoked many times, and it is a description which came to mind as the Flying Dolphin skimmed over the water. Small islands, some consisting solely of barren rock, others with scrub bushes, a few with trees, provide the string of pearls on a velvet blue highway.

It takes forty minutes by hydrofoil to reach Aegina, the nearest peopled island to Athens. Speed was important to me that day, but it was a barbaric way to travel, huddled inside a caterpillar-like structure, looking through airplane windows, skimming the water at sea-level, seeing the view a three year old has of the world around her. More civilized and more glorious is the ferry boat which takes three times as long, but has the charm and excitement of throbbing engines, the smell of oil and salt, the voluble crowd on deck, the array of bags and parcels scattered around, and the chance for a leisurely ouzo with its accompanying small plate of salted appetizers.

Coming into the port of Aegina on a ferry boat, one gets a glimpse of the remains of the once magnificent temple to Aphrodite, the goddess of desire who caused grass and flowers to spring from the soil wherever she trod. The port, bustling, noisy, dusty, yet proud and elegant, brings tears of happiness to the eyes of those of us afflicted with what Lawrence Durrell named "islamania."

Although on the day I was travelling my mood was considerably improved, I needed the diversion of the conference and time with my co-workers. I asked that my normal greeting to the gathering be moved from the beginning to the end. This is what I said to the women of EGE on Sunday, the second and final day of the conference.

During a very difficult time in my life, I felt the warmth, the commitment and the support of the women of EGE, in all parts of Greece. I have been tremendously moved by your solidarity, and it has given me courage to hold my head high when I had no mood to do so. What I am going through is a cyclone, a storm, and it will pass.

It was stated recently that we are planning to form a political party. And much fuss and attention was given to this possibility. This simply confirmed what I always believed:

women in Greece have great political power, and especially the women of EGE. How can we exploit this power? By founding a party? And calling it the Party of Simple Citizens? This idea we have rejected.

It is not necessary for women to follow the male prototype to affect the direction of our society. What we need to do is infiltrate, to capture positions in the governmental bodies, in local administration, in business, in education, in the arts, bringing our socialist-feminist ideology and positions with us, and holding on to the vision of the kind of society we want. This society will have the human being at its center, where every decision and every act of the government will be taken together with the people, men and women. Women will secure the emotional and psychological tranquility needed to promote the proper environment for creative work and a creative life. In this type of environment there will be no room for violence, and the soul and spirit will be liberated from every form of oppression and fear.

The women of Greece must play an important and significant role in the development of our country – development which will lead to a humane society- democratic, independent, and feminist- that will have as its aims equality, social development and peace. We are moving ahead to the place we deserve in the community. This means many responsibilities as well, but our star is shining bright in the sky. All of you here today, along with members from our other chapters, should participate in our campaign for disarmament which begins on Friday, the 23rd of October, the first day of the United Nations Disarmament Week."

I yearn for success in our struggle. I thank you again for standing by me, and for your love, and I make one wish: that we continue to work together for many years in our common struggle for justice and a better quality of life.

Quite a few papers called our gathering "a meeting with tears." Several said I broke down and sobbed. I did feel emotional, but I was in control, spirits rising, knowing something no one else knew. My interview would be out on Monday.

Chapter Twenty Five

Diplomacy at Home and Abroad

The next day – Monday, I asked Panayiotis to pick up copies of *Mesimvrini* as soon as they were delivered to the kiosk. Afternoon papers arrive around noon. There was a picture of me on the front page saying "Margarita Breaks her Long Silence and Gives an Exclusive Interview." The interview inside covered two tabloid pages, with two pictures of me and the headline "I AM NOT DIVORCING ANDREAS." In smaller letters under the title "Neither Has He Asked for a Divorce." The interview began with questions about EGE, the women's movement, and its effects on society, then slowly built up to the part the whole country was scanning for.

"Question: How do you see the evolution of the traditional institutions of the western society (home, family, etc.)?

"Answer: No doubt the traditional family, (father, mother, children) is undergoing tremendous strain and is no longer the strong institution it once was. Many times the Women's Movement is blamed for the break-up of the family. But the reasons are more complicated than that and involve the role of the State, the level of economic development, mobility, mass media, rising expectations, alienation, community disintegration. It is hard for me, however, to imagine what kind of society we might develop not based on the family unit. This may sound like a conservative assessment. I have examined other forms of human organization, and I do not see any that offer the emotional security and emotional stability that can be given by the family unit.

"Question: What is your opinion regarding the problems created between husband and wife? We see more of this in all societies.

"Answer: I know why you asked me this. I did say that marriages are under stress. Ours is no exception. It just happens that the foundations of our marriage are very strong. We have gone through many difficulties and common struggles. Marriages of long duration go through crises. It depends on how you view the crisis and how serious you judge it. When you both have confidence and faith in your common love and affection, you know the relationship will survive.

"Question: The press says you have filed for divorce; you are leaving for a year to the States, etc. From your response to my previous question, I presume this is not true.

"Answer: The press seems to have a wild imagination. It is more likely this is being done on purpose for political aims, to "put oil on the fire," to confuse the public, to create additional family conflict. The situation has been exaggerated out of all proportion to its significance. Most of what is written is a series of lies. First that I was going to form a political party. Absolutely untrue, and as I said, "nonsense." Second, that I have filed for divorce in Minnesota. Andreas and I were never married in Minnesota. Our civil marriage was in Nevada and our orthodox ceremony in California. Neither of us has filed for divorce, and we do not intend to. Third, that I am leaving for a year to help in the Dukakis campaign. I would love to see a Greek-American win the presidency. But my political base and activities are here, both with Greek women in the Women's Movement and as international liaison for the global organization WMS. I am committed to these causes and have never considered for one moment giving them up.

"I hope these responses clarify this issue. This has been a difficult period for our family with the spotlight of the press turned on us and poisonous pens distorting the truth. Is it too much to ask to be given some respect and time to sort out our personal problems and to be judged on our political contribution to the society?"

(Diary Entry) *October 25th, Sunday, Kastri, 1 A.M. in the morning*

Talked to Andrikos in Boston and to Nikos in New York, my attractive boys who turned into handsome men. Both of them seem in a good frame of mind. Andrikos has a lingering chest cold. I asked him to check to make sure a pneumonia hasn't set in. He said he wanted to wait until next month when his health insurance goes into effect. I gave him motherly advice: health comes before any money considerations. While working on his thesis he is following a class on famine by his thesis advisor, Amartya Sen. When Sen accepted an appointment to teach at Harvard, Andreas trekked along with him from Oxford.

Andrikos told me he feels at home in the U.S., although he was only three when we moved from California to Greece. He felt more of a foreigner in England, although he did all of his university work there. I guess the old American training from an old American Mom produced a child who feels comfortable in two countries, like his mother.

Niko's professor at Princeton told him not to go on the job market but to search for research funds, that there are many interesting things he can do. He liked the idea because it would give him freedom of movement; he can do his research both in Greece and the States. He also has an offer for a job at the World Bank. Although I believe he has a good future, he hasn't found himself yet. He is a talented person with many interests. Anything he tackles he does well. Because of that and because he sees many roads open to him, he hesitates to choose one road which may foreclose the others. He is emotional and sentimental and vigorously loyal to friends and spends much time helping others, often an exploitation by his friends of his character. This is uncompensated time, but does apparently give him satisfaction. I am very sensitive to the problems of this brilliant son of mine and hope he soon finds his direction.

Meanwhile I had decided I would not go to the States if there was no summit meeting. The exact time had not been fixed, and there was talk of cancellation. Initially I was planning to use the trip for other peace activities as well, to set up my speaking tour after Christmas, and to iron out organizational problems for WMS. Given my personal situation, I hoped the Summit would be scheduled for a later date. The situation was tenuous, and I felt the need to stick around. All the children felt relieved about the family situation after my interview. I told them to keep their fingers crossed.

I had not seen Andreas since the publication of the interview, nor talked to him. The family lunch was changed from Wednesday to Monday, and then back to Wednesday. According to the newspapers, there was a "climate of reconciliation." Sophia told me The Hostess was fighting – she would not give up. Her father will have difficulties. And unpleasantness. That will be nice. Let it be on his side for a change. I asked her, "Is this irrevocable change? I hope there are no second thoughts now." "Oh, no, no," she said, with her sweet sincerity and conviction. "He just wants to do it softly, on tip-toe, so to speak."

That reminded me of a time when my friend Marjorie Schachter, who was staying with me when Andreas was in jail under the dictatorship, came tip-toeing into my bedroom one afternoon when I was napping. Kyveli had telephoned to say her husband Tito, who gave me stalwart moral support and drove me to jail each day to deliver Andreas's food, had been picked up and jailed. She didn't know where he was being kept. "Tell Margarita," she said to Marjorie, "but break it to her softly."

Marjorie woke me up with a tug on my shoulder and said, "I am supposed to tell you softly that Tito has been jailed, and I don't know how to tell you softly." She was absolutely right. You can't tell harsh news in a delicate way. It's better just to tell it. And that holds for Andreas. Just tell The Hostess to disappear. It's over. Period.

During all of this fanfare the day arrived for EGE's big campaign to distribute our printed positions on disarmament and peace. We gathered in front of the University of Athens, downtown, and after a few speeches to those who had stopped to listen, we spread out into the streets of Athens, into stores, into buses, down to Omonia Square and the underground tram station – all over the place. One woman hugged me, held me tight and said, "We are with you – all the way with you." She was not referring to our efforts for disarmament. I heard such statements a number of times, mostly from women, but from a sizeable number of men as well. It was a human phenomenon, not a political one.

My popularity was higher than when I was doing serious positive things. Eleni Vlahou, a respected newspaper editor and columnist, wrote in her column: "It seems the first scenario is winning ground – that he is coming back to the house. What has helped has been the intelligent and serious management and manner of Margarita. This certainly makes her the most worthy and dignified member of PASOK." And as far as I was concerned, it made Vlahou the most worthy and dignified member of the press.

On October 26, 1987, I talked to Evelyn. "We call it a transition stage, Evelyn. Things are shaky as yet. He has made up his mind to quit the other relationship. It's just a process of winding down. Yes, she will make a great fuss. I get the message quite clearly from him and quite clearly from people around him. Tomorrow we have a family lunch here in Kastri. Our children and the two grandchildren. Next week we will be going to memorial services for George Papandreou- a public appearance. So far I am pleased. My soul is at peace. I wish it was a cleaner and quicker break. No, I don't believe it is being done only because of political pressure. I think this is the way he feels inside himself – and that's the important thing to me. If it is not an internal decision then there will be ramifications and complications."

Life can behave as ruthlessly and sometimes as magically as fiction. I happen to be a character in the serial, and an observer of the serial. Becoming an observer was a technique I learned in order to withdraw from a painful situation and watch it develop. Serials are made from life, not the opposite.

I awoke the next morning to the sound of marching band music. It was the local high school practicing for the annual "OXI" day parade. OXI means "NO" in Greek and refers to the historic moment when General Metaxas, the dictator of Greece, said NO to the invading Italian army's ultimatum to surrender on that day of October 28, 1940. The one word answer to Mussolini was true to Greece's Periclean heritage.

On that day of October 28th, 1940, Andreas had told me in the past, he walked to the Square of Psyhico, in the suburb of Athens where he lived, and found a cluster of people reading a poster stuck up on the Square's bulletin board. It was the announcement of the suspension of the articles in the Constitution, a declaration of a takeover of the country by a dictatorial power. Voices were muffled; the citizens were scared. Andreas went to the board and ripped down the poster. This was his first act of resistance. As a law student at the University of Athens, member of a Trotskyite organization, he was a natural target for the new regime, and when he started other acts of resistance, he was arrested and tortured.

Andreas had told me about this when we first met. Metaxas and OXI day were entwined with my early encounters with Andreas. The peal of church bells, the music of the proud national anthem, the smell of Greek (we don't call it Turkish) coffee wafting up from the downstairs kitchen – all mingled together and formed a lump of nostalgia in my throat as I fumbled for my clothes. I longed for the early Andreas. I had come to his country; I had grown to love it deeply. Would it seem the same without him beside me? I wondered if today would be a day of "no," or a "yes," affirming that we continue our life paths together.

The family lunch on OXI day mostly started out well, not exactly joyous – talk about international issues, recent government problems, even the weather. There was an underlying tension, but a clear sense on the part of the kids that "Dad is home – almost- and it feels good." All was spoiled at the end. I asked him when I would see him next. He said he supposed when I returned from Thessaloniki. I said I would see him before that at the memorial service for his father.

"You know," he said, "I think it would be better if we didn't have a memorial service – at least not at the cemetery. I think we could have a service at Kastri, just the family and Karatsis – because, you know, everybody is expecting us to be together there – it will be a display, uh, a sign of our reconciliation."

"I thought this was part of the plan, a way in which we would signal we were getting back together. Where else better to do it? It's a service for your father, it's an annual family event, and it's the most natural activity to appear at."

"Yes, yes, but you know the newspapers have made such an issue out of it- all eyes will be on us…" He was not looking at me but down on the table.

"Right," I answered. "Of course, it is what one would expect. In any case what's wrong with the press being focused on this?"

My question created a storm. He started shouting. I don't remember his words anymore because anger was rising in me, igniting my body. He raised the question of his "manliness" - that it would appear he was not a man, that he had succumbed to pressure, the old story. I remember saying he was not a man when he couldn't take a decision and carry it through; to come out aggressively and say "this is it." The children said that the idea of having a memorial service, private, in Kastri, for a man of George Papandreou's public stature, was not feasible. The children not supporting his view made him furious. He walked out of the dining room. Sometime later I realized we were having a cultural battle. Manliness in Greece means control of women – and total respect from children. I wasn't brought up quite that way in America. And my feminist commitment was strong.

At the time, however, I simply sat at the table dumbfounded. So soon we were having a conflict in what had appeared to be a major step toward reconciliation?

"Mom," said Nikos, "Why are you so angry and surprised? That's Dad – you've known him for years."

"No-o-o-o" My voice came out like a wail in a barrel. "He's not that way. He's made a sea change – he worked with me to set the stage, to write the scenario. I did a whole goddamn interview in Kathimerini as part of this – to pave the way for the next developments – one of which was this lunch, then the memorial service."

By now I was pacing around the room. I couldn't get my breath. Finally the kids got me to sit down in a chair and handed me a glass of water. Sophia was stroking my arm as if she was trying to get the blood circulating. George was caressing my hair. My head felt like an exploding missile about to take off from a launching pad. At that moment Kostas, the psychiatrist, walked in. One of the children had called him to hurry over. I heard Sophia say, "She's better now," as if I'd had a heart attack. Or an anaphylactic shock. Slowly the room temperature was brought down. Kostas let me run on, repeating myself.

Finally I turned to them, calm and sober, my juices dried up, my body wheezing with exhaustion. "Kostas, George, Sophia, Nick – why are we all trying so hard to put something together, to patch something up – that isn't patchable? Why don't we just be honest about this thing? That Andreas and I can't get together again...Despite all the political pressure and family pressure – he can't do it. He can't come back. Why don't we accept reality? The truth. The relationship is dead. If not completely dead – in a coma. It is not possible to give oxygen and blood transfusions and food through the veins – to bring it back to life. Kostas, why do you insist? Why don't you say to me his emotional needs are satisfied elsewhere? Why don't you let him proceed? Why don't you support him rather than put obstacles in his way? What kind of a psychiatrist are you?"

Kostas flushed. "I do it for him. He is not in a position to take the right decision. He will regret it someday. It will not last; it will fall apart – and his health will deteriorate, if not immediately, soon."

"Okay, you can treat him as a patient. But the rest of us…why do we all think we know what's best for him? He's not a child. Who knows better than himself what he wants?"

"Look, Margarita, he's reached a very important stage. There has been a turnaround. Don't quit now. He's having problems with it, and he's getting tremendous pressure from the other side."

I told Kostas I had to deal with the situation differently. I was the one to make the decision, not him. The children told me not to make a decision in a moment of emotion. I said, "What moment of emotion? This moment is a culmination of everything I have been going through for the last nine months. It's not a moment of emotion; it's a 'gelling.'"

"Mom," spoke up Nikos. "You know I've been one of the first to say get out of it, but it should be what you really want. Will it be right for you?"

"I know what is right for me. I know the difficulties I will confront by leaving him, but I know I cannot, just cannot, continue living this way. People tell me I can't foresee how different life will be after a divorce. My status will change. But even if I'm just a small struggler in the women's movement, I won't die. I won't be overwhelmed by a diminution in my status or a demotion in position. I have the capacity of adaptability. Anyway, life after divorce cannot be more difficult than what I have been going through."

I had come to the final realization that there was no more chance for a reconciliation, I was saddened by that – yes. On the other hand, when I envisioned him back in this house, no, it was over. The day after my explosion Panayiotis brought me a copy of *Eikones*. The cover had a photo of me carrying a platter. On the platter was the head of The Hostess! The sub-title was "These things happen once in a while," a paraphrase of what I had said in my newspaper interview. I was disgusted and appalled. The magazine depicted this whole ghastly affair as a deadly battle between two women. Me, a feminist, fighting with another woman.

Two weeks went by and then I phoned him, "I have not heard a word from you. I can't trust your promises, so I have seen a lawyer."

"For god's sake, Margarita, what more can I do? The memorial service is coming up and the trip to Patras. Isn't that an indication of something?" So he had calmed down.

"Aren't we pretending, Andreas?"

He paused. "I don't think so. Time will tell. Meet me at Maximou for the service. We'll drive over together." I surprised myself by immediately accepting.

Our appearance at the memorial service for George Papandreou, and our trip to Patras for the Saint Andreas Day ceremonies, both with family in tow, was called "A New Beginning" by the periodical *Eikones*. We marched together in the annual parade in the streets of Patras. Newspapers called this "an impressive show." Andreas, one article said, was extremely happy and declared "I return to my roots and to my family." I didn't hear him say it.

After two public appearances together Andreas returned to the house. The morning he moved in, with two security guards behind him carrying piles of clothes, he wore a big, broad smile. I was at the breakfast table and he told me, "Just a few seconds and I'll be down." He proceeded to the room upstairs where flowers had waited for so many weeks almost a year before. His face was flushed when he came down, looking healthier than I had seen him in months, and he sat down at his old place at the table, a tiny bleat of air passing through his lips.

I sensed he was present as a person, but not in spirit. There was a thickly-meshed screen between us, like the one I used to talk through when he was in jail under the junta. I had, during this period of "transition" become a zombie going through the rituals of everyday life, and waiting for the other shoe to fall. I had made a decision to divorce. I was confident it was the right thing to do. My inner voice told me this is not an authentic reunion.

On my agenda prior to Andreas's return to the house was the trip to Washington and the summit meeting. I had hoped it would be postponed; now I was seizing it to run away. When I arrived in Washington it was cold and bleak. It matched my mood. I was unable to develop enthusiasm for this historic event: Gorbachev in the United States for further discussions on nuclear disarmament. Earlier in the year I became very excited by the Soviet Union's deputy minister for foreign affairs Vladimir Petrovsky's new language on the question of war and peace. He sounded like those of us in the women's movement saying that warfare as an instrument of policy should be shelved once and for all. Such stereotype thinking, he argued, intensifies the atmosphere of fear and mistrust. He pressed for a new mentality not based on artificially inflamed emotions and prejudices. Changes were taking place of momentous importance, and I wanted to be part of them. Yet there I was, a depressed peace activist, unable to feel much of anything.

The Guardian wrote, "The euphoria of pre-summit Washington will be punctured this week by the appearance before Congress of women parliamentarians, women's organizations and leaders from NATO and Warsaw Pact countries, testifying on what they see as the reality behind the INF agreement."

WMS was collaborating in this peace action with Women Parliamentarians of the World for Peace. A common meeting for all the participants before the summit talks was scheduled in order to refine and detail a program of action during the Summit days. Bella Abzug of the big hat was coordinating the activities of WWPP with our network, but as it turned out, her concept of coordination was to invite the members within our organization who were parliamentarians to meetings, leaving the other members out. This created confusion, and hostility.

We wanted a melding of all members of the two groups, regardless of their career roles. It was as if women who were not elected members of their country's legislative bodies were an inferior category. I loved the gruff - voiced Bella with her crusading zeal, but this was, in simple words, elitism. Many of the NGO women were dedicated peace activists whose entire lives had been given to the struggle for peace. Their contribution to de-militarization and de-nuclearization probably outweighed that of the parliamentarians.

After the first meeting was held separately, we managed to coordinate our efforts. We had an unprecedented audience with Congress and presented evidence that NATO governments were taking steps toward introducing new nuclear weapons to replace the Pershing and cruise missiles. We described the three options under consideration by the European and North American defense ministers of NATO's High Level Group. We put specific questions to Congress, without mincing words. We also sent delegations to meetings with ambassadors of countries key to the nuclear question and managed to get a WMS member into a session with Gorbachev (where she pinned a WMS peace bird on his lapel); tried to see Raisa Gorbachev and Nancy Reagan – unsuccessfully; met with journalists; got interviewed on CNN; and participated in a big march of peace organizations which started in Lafayette Square.

I had a chance to address the crowd prior to the march. From the platform I announced the countries represented by women from our network working toward de-nuclearization, and each announcement seemed to bring louder applause than the previous one, especially when I announced names from the Soviet Union and Eastern Europe. The general atmosphere was positive, and would, we thought, convince the decision-makers of vast popular support for reducing nuclear weapons and opening up to the East. We made it clear that this was just a beginning, and we would be tough watchdogs. Our strength could save lives and shift the diplomatic focus if there was a wavering toward the goal.

From Washington I went to New York where I had an appointment with the General Secretary of the U.N., Javier Perez de Cuellar, to discuss the U.N. role in nuclear disarmament, and also reforms in the UN which would give it a more significant role in peace making. The General Secretary's position would be open in a few years. I thought it inadvisable to tell him we were putting on a campaign for a woman General Secretary.

Chapter Twenty Six

The Deeply Personal, Palesting and the Warsaw Pact

(Diary Entry) *December 14th, 1987, flying back to Greece*

During the twelve days I was in the U.S., I talked frequently with Andreas. He was warm and communicative, told me about his doings and listened to mine. He had been on my mind every day. I remembered pieces of advice often given under these circumstances: "Learn to love what you have instead of yearning always for what you're missing, or what you imagine you're missing." As I walked up the steps to the plane, I felt a spring in my legs. Now, gliding high above the ocean, I find myself eager to see him. I imagine myself smoothing the wrinkles around his eyes and softly kissing the lobes of his ears. I wondered if I stayed away on this trip too long. I never believed, however, that you can put a cage around a man. If he is going to wander, he will wander whether you are at home or not. But might it have been less tempting if I were there? I am going to banish such thoughts from my mind. He's not the person I thought he was; he's changed, and I've changed, but he is my life. So much of my actions, my thoughts, are built around him; my history is with him. If I turn away from him, it's like editing an 8 millimeter film of our lives together and whenever he appears on the screen, I cut – and then what is left?

The rest of the month seemed quite normal. I didn't touch his face with my fingers, nor kiss his ear lobes. The feeling of closeness was still not there. The past year had taken its toll, and the patches I was trying to sew on the relationship did not cover up the jagged rips. We spent New Year's Eve at a friend's home, leaving around 11:30 to attend the annual Army Club's gala. As we toasted each other and kissed at midnight I resolved to fight, to do whatever was humanly possible to keep Andreas with me. I sensed I was not only up against his own ambivalence, or uncertainty, but was confronting a diabolical scheme to break up the family. The Hostess, I learned, had already tried twice to commit suicide. She was also on a hunger strike. This demonstration of deep anguish, although a ruse, was undoubtedly flattering to a man who likes romance and dark, deep, irrational passions. Her circle of advisor-friends had smelled the potent and heady aroma of power and were not about to give up easily. There were others in the political party toadying up to her and encouraging Andreas to reestablish a contact, believing that their own careers would benefit more under her influence than mine.

The next meeting of the Initiative of the Six was being held in Stockholm from the 20th to the 23rd of January. This was the first official trip since the break-up. I asked Andreas if The Hostess would be on the plane and told him this would be a disastrous mistake and would start a plethora of rumors again. He told me he had heard she was making a big fuss about not going on the plane, because her career was at stake. He looked at me as if I might give my permission. I did not. She did not appear. He was distant and distracted on the trip and during the few days of meetings and events in Sweden. Pierre was supposed to attend, as he had in Mexico, with the "Friends of the Six," but called me a few days before to say he could not make it. He knew Andreas and I were trying reconciliation. He had the good sense not to complicate our lives.

On my return from Stockholm I flew separately in order to stop in Prague to talk with WMS women about the possibility of a meeting with Warsaw Pact foreign ministers and to determine the substance of our discussions. We had already organized to bring a delegation of Warsaw Pact women to Brussels on May 24th, 1988 (I disliked calling them that as I also disliked being called NATO women, but it simplified our communications), for talks with permanent representatives of NATO countries who carry the rank of ambassadors and with military attaches. Having invited Eastern European women to join us on one of our forays into the halls of NATO, we now were organizing with them to bring Western women to discussions on the other side of the Iron Curtain. This was the first time such an attempt was made for direct contact with decision-makers from the two military blocs. All of this was in connection with our effort to break down barriers, establish a line of communication, and develop confidence and trust among the peoples of all the countries. When I talked to Andreas about this plan earlier and asked him what he thought of it, he replied, "fantastic."

I should have said that we were not so naïve to believe that such actions could prevent the special interests community from getting their way. NATO had developed into a huge machine, creating riches for favored business corporations and jobs for the military. What was important was that we developed doubts in the minds of the public – the only force the peace movement had.

My plane was unable to land in Prague because of fog, and I found myself coming down in Bratislava, leaving a delegation from the Czechoslovak Union of Women waiting at the Prague airport to meet me, freezing along with their flowers. The officials directed me, as the only VIP aboard, to a huge, empty hall at the airport where American music was blasting from a large hi-fi set, to wait for the fog to lift, or to find sleeping arrangements in Bratislava. During the several hours I was there, I read, wrote, hummed and danced alone. My prime motivation was to buoy up my spirits once again to stay in the personal fight that I sensed was more and more a losing battle.

I arrived in Prague around 4 o'clock in the morning. The delegation had been reduced from six women to one dear soul who was assigned to be there at whatever time I arrived. The following evening I was complaining at a dinner table at the Palace of Valdstejn about my difficulty in making contact with the head of the Warsaw Pact. Although their central office was in Poland, it was only a small office with a secretary, who was not in a position to make any decisions or commitments for extraordinary meetings. The contrast between the vast NATO Headquarters in Brussels and the Warsaw Pact miniature space in Brussels startled me. A government official at the table suggested I get in touch with the Foreign Minister of Bulgaria, where he thought the next Pact meeting would be held, to make our request. This I did.

During the next month, in addition to preparing speeches for a U.S. speaking tour, I steeped myself again in military doctrine, reading up on mutual and balanced force reduction, on conventional stability in Europe, on the NATO high level task force, the Stockholm CSBM regime and, more to my liking, practical steps for building confidence in Europe. Much of this we had gone through in our discussions with Platias. This time, however, we would be facing people familiar with both the political and military side, and we wanted to sound knowledgeable and reasonable on military matters in order to be effective on political matters. We were helped immensely by Randy Forsberg and her Institute, particularly since her approach was a woman's approach with emphasis on downgrading the use of force in international conflicts. Although we had no confirmation from the East about a meeting, I was getting bits of information from Eastern European women that their governments were intrigued by the proposal and the Soviet Union especially found the idea in line with Gorbachev's new thinking. It went without saying that the Soviet Union's blessing was key to our project.

As a beginning I telegraphed questions to the women from NATO countries about their government's reactions on three issues: the Jaruzelski memorandum presented to CSCE states; in-depth discussions between the two blocs on military doctrines, a proposal made by the Warsaw Pact; and the suggestions made by Gorbachev for the Mediterranean area during his recent trip to Yugoslavia.

On February 17th I headed for the States, leaving a tenuous personal situation behind. I kept in touch with Andreas during the period of time I was gone, but never knew at the moment he came to the phone if it would be a warm or a cold communication. Prior to my departure I got in touch with Pierre and told him my trip schedule and asked if he could join me somewhere in order to talk. He suggested Boston.

Pierre arrived at the Four Seasons Hotel in Boston on the fourth day of my stay there. He strode in, cheeks ruddy from the cold, a hesitant smile on his face, shook my hand solemnly and waited for a cue from me. I felt a surge of attraction, but quickly and deliberately snuffed if out.

"Shall we have a drink?"

Before or after?" he said, trying to be clever, and natural.

"Now," I answered, somewhat curtly.

When we had ordered our drinks, Pierre spoke, "You know, I did not come to Stockholm because…"

I interrupted. I was sure he was going to say because of his sensitivity to my marital situation. "Please, let's just talk for a while, about other things, about what you've been doing, what I've been doing, how you feel about the INF Treaty, about the weather; anything that is not deeply personal."

"Well," Pierre was stumbling for words, "let's talk about your peace concerns. Are you still going out in the world like an apostle seeking misery and ugliness?"

I was taken aback. He often teased me, but this question had bite in it. I felt anger and momentarily wanted to lash back with equivalent nastiness. Then I remembered all the wonderful moments we had shared. I had not brought him all this way to start an argument. I decided to treat the comment lightly.

"Yeah, man, and finding a lot of it, to my great joy. When was the last time we were together? Months ago?" Pierre nodded. "Did I tell you on the phone about my summit experiences?"

"You told me about the struggle for power between two women's organizations."

"It's one of my least favorite subjects of conversation – rifts and battles among women. It makes me question what I say about women's way of ruling the world and challenges my beliefs."

"Challenges like that are healthy. We wouldn't be rational human beings if we didn't look at our ideals and values, our methods of operation, from time to time. What do you think I did, a military man who became a worker in the peace movement?"

"I have enough dilemmas in my life right now. I can't tolerate another one."

"Aw, come on. I don't really believe this shakes your solid feminist principles." I looked at him quizzically.

"Are you…" I struggled to complete the sentence.

"Making fun of you? No, well, maybe yes. The truth is, Maggie, I 'm trying to lighten up the conversation. I've been dying to see you, but I sense there is a moot purpose in your calling me to come here, and I am, hmm, let's say, uncomfortable. And I guess I'm not sure I want to hear what you have to say. I prefer, well, I prefer you in my arms." He said this in such an endearing way. I felt a rising desire to protect him, to take care of him.

"I'm sorry. I don't want this to be awkward. God damn it, Pierre, it feels good to be with you…you mean much to me…" I was going to cry. I strained to keep my voice under control, to keep my composure. My insides were screaming, the flood gates opened and tears slid down my face. I grabbed the cocktail napkin at the same moment Pierre put his hand on my shoulder, and that tender gesture made me sure I would collapse in a quivering bundle on the floor.

"Maggie, it's alright. It's okay. Here, have a sip of your drink. I'm doing everything wrong. No I'm not. You're doing everything wrong." His arm came around me. "Imagine you, a grownup woman, crying in Boston…In the Four Seasons Hotel in a cocktail lounge with a man!" A giggle burbled through my choked up throat. I took hold of his hand and held it close to my cheek.

For the next few minutes we sort of just sat there. He said a few more sweet things, and some funny things. I don't remember what finally got us started on other subjects. In the end we were talking about the role of non-governmental organizations in social change. It was a long conversation, and as always with him, an interesting one. He believed, as I did, that the glue holding such organizations together was a shared vision of a better world. Their strength was in a commitment to similar values. And this makes those of us in NGO's relatively immune to faction or fortune. We cannot be squelched by parties or political agendas of governments. (or by private life agonies?)

He pointed out what important roles NGO's play by supplementing political parties, by being mechanisms through which citizens articulate their needs, and make demands on the government. They educate the public and play a watchdog role, reigning in the expansionist tendencies of the political elite for more power, and demanding accountability in their actions. I told him how I disliked fund-raising and how we were in a constant scramble to survive financially, but I thought this was in the end a good thing. We did not become bureaucratic and didn't have enough money to worry about corruption. We were not dependent on the organization for our livelihood, and this allowed for independent thinking and independent expression of opinion. I started feeling better about myself, and my continuing efforts to organize for what I believed in.

Finally we were talked out. Pierre said, "Now, how about the deeply personal?"

"Yes," I answered. "It is time for that."

"Should we go up to your room?" I had planned differently. I didn't want the atmosphere, nor temptation, to influence my talk with him. By now the bar was full, noisy and smoky. Intimate talk was incongruous with the environment. And I did want to feel close to him.

"Yes, let's go."

As soon as the room door closed behind us, I started to speak.

"I won't give a long introduction, just that you know Andreas and I are trying a reconciliation. " He nodded his head. "We are working at it, and I am trying to do everything I can to recover our old relationship, or to start up a new one on a different basis, but to keep the family intact.

"Sit down, Maggie, don't rush, we have a little time." I realized I was acting nervous.

I am not just doing this for the children. They are grown and will find a way to handle a separation. I am doing it for me. I still need him, not as a prime minister, but as my companion. I always believed there was a solid, deep, untouchable connection between the two of us – and up until now this had been the case. We have gone through many fires: sickness, a coup d'état, imprisonment, extra-marital affairs. Andreas always came back to home port. He has done so again, but the waters are choppy, and I feel the anchorage slipping."

"You see me as somehow a bad element in the picture?"

"I don't know. I don't think so. What we've had together has been beautiful, but maybe, just maybe, I rearranged my feelings to accommodate this relationship. At first it was an adventure, and a flattering balm to my tortured ego. Then it started to have meaning." I looked at him sitting next to me. His expression was mournful. In the lamplight his skin looked unwholesome, like the pink skin under a scab.

"Look, Maggie, before you continue, I want to say something. I think meeting you and loving you has been one of the most important happenings in my life. Just recently one of our best French writers asked if he could do a profile of me for a magazine. He said he wanted not just my philosophy and descriptions of my peace work, but background material on my personal life, childhood, family, friends. I thought about it for a while. Then I realized I could not give a true account of my life without including you. We haven't talked much about our feelings toward each other. We do not engage in love chatter…but this is something I had to say."

"I am glad you said it, but you are right, we don't do those whisperings, those revelations. They seem childlike and reduce feelings to sound bites."

"I have never told you how precious you are to me. That you became the core, the centerpiece, of this space of time we have known each other."

"Please don't say any more. I will start to become teary-eyed again." This time I put my hand on his arm.

"I knew the day would come when we would say good-bye. I had hoped not so soon," Pierre was looking somewhere else, not at me.

"I cannot cut you from my life with a knife, Pierre. I guess what I am saying is that I want us to see each other less frequently and with a new understanding. I cannot – even if perhaps I should – see you walk out that door, looking at your disappearing back, and say that's the end, that's the last time I'll see him."

We talked on into the night, reminiscing, joking, laughing and crying. It started to be inevitable that we would end up in bed, so I gathered strength and took the decision to say good-bye.

The next day I felt emptiness and a longing. I was wondering whether Pierre could ever really be out of my life. I went through my various contacts and activities with little excitement. Pierre wanted to take me out for lunch, or dinner and I said no. On the following day I was leaving for New York and on to Athens. He wanted to fly with me to New York. I said no. I was being little Miss Goody Two Shoes, or some such thing, putting into practice my request that we not see each other often, thinking at the same time, my god, I am an absolute jerk.

I arrived in Athens on the morning of the 7th of March and had lunch with Sophia, Nikos and my husband. It seemed like a normal lunch. In the evening Andreas went out for dinner, not telling me where, and arrived in Kastri late at night. That same evening I rifled through newspaper clippings which had piled up on my desk during my absence. There were comments about my trip to the U.S. '*Ethnos*', the least friendly of the newspapers, said it was my tenth trip since the party took over the government, and that the prime minister had not gone once. Nor had he been invited on an official visit by President Reagan. To this reporter it was unseemly that I travel and be involved in international politics. Men do the travelling and politicking in this world...I wanted to tell the fool that it is not chromosomes which put men m the middle of international politics but the creation of social processes and institutions over generations which keep women out of any political role which affects state actions. The article indirectly said I was usurping Andreas's role – a male role. This hardly helped my cause. '*Vradini*' wrote: "Margarita will explain her husband's philosophy to Reagan, 'Make love, not war." And the most ominous, a columnist for '*Eleftheros Typos*,' indicating he was in a position to know, wrote that Margarita would soon again become a "Simple Citizen." None of these things bolstered by sagging spirits.

What did give me a boost was throwing myself into the preparations for "A Day of Solidarity with Palestinian Women." Before my departure, and because of the Israeli bombing of Palestinian camps in Lebanon, EGE had decided to put on an international event to bring the Palestinian cause to the forefront.

Women came from all over Europe, the United States, Soviet Union, from Israel and Palestine, personalities, politicians – and adults and children from the neighborhood of Nea Smyrni, where the large, enclosed stadium opened its doors to them. The best of our musicians gave of their time and talent to play at the gathering. Andreas sent a warm greeting, as did Arafat. Melina Mercouri spoke and said, "Every time a Palestinian child is hurt we women feel one of our own children has been hit. We feel pain and rage, because our people have gone through similar bitter experiences."

I told them, "Now is the time to call an international conference with Israel and Palestine, the two super powers, and whatever other agencies or nations could contribute to a peaceful resolution of the conflict. The Greek government has indicated its desire to be the host and to facilitate every effort toward this aim." This latter Andreas had instructed me to say.

The star of the show was Michel Schwartz, editor of *Tarak Al Sarara*, the sole Arab - language newspaper in Israel. She introduced herself as a member of a non-Zionist collection of Palestinian and Israeli women, living in Israel, who, along with other women's organizations, were shocked by Israeli barbarism. "The Palestinian woman," she said, "bears the burden of the occupation. We find her in all the hospitals, full of black and blue marks from beatings by Israeli soldiers. In the Sifa hospital of Gaza, I saw a young woman whose ribs had been smashed when she was walking to her engagement party. 'It doesn't matter,' she told me, 'I'll have a new opportunity to get engaged during the coming general strike.'"

When Michel returned to Israel she was put in jail.

Between this demonstration of solidarity with Palestinian women and my departure for Bulgaria, life continued in its routine way. We had an official visit from the President of Cyprus and his wife, some embassy receptions, and family lunches. I saw less and less of Andreas, however, and not because of my own activities. True, I had a lot of work in preparation for our meeting with the Warsaw Pact, the mirror organization to NATO, but I was available at all times, and willing to rearrange my schedule at his request. His requests were virtually non-existent.

At this particular time, my thoughts were riveted on the discussion coming up with the Warsaw Pact. This was, as far as I knew, the first attempt to establish a channel of communication between NATO and the Warsaw Pact. And women were doing it by making direct contact with military bloc decision-makers on issues of disarmament, defense strategies, mutual security, etc. We were prepared to become a conduit between the two, and would so indicate in Bulgaria. Being messengers was not, however, our main aim, even though this could be seen as part of the wind of change, blowing away the confrontational stance intrinsic to the Cold War.

Men don't like us traipsing around on their territory. They find a way to make us feel dumb or silly when we talk about militarism and sexism, or when we reveal the gender-colored strategy, doctrine and attitudes of the military. When we talk about de-militarization, we are really talking about de-masculinization, or, wow, feminization of the military. Feminization would mean not allowing the vested interests in arms production to control our political choices. It would mean using technology to achieve human-defined goals. It would mean replacing force with cooperation and dialogue. And it would mean a women's strategy for peace, for common security. It required a different vocabulary. Our task was difficult because we were trying to make them understand by using their vocabulary.

While it was difficult to ask questions with a feminist vocabulary to NATO representatives, I thought we might have more problems with representatives of the communist nations. This was so because while their rhetoric claimed the equality of women, they have mentally compartmentalized women to the female role, extolling their mission as mothers and providers of emotional support. This patriarchal mentality, which is cross-cultural and trans-national, says that military policy is too complex, too tough and too remote for the feminine mind to understand. Because of this, my position has been that even though we cringe when we hear words like megaton, blast facilities, third generation nukes, and other vehicles of violence, we should not be intimidated by the lingo, and we should learn military concepts in order to re-interpret that lingo, change those concepts.

I urged all women to come a day or so earlier than our scheduled meeting at five o'clock on Monday, the 28th of March. Most of them did, representatives from our ten NATO countries, and from the Warsaw Pact side, Czechoslovakia, the Soviet Union, Bulgaria, and East Germany. We were missing three: Romania, Hungary and Poland.

After a day and a half of sessions among ourselves, we arrived at the meeting crammed with information and knowledge and hyped up for this historic event. The Soviet foreign ministers were lined up along one side of a long table. Because of the width of the table, handshakes across the table had us almost flattened belly down to reach their outstretched hands. There was a slight skirmish on our side about seating arrangements. We were more than they, and only seven of us would be sitting directly across from a minister. The rest would be at the margins on either end. I asked the president of the Union of Bulgarian women to arrange us appropriately. That created a momentary altercation between her and the American representative, but it soon subsided.

Shevardnadze started the debate. He was cordial and not at all patronizing. I responded to his initial remarks, and told him we would like to ask them a series of questions, state our opinions, and because we were sure there was not enough time to cover all the issues, we wanted their agreement to answer the remaining questions in writing. I emphasized the centrality of women's issues to our mounting global crisis, for example, that population growth created pressures which aggravated conflict. Arresting this growth hinges – among other things – on sexual equality, education for women and training for jobs and careers. We pointed out that people involved in the military who use the threat of war to establish peace should be aware of methods of dealing with the causes of war, and should feel responsible for helping create preventive measures to the use of force. I am positive WMS established a "first" in a Warsaw Pact meeting talking about sexual equality.

Shevardnadze determined which member of the Pact would respond to which question, giving us a chance to size up the ministers. What was eminently clear was who ran the show. The term "satellite" came to my mind as I watched the functioning of this alliance.

Towards the end of three hours of talk, we made four proposals for action; (1) A percentage of funds which go to military hardware for each bloc be diverted to develop "sister" peace institutes, West and East, for research and peace education. (2) Funds from both blocs to be made available for a Women's Commission on Mutual Security and Peace Partnership. The Commission to be made up of prominent female personalities who would have the responsibility of drawing up a peace platform which would reflect women's practicality, realism, understanding and vision of how to reach a world where conflict is resolved without violence. (3) Declaration to be prepared by all the women present at the dialogue in Bulgaria to pledge to work for a nuclear-weapons-free country- their own, and to get it published in their own countries. (4) An agreement to continue the dialogue with the Warsaw Pact during their next official meeting, and to organize similar opportunities the other way around.

When I returned from Bulgaria, Andreas had taken his clothes from his room and moved out. No explanation. I watched him on television in the official box during the March 25th National Holiday parade, something he did every year. Women were not included in the box, so I was not expected to attend. He looked puffed and tired, and I was dismayed to see him falling asleep at various moments during the parade. This was not natural for him.

Two themes ran through newspapers during the next several months. First, Margarita's feminism created problems for Andreas. His clothes were not pressed, his food was casually prepared; essentially he was uncared for. Second, a speech given by Nikos was considered his political debut. He was following in his mother's footsteps (not father's). Interest in Nikos heightened.

(Diary Entry) *May 20th, 1988, Kastri*

From the point of view of my public career, this year so far has probably been the most productive and successful of my life. In April I flew to New York to speak at a UNICEF function, held in the auditorium of the U.N. Our women's organization conducted its seventh congress, a lively, well-organized event. I was again elected president. WMS held a "women's summit" on a boat with the cream of Soviet and American women in the peace movement, and with two "stars" from the U.S. Coretta Scott King and Maxine Waters. We received a lot of publicity by our call for a Pan-European Women's Peace Institute. We also developed a women's peace program to take to the Summit in Moscow on the occasion of Reagan's first visit to the Soviet Union. The dialogue on the boat was fascinating, tough, but always convivial. Today I returned from an Australian speaking tour, invited by the Australian peace movement.

Chapter Twenty Seven

Smoke Around the Papandreou Story

(Diary entry) *June 2nd 1988 – Kastri*

During this time Andreas and I have had lunches together, sometimes with the family, sometimes alone, and an occasional dinner at Kastri. This Easter we did the rounds together. Several newspapers called it a "charade." I have done the maximum to rebuild our relationship except to withdraw from all my political activities. Whenever I brought up our difficulties and held the door open for him to spurt out whatever he wants to say, including let's terminate our marriage, he never says it. Quite the contrary, if I mention divorce, he says, "I haven't used that word."

Yesterday's lunch, however, with him and Sophia, had a different flavor. He congratulated me on my Australian trip, saying I had certainly proved I could function independently in the political arena. Whatever else we said, there was an air of finality hovering over the table. Sophia looked anxious. Her presence forced me to keep the talk low-key. It felt like a re-run of last year's soap opera. I guess every unraveling of a marriage, every divorce, is like a soap opera. Clearly, the struggle is not worth it anymore. I have ceased being an active participant. I am watching a drama unfold, uncertain of the scenario, letting the leading man make the moves. I have a macabre kind of curiosity as to what will happen next.

From May 27 to June 3 I was in Moscow with a delegation of WMS women for the U.S. Soviet summit meeting. Together with Raisa Gorbachev I unveiled a replica of a 5th century B.C. Greek statue of peace donated by the Greek sculptor Stavros Georgopoulos who was present for the ceremony. It was placed in a prominent spot in a square in front of the hotel Cosmos in downtown Moscow. A large crowd gathered for the ceremony. The atmosphere was enlivened by American women holding patches of brightly colored cloth with designs made by American children declaring their support for the summit peace initiative. Our entire delegation had a meeting with Shevernadze. His first act was to present us with 15 pages of answers to the questions we had left unasked at the Warsaw Pact meeting. He told us he had looked into the contents of the manual for soldiers and changes were being made in response to our criticism that the language reflected an offensive military policy rather than defensive. We commented by saying we didn't want just the language to change, but the policy.

A smaller delegation was invited to meet with Ms. Roxanne Ridgeway, the State Department assistant to Schultz on NATO affairs. This was in response to our request to see President Reagan to deliver our Women's Peace Program, the pages now displayed within a lovely glass container decorated with metal by one of Greece's well-known artists, Dimitri Talaganis. I was interviewed on Russian TV, and one question stopped me short. "How does your husband react to your extensive involvement in politics?" I answered honestly, saying he wasn't very happy, but we each had our independent lives, and this was understood by both. At the end of the summit meeting Gorbachev invited all NGO's to a large assembly hall, and after a statement by him, opened up the microphones for our participation. When the meeting was finished he walked over to me to give me greetings to bring to the prime minister.

A reporter who asked Andreas at a press conference about my activities, brought this remark: "We make no comments on her activities and neither PASOK nor the government coordinates her initiatives, nor controls them." This inspired a newspaper headline: "Margarita Out of Control." When I returned from Moscow I discovered an embargo had been placed on publicity on my trip on state television. I further learned Andreas was furious about my meeting with Gorbachev. I don't know what he fantasized – that I had a one-to-one tete-a-tete where we discussed affairs of state? I was one of 300 people.

While state TV ignored my visit, most of the Athenian newspapers carried stories about it. The photograph of me with Raisa at the unveiling got international coverage, probably because Raisa and Gorby were new to the international scene and were considered newsworthy. Interpretations of my visit and what was said were a series of fantasies. One newspaper said Gorbachev congratulated EGE and my role as president on our peace initiatives. Another said I managed through Raisa to accomplish something the diplomatic office had not been able to do for Andreas: a meeting with Nancy Reagan and the President, where I would give Reagan a red rose. In addition, I supposedly had arranged a date for a meeting between Andreas and Gorbachev. The headline on that story was "Margarita Again Opens the Road. " In fact, none of these statements were true. I was just being ground to pieces

My clipping service, reviewing 17 newspapers in Athens, sent boxes of clips daily with articles concerning me. One general comment I can make is that the male-dominated media is deaf, dumb and blind to the way women experience the world. Several people wrote open letters asking me to form a national party in which women would be prominent. This fascination with me had to do with the interest in the not-so-covert story of Andreas's relationship with the blonde stewardess. Much was deliberately done by the opposition, as a way to undermine further our relationship by depicting me as an effective, but uncontrollable, ambassador for Greece. Unfortunately The Hostess knew his psychological world and had ample opportunities to point out things to contribute to my overthrow. I had no public relations person, and no way to stop this barrage – except not to exist.

In early June I learned that Ozal, the prime minister of Turkey, was making an official visit to Greece, along with his wife. Because I had been publicly vocal on the necessity to resolve problems of conflict through dialogue, it was assumed that in addition to my role as wife of the PM of Greece, I would be present at the meetings of the Turkish congregation while in Greece. In other words, my effectiveness in establishing better Greek-Turkish relations was considered almost equal to the prime minister's. The protocol officer from the Ministry of Foreign Affairs asked me to propose activities for the wife during the times the two leaders were dealing with official business. The truth is I wanted very much to talk with Ms. Ozal, woman to woman, on behalf of the mothers in Cyprus whose sons had disappeared during the invasion of Cyprus by Turkey, they were presumed to be in Turkey as hostages. Once I tried this with a Turkish woman M.P. attending the UN Decade of Women's Conference in Nairobi, in a private conversation at my hotel, and got showered with ice. This is an example where sisterhood did not work.

I decided to plan for the usual diplomatic lunch with top wives in the government at a lovely restaurant with a view of the Acropolis. Meanwhile, I checked with a ship-owner about the use of a cruise ship for a day's cruise with the Turkish women visitors in the contingent from Ankara, and whatever other Turkish women were connected with the Embassy. On the Greek side, since the question of relations with the "eternal enemy" was a national question, I invited women from all political parties. We began to draw up a list and started making the calls. The response from all the women was stupendous. Women were eager for a chance to dialogue with the other side.

Then things started going sour. I was told I was not to go to the airport to meet the Ozals, but Melina Mercouri would go. Melina was Minister of Culture, and a friend, but it was protocol for the Turkish prime minister's wife to be met by the Greek prime minister's wife. Of course, I knew what was happening. I was being kicked publicly downstairs, again on my way to becoming a "simple citizen." Because I refused this order and said I would be obliged to go, another tactic was tried. People in the foreign ministry told me there would be no official program for the wives, or other female members of the entourage, in order to diminish the importance of the visit for domestic consumption. Although I didn't know the details, this was enough for Ms. Ozal to announce she would not join her husband on the trip.

A deluge of stories speculated on the reasons for her cancellation. One was that I rejected the traditional role of wives meeting wives at the airport, supposedly as a feminist protest (!) Another was that the cruise I had organized was on the Aegean, a sea whose continental shelf was in dispute by the two nations. It was further suggested I didn't agree with Andreas's line vis-a-vis Turkey and since I was organizing my own party, did not want to get sucked into a failed friendly initiative. Another, and more realistic explanation was that the prime minister did not want my political profile to be enhanced by successful meetings between Ms. Ozal and a broad spectrum of Greek women. In this case, the "personal is political" was literally true. Dealings at the level of international affairs were being affected by the messed-up personal life of the couple Papandreou.

At the same time, word was out about a reshuffle of ministers in the government. When this happens, speculation goes on for days or weeks beforehand and political commentary for days or weeks afterwards. Newspapers are full of it. This game of musical chairs, because it involved personalities and had a lot of human drama, began at the time of the fuss on the Ozal visit and was occupying much of the month of June. I should have been clever enough to foresee that it might have had something to do with me, a means of turning attention away from the screwed up meeting with the Turkish Prime Minister. By now my firmly installed indifference and "spectator" role meant little reading of newspapers, little watching of television news shows, which in Greece are full of the stars of the theater of politics, and little thought about Andreas. I shunted off the Turkish fiasco and got on with my own activities and my life.

On the 23rd Andreas left for an official trip to Germany, taking Sophia with him. On my last trip to the U.S., I had purchased a handsome sports jacket with shirt and tie to match, and I suggested to Sophia that she take it with her and surprise him with it in Frankfurt. On the 25th I left for Volos, with my good friend Anna, and a meeting with the local chapter of EGE. Sunday morning, the 26th, I was scheduled to give a speech in Larissa, a town two hours from Volos in central Greece. On the way leaving the hotel, we stopped to pick up the Sunday papers. A headline in Ethnos caught my eye: "Separation Definitive." A large picture in the top right corner of Andreas and me dancing had the title "Andreas-Margarita at Their Last Tango."

I was shocked. No, upset – I could no longer be shocked. The large black letters of the main headline occupied a third of the tabloid page. Of course things weren't going well for us, and the little acts of unkindness toward me had been growing. On one occasion I told Andreas if the time comes for a divorce, I would like us to do it in a joint press conference in a civilized fashion. It was one of the many times he said he was not interested in a divorce. Because I had become a bystander to my personal life, I looked at this inconsistency with Andreas' behavior as part of the merry go round life the couple was living. Anna read the other sub-title to me as I looked out the car window at a fabulous landscape, which I could not appreciate. "Margarita tried to get her friends on the list of PASOK." This was the parliamentary candidate list. And under a small picture of Sophia, "Ill-fated attempt to get them together."

More surprising was that on the list of reasons for the separation there was no mention of Andreas's affair with another woman. The old boys club was working well. PASOK newspapers wanted to protect him from a marital scandal and were conjuring up the explanation which could justify our separation in the eyes of a patriarchal society. A few of the sentences gave ample proof of their intent. "The whole thing started in December of 1986 (interesting that the date coincided with the London incident) when Margarita began to take autonomous actions, making political statements and joining political activities which were the purview of the prime minister." The story continued by saying "she made trips outside and inside Greece which were neither announced nor agreed upon by the prime minister." "This right she certainly did not have because she wasn't even a member of PASOK." (This was a fabrication. For years I was a member of the international relations committee in the central offices of the party.)

According to this paper, the straw that broke the camel's back was my insistence on putting women on the parliamentary list for the coming elections. In order to verify this, the writer took the names of the members of the Executive Board of EGE and presented them as "Margarita's list." Although I promoted women in general, whenever I could, I had only once given Andreas names – when he asked for them in the elections of 1981. The newspaper continued by harping on my feminism, called me a controversial figure, ambitious and involving myself in matters not of my concern. "Margarita did not accept Roumbatis' description of her as a 'simple citizen,' and at this very moment she is travelling with members of EGE in Volos and Larissa, where she will baptize a child." How this latter activity was outside my traditional realm, I failed to understand.

Finally, the newspaper raised the issue of The Hostess, saying that friends of the prime minister do not give as a reason for the separation his relationship with her, and this because her designs were not so strongly ambitious as to break up the marriage. This was meant to belittle his extra – marital affair, and to give a favorable image of The Hostess at the same time. The article concluded with passages from interviews or speeches I had given over time. "As a woman I believe I have something special to give in the political sphere, a feminist perspective, or if you prefer; more concern for the effect of political decisions on the human being."

"Perhaps I am more radical than Andreas because I am not in government." "Naturally, when it comes to questions of equality, I am considerably more progressive." "As a feminist, I have not discovered a capitalist system which satisfies me, nor a socialist one." "We have managed to develop an independent women's organization, both organizationally and economically." "We take positions according to our feminist-socialist ideology, and when those positions are opposite to the positions of the government, we are the first to emphasize this and to try to change the policy of the government." "I truly believe women are the real change agents in a society."

Reciting these statements was meant to ring the death knell of the marriage.

The large hall for my speech that night was overflowing. My talk was entitled "A Feminist-Socialist Proposal for the Upbringing of Children." I had been trying for some time to put the ideology, or philosophy, I wasn't sure which, into practical terms. Ideology sounds too doctrinaire; feminist-socialist philosophy sounds too grand. Perhaps the word "theory" is more apt. We had developed an understanding of the system of power deriving from the capitalist patriarchal system. Although male supremacy existed before capitalism, it existed in socialist systems as well, so it is the present situation which must be understood if we are to change the structure of oppression.

What I had been trying to do was to look at a foreign policy which would change the situation to better the condition of women in the world. Or a development program which would do the same. (One could paraphrase the well-known saying, "What is good for Ford is good for the nation" by substituting for Ford the word "women.") In social change one has to break down the barriers, develop a new awareness, a new mentality, and change institutions. In Larisa I was talking about the education of young children within the family during the pre-school age where women have considerable control.

No one present referred to the *Ethnos* story either publicly or privately. When it came to the banquet later in the evening, however, I discovered that several local PASOK personalities and functionaries had cancelled their reservations. I was entering the period where friends and colleagues would avoid me and when necessary, cross the street so as not to say hello to me. The next stage would be to abandon me; the final stage to speak against me. I remembered Melina's admonition about losing power.

At the same time I thought perhaps an old story was being rehashed for newspaper circulation purposes. When I returned to Kastri I called Sophia in Frankfurt. She had telephoned prior to the article in *Ethnos*, leaving a message at the house, saying her father had told her to buy a lovely gift for her mother. I was puzzled. This sounded so positive, and the article so negative. Also, apparently she had given him the jacket gift before they left because I found a short note from Andreas. "Dear Margarita, many, many thanks for the beautiful coat and pants, ties and shirts. I will take them along on my trip to Germany. Yours, Andreas." Messages were coming from two different poles.

I didn't have to wait long to know which pole was in the ascendancy.

With a gorgeous turquoise lamb's wool sweater delivered to me by a sad looking Sophia, came this letter in Andreas's handwriting.

"Yesterday's Ethnos came out with the news that we have split up and that this is definitive. It was difficult, indeed impossible, to have Maroudas deny the basic fact- the fact that we have been apart for almost a year and a half. It was absolutely essential to 'clear the air.'

"Now that this is out of the way, I am convinced it will be possible for us to develop a friendly human relationship- something that is also very important for the children, and especially for Sophia.

"Also, you will have the opportunity to develop fully – and independently of me – your course in public life with your personality in the center of your activities.

"I have no objection for Sophia's plans for the development of a suite on the second floor. And I am prepared to proceed to put up a pre-fab in the garden for your office facilities.

"In the hope that both of us can achieve emotional peace – I send you my greetings from Germany, and look forward to meeting with you soon after my return."

(Diary Entry) *June 30th, 1988, Corfu*

As soon as I read Andreas's letter, I fell apart. My facade of indifference cracked. Underneath is still a layer of hope. And underneath that, love. I called Evelyn, speaking incoherently into the phone. Before I could describe what happened, Evelyn said, "I'm on the way over." She had foreseen this likelihood and kept her bag packed. She arrived a day later in the morning, and we were off in the afternoon for Corfu. Effie Zianga arranged with Anna Panagopoulou and several other women to join us – all of this to build up my sunken spirit. I truly needed a morale boost.

I know these are the thoughts going through the heads of discarded partners in many parts of the world, both men and women. Knowing we form a vast population was small comfort. I am trying to lift myself out of my depression, carrying out normal activities, laughing when it was appropriate, drinking with relish, dancing under the moon, talking endlessly with my sister. There are some things I can't act out – eating and sleeping. Nor can I rid myself of the feeling I am sinking in quicksand. I've been trying not to say it – I will write it first: this is it, this is the end. No, I am still in the process of dying. When I am totally dead, I will await a rebirth. There has to be a rebirth. There WILL be a rebirth.

I flew back to Athens just in time to get a bag packed for workshops on the island of Spetsis arranged by the Center of Studies on Mediterranean Women which EGE had spawned in the mid – 1980's. I scrawled a note to Andreas who was somewhere cruising around the Aegean and left it under his door at the ranch house. It said simply that we must have a meeting.

On the island of Spetsis were several women from the board of EGE who came to me to say they had been authorized by the rest of the board to write a response to all the newspaper coverage of recent vintage. Personally I didn't want it. I told them I would not intervene, but I would like to read it before its submission to the newspapers. Always I had insisted on a bold approach in the fight for women's rights and dignity. The Board seemed to have picked up this practice.

After several revisions, and over my objection to a phrase which described me as a loyal wife and good mother (as if I were not loyal and good there would be justification for abuse) the statement came out as follows:

"For many days now, we have been witnesses for the first time, given Greek mores, of a patriarchal attack against our president Margarita Papandreou, with the aim of blemishing her reputation gained in our society since 1963.

"It is unjust that a personal situation becomes the origin of a backward turn in our society. Margarita is being attacked because, besides being a loyal wife and good mother, as well as a valuable and esteemed advocate of women's rights, she wanted to struggle to change the fate of women in order that our society become a society of equality and progress. Her love and her struggles on behalf of women and her work in founding a world network for peace are known both here and abroad.

"What circles and based on what standards do they set about, dictate and justify publicizing false facts on a clearly personal matter?

All of this makes us more determined to continue to struggle for equality, to support peace initiatives and for an establishment which does not use its power to batter and oppress women. We call the members of EGE to gather around our worthy president, and for the Executive Board and the entire organization to reject the lies and the distortions, to protect our organization and to maintain – all of us, as we have done up till now through struggle – the rights we have earned."

EGE, a women's organization was obliged to look at this as demeaning women in general. All the work we had put into raising the status of women, of giving them a role in the decision-making process of the state, of expressing independent thoughts, was being undermined.

An announcement of a divorce would have been acceptable. What I knew, however, was that the people loved Andreas. They were under the spell of his charisma, as I had always been. And, to be honest, he paid attention to their interests, and had fought the special interests on their behalf. He was in essence a good person. My attributes by comparison were limited – a foreign lady, a feminist, and a person of independent thinking.

The initial intentions of the EGE Board had a good deal of bravado. They sensed from my attitude that it was a losing battle. Then, each woman looked into the "political cost" or perhaps the personal cost of signing the document, evaluating such an act in the light of her own ambitions and aspirations, or in many cases, of her husband's ambitions. Within the Board, women of daring did exist. In the process of getting consensus, they were outnumbered. The letter was not sent.

A curious thing happened as a result of my Spetsis speech "A Feminist Security Policy." It proves how delicate making public statements can be in political life. The speech was an older one. I had used it, or something similar, on several occasions outside of Greece. Given my mental state and my concentration on my own problems, I failed to reread it before presenting it. In an effort to describe in simple terms non-provocative defense as part of a mutual security system in international matters, I developed examples. In the real world, I explained, as it presently exists, when we see married life between human beings as a partnership, we must move in the direction of seeing life among nations as a larger partnership. "Since most marriages are not partnership marriages and most countries not in a partnership relationship what rights to security, to defense against an attack do we have?

As a person, do you have the right to protect yourself against blows from, a husband? What if a husband knew that each time he battered you he would get a powerful electrical shock? Or that ten female friends would automatically appear and form a protective ring around you, or pin him to the floor? This is a defense system that could be called non-provocative, but would still give you a sense of security.

Oof! Even before I finished my speech, I saw several journalists in the room scrambling for the door, and suddenly I visualized what mischief the newspapers would make with these blunt comments. A real foot-in-the-mouth blunder!

When I returned home, I went to see a lawyer about getting a divorce. I was fairly familiar with the law because EGE had been instrumental in changing features of it during the revision of the Family Code in 1983. When both spouses agreed, the decree could be handed down in only a few months' time. If the divorce was contested, the process could drag out for as many as four years. This applied to ordinary citizens. I understood the power of power. The dictator Papadopoulos divorced his wife virtually with a wave of the hand. We were no longer living under a dictatorship, but the head of government was strong, and now apparently determined. I had advisors who wanted me to make a battle out of it. I didn't. I preferred a divorce by consent.

Although a lot of sympathy existed for me on the part of the public, PASOK newspapers now had to justify my husband's Frankfurt declaration in readiness for the next year's elections. I had to be visualized as a power-hungry, overwhelmingly ambitious female, messing around in public affairs, denying Andreas the solicitude and warmth of a true wife. One newspaper said I didn't wash his socks, nor did I know how to boil an egg. I would have enjoyed that as a satirical justification, but it was meant literally.

The rest of the summer I kept in motion with my women's and peace commitments, dodging the "slings and arrows of outrageous fortune." Meanwhile, a letter signed by his political office was sent to all embassies saying my name was not to be included on any invitations sent to the Prime Minister. After shooting this pellet, Andreas went back to cruising on the Aegean, considering himself free of marital ties or obligations. He had not called me for a discussion, avoiding, as usual, confrontation with the unpleasant, and his resistance to being pinned down. Finally, after my prodding, it was about to happen. A meeting was set for the evening of August the 2nd. When I walked into his office late that evening I found him with his personal secretary, Mihalis.

"I didn't expect there would be somebody else here for our conversation," I said.

"Mihalis will leave," he said. And he did. We waited for the door to close.

Andreas began, "As I said in my letter, I think it will be possible to have a new situation." Before I could respond to this remark, Andreas continued. "The fundamental thing is that my basic decision is given and final. And then we can discuss everything – financial support, as much as in the past, and maybe for life. It is my intention, if I can, for life. There are some other things. I don't want to have other persons intervene in my opinion."

"Come now, Andreas, you don't expect people to hear such an announcement and then to say, 'that's it.' People have their reactions too. Are you implying that I have given orders to them?"

"Yes, tell your friends to stop intervening."

"Look, Andreas, I don't control my friends any more than you control yours – and people you think are your friends. I can tell you many things your so-called friends have said about you that would knock you off your seat."

He was somewhat intrigued with this statement. "Hell, if they don't want me, they can leave the party."

"Frankly," I said, "I don't want to overplay this theme, but I would have liked to have the chance to defend myself against unfair statements."

"There is nothing to defend…it's an emotional thing."

"Then why did you use political methods to get rid of me – calling me a 'simple citizen,' writing letters to embassies…"

"I didn't use any…"

I interrupted, "my political activities were disturbing you."

"Yes, they were…and this is something, however, this was a situation which developed and mushroomed, and had it been up to me…There was an article by Marangopoulou in the newspaper – and that was an ugly thing – and this was the impression that was obviously being created…"

Marangopoulou was an older woman who had been active in women's issues years before I came on the scene, one of the few, and, I would say, a pioneer. She was working at the theoretical level primarily, having organized university graduates to write on feminist issues. I was working organizing women to take an activist role in fighting for their rights. I said to Andreas, "I was treading on her territory. I am not concerned about what she wrote. It was a very anti-feminist argument. She said, presumably as a feminist, that I should have thrown you out the door. I don't believe that feminists use violence, but they do insist on their rights before taking action."

"I'm sorry she wrote about you in such a manner," he said more softly now, indicating a kind of solidarity with me. He didn't return to the theme of my political activity bothering him.

"And I am terribly sorry about all the ugly attacks on you, which often makes you appear ridiculous," I declared softly. We were talking earnestly, like people who care for each other. We talked a bit about some of the things we had done in our life together. Then suddenly he said, "You make me feel guilty; is that what you want to do?" Then he hardened up. "I don't want any more to be officially related to you. Officially I want to finish. And I know it would never happen if I didn't do this."

"Did you ever think we could sit down together and talk seriously about a solution that would be satisfactory to both of us?"

"Like what?"

"I was ready, if you want to know, to join you and publicly declare that we were separating, be a cover for you, to even do that, instead of having all these things spread out in the press. My friends know that too."

"You would have done that?"

"Yes, with difficulty, but I would have done it."

"I don't believe you."

"I said to Kostas many times that if that man is really in love with that woman…"

"It has nothing to do with that woman. This is what you have not understood. I told Nikos to tell you…told him to tell you that I won't be with that woman. And I do not, will not, continue that relationship."

"Why is that? Because of me…"

"It is not in my soul."

I let it go at that. I changed the subject and asked him about his health. He gave me a rather long story about having taken wrong medication that caused him many problems which he blamed on the psychiatrist. When he described the symptoms they sounded to me like the symptoms of a heart and circulatory problem, not something from medication.

"It's not a very good period from what I can gather. Are you better now?"

His answer was "yes." I decided then to raise the issue of my political activities. I told him how I believed that my political activities had been helpful to him. I didn't like the impression that I was doing things politically which were in contrast or inconsistent with what he was already doing, or saying.

"I supported the Davos statement; I supported the Initiative of the Six; I couldn't figure out where I had taken positions in opposition. I also saw in an article in *Ethnos* that I had given you a list of women candidates for Parliament. Did I ever give such a list to you?"

"No."

"These lies were designed..."

He interrupted, "Not by me..."

I was thinking at that point how a relationship can get screwed up when there is little honest discussion between two people that had drifted apart. He returned to the question of my health and gave some advice, trying, I believed, to ovoid a discussion of my political activities. Then he moved to the subject of the terms of our separation. I told him I hadn't given it much thought, that I was puzzled by what he meant by 'separation,' and I suggested that we both take a deep breath and prepare our terms.

"Yes, we'll talk again, Margaret." He wanted to make sure he did not say 'Margarita, or Maggie, in order to indicate to me we were not functioning on any affectionate level, but on a strictly formal level. Still, he came and kissed me on the cheek as I got up to leave, something that suggested to me that the bond was still there. .

Chapter Twenty Eight

What is This Thing Called Love?

I had a week to think about the next meeting. The only thing that perked up my spirits during this time was when I heard someone in Greece had named a horse after The Hostess, using her nickname "Mimi."

On August 10, I walked over to his house/office around 7 in the evening with trepidation and feeling of sadness. This was to be the final meeting of clarification of our relationship from now on. As I entered the room Andreas said, "I see a bit of nervousness." I wondered what in god's name he expected, a woman riding a cloud of happiness? I ignored the remark.

"How is your health?" This was the subject that created the least problems between us, but in fact, I was seriously concerned about his health. I know some women who during a pre-divorce conflict period would like to see their husbands in jail, or to have a serious accident, or to become sick with a debilitating disease. Such hate I have never experienced – for anyone.

"My basic health seems to be alright, but this medicine that Kostas gave me – he denies the possibility, of course, seemed to have toxic effects on my heart muscle."

"Oh, my god!"

"And it's from there that all these things have come."

"Really? Andreas, I can't believe that. I talked to Kostas, and he says there is no way the medication could have created your health problems. He even did a survey of all the medical literature through the internet. No one has ever had side effects from what he gave you. Anyway, has it finished now?"

"I have had everything checked out, and the situation is better. But I have this swelling, and they are working with stronger drugs to bring about dehydration. So I think there is some improvement in terms of mobility and so forth – some difficulty…"

"Have you done a thorough examination – your heart, circulation, arteries?"

"I don't need it. All of this, as I said, was from the pills I took."

Clearly he refused to accept the truth, and I decided to change the subject and get to the core of our so-called separation. What followed was a serious talk about my future. At some point I returned to a statement I had made in a much earlier confrontation "I understand that this discussion we are having is because you fell in love."

"No, I didn't fall in love. Here you are wrong."

"I can understand it because we fell in love, and I know what it is like to be in love with you, and how you react under those circumstances." This latter was a play on his emotions with a kind of cunningness – not characteristic of me. Somewhere in the corner of my personality such a trait must exist, and I had opened the door and let it slip out. "In any case, I am glad to know it is not serious because connecting yourself with her would be a disaster, for you, for the country. And I say this not because I see her as a rival, but because it is the objective truth."

I saw him thoughtful.

"Let's get on with the main subject. I am not an 'independent' woman, as you have described. Independence requires money. I will need help from you, and a commitment that you will support the children who have as yet no income of their own."

"Do you think I would do otherwise?''

"No, I am just trying to be clear about the conditions. I am talking as a woman who must ensure her future…I did the stupid thing that I tell all women not to do. I never tried to gain economic independence. I have no health insurance. I have no job. I have no pension. If something happens to you, she will get your pension," according to a very unfair law.

"But she won't be married to me."

This was the second time he denied he would marry her. I was beginning to understand that he wanted an arrangement that we would share the house at Kastri, would be officially separated, but not divorced. He mentioned at some point a change on the second floor of bedrooms, more like an apartment. Since he had the ranch house that he used as an office, and it was a bona fide house with bedrooms, living room, bath room, kitchen, and a big playroom in the basement, I wondered what exactly he had in mind. He was not thinking clearly, but neither was I.

I needed air. We covered most of what I came to say and agreed on financial matters. I told him that I was considering developing a small business on the land his father had given to me when Andreas entered parliament. There I would need financial help. He simply said, "of course." Yet when I left, and he got up to walk me to the door, I still felt a strong bond still. With him I sensed he cared about me; he didn't want to "crush me," but his mixed up, conflicting feelings didn't permit any back sliding.

Twenty-one days passed before I saw Andreas again. It was summer stand-still time. Family and friends were scattered around the Mediterranean, the phones stopped ringing, newspapers ceased their screaming headlines, and the bugs and the birds took over the outdoor air space. People were waiting for the next chapter of this headline story, but not holding their breaths. I also scattered myself to the Sea in the company of American friends, Ruth and Phil Anderson, and friends of my son Andrikos, along with his professor Amartya Sen and children. We droned lazily on a lovely yacht (with plumbing problems) around the Ionian, touching base at

Skorpios, the island owned by Onassis where he and Jackie Kennedy got married, Lefkada, Ithika, Kefalonia and then back to the Peloponnesus and my favorite beach area- Akrata, near the town of Corinth.

When I returned to Kastri, I found a letter awaiting me from a man I had almost forgotten – Paul Olum. It was a lovely support letter and injected a spec of spirit into my embattled psyche. He addressed me formally as Ms. Papandreou, but the letter was informal, chatty and sensitive.

"I am writing this on an airplane returning to Eugene from our new Soviet Sister City, Irkutsk, in Siberia The visit to Irkutsk was in many ways a mission of peace, and during the trip I have thought from time to time of our meeting and conversation in my office when you came to the University of Oregon to give a talk around a year ago. I don't suppose you are likely to remember the occasion as well as I do, so perhaps I should re-introduce myself. I am president of the University of Oregon. We talked for perhaps an hour, and when you left you gave a set of worry beads with a medallion bearing the symbol of your organization and also (which you doubted I would have need of) the likeness of the goddess of fertility. It sits now on a low table in my office and often reminds me of your visit.

"We talked of your work for women's rights and above all, your work for peace and for the achievements of a meaningful summit. Since I spent the war years from early 1943 to the beginning of 1946 on the Manhattan project at Los Alamos, I spoke of my own similar commitment to working for the end of the nuclear arms race and of the time I spend (my principle extra-curricular activity) giving talks about the history of nuclear armaments and about the desperate importance of bringing to end all of the machinery of war.

"Our visit to Irkutsk…represented the desire to establish bonds of sisterhood and cooperation with a Soviet city, something we see as a small step toward creating a world of friendship and peace…It seems to me the great hope of peace

in the world today comes out of the Soviet Union, specifically Gorbachev. His commitment appears to be genuine, and I gather he has the backing of the party leadership, if not the entrenched bureaucracy.

"I'm afraid I'm going on at great length, but I have wanted to write to you for some time. I could hardly have missed reading about your own personal travails over the past months, and I wanted to tell you both how sorry I am (angry, too), at the unpleasantness you have had to experience and also how much I admire the courage and dignity with which you have handled it. You are, in very many ways, an extraordinary person.

"I would like so much to be able to see you again. I know you occasionally give talks, attend conferences, etc. in the States, and I usually find out about it afterwards through some article in the newspaper. If you are going to be in this country in the near future, especially on the West Coast, but perhaps anywhere, and you would be willing to meet again, please let me know your schedule. I would hope we could spend some time together."

It was signed with the word "Warmly." I didn't know then, but this contact was destined to mean much more in my life than a morale boost.

On August 23rd, Andreas called me over to his office around 5 o'clock in the afternoon. I found him with his legs up on a footstool, his feet stuffed into shoes, flesh lapping over loosened shoestrings, and a face bloated, with a grayish tinge. I was shocked. I asked him what in god's name was wrong, and he replied that he was still getting over his bout with drugs, but was on the way to being alright. I knew he had a cruise scheduled for the weekend and was determined to keep it. He said he was going in for further tests late that night in a hospital, scheduled at that time in order to keep the visit a secret. I was against secret medical check-ups, arguing about the naturalness of people our age having regular check-ups and the responsibility of a prime minister to have such check-ups. They never remain secret and the mystery provides much more room for speculation than an upfront announcement. Then I left.

I had a feeling he wanted to see me because he wasn't well, because I had always been his pillar of strength and optimism in times of difficulty. Sub-consciously, he wanted me near. That was my interpretation. He said nothing of the kind. He mainly wanted to tell me he was giving thought to my conditions and by the end of the summer would be able to make a proposal. The most astounding thing about the three discussions having to do with our personal lives was the absence of the word "divorce."

The more I thought about it, the more I realized the arrangement he was proposing was unrealistic. The word he always used was "separation." Without a legal settlement, I would have no guarantee of anything we agreed upon. Furthermore, what was the point of being married in name only? And the bigger question – is my love for him strong enough to let him go?

I sat down the next morning and wrote a brief note with a few comments of regret and about being available in time of need, then underlined the simple sentence – <u>I want a divorce.</u> As I had always predicted, I would be the one who would make the proposal. While I was sealing the envelope whales of tears spilled from my eyes, my throat choked up – not only because of the decision, but because of the physical condition I found him in. He was precious to me, my love was still there, and I had no feelings of ill will. I took the envelope and slipped it under his door.

Late that evening, Mihalis came to talk to me. He told me the tests had shown a serious circulatory situation, and a heart condition. He had been advised to go to London, probably for a bi-pass. Mihalis was exasperated because Andreas argued for a departure on Monday so he could have his cruise. I suggested that he urge him to talk to his psychiatrist. Kostas was clearly not on good terms with Andreas because of the accusation of causing all of these problems. Yet he was the only one who could find a way to persuade Andreas to do the right thing.

Kostas, after hearing about the condition of Andreas, couldn't sleep that night, he told me later, and very early in the morning he went to Andreas's house, unannounced, and convinced him to leave for London within twenty-four hours, insisting that time was of the essence. That evening of the 24th I talked to Mihalis again and told him I would be willing to accompany my husband on the trip, but could not impose myself, given the personal circumstances. The children would be with him, and I only hoped he would not take the Hostess. Mihalis told me Andreas had promised he would not. Mihalis, however, believed she would inveigle her way in during the time of preparations. Andreas was too sick to impose his own desires or views on this matter.

The departure of the Prime Minister for London had all the elements of a television scenario or a secret service design to fool the enemy. Angela, his secretary, was asked to reserve eleven seats on the Olympic Airlines flight leaving at 2 p.m. on the 25th under the name Akrivakis, who was the director of the Olympic Airport. A programmed meeting early the next week with the president of Cyprus, Mr. Vassiliou, was cancelled with no explanation. Around 12 noon a call from the office of the prime minister was made to Central Police Headquarters to send security police out in force to the airport without further details. Ministers of the government were kept in the dark.

Around 12:15 it became known that Andreas was going to London for a check on a problem with his heart. Reporters and photographers gathered in the VIP lounge to await his arrival. At 1:40 they learned that he, with 10 additional people, was already in the plane. He came without the normal fanfare of motorcycles and black Mercedes security cars accompanying his departures, driving to the area where commercial vehicles arrive, and from there made his way to the plane without being seen. No flash bulbs, and no questions. The newspapers printed the name of the eleven passengers the following day.

Among them was the name of The Hostess.

The following day I drove Nikos to the airport to be with his father with last words of encouragement from me. The next day Sophia left and on the 31st Andrikos left. George cleared his desk at the Ministry of Education and took off for London on September 2nd. A barrage of news stories ensued concerning everything from who would be in charge of the government during the operation and convalescence, who would take over in case the procedure was unsuccessful, whether or not Margarita would go to London to assert her right to be near him as his wife (throwing The Hostess to the wolves), and Sophia's anger and rage at the unwanted intruder, and the Hostesses' dominating presence. We learned that Andreas needed a triple by-pass and replacement of the heart valve. Because of his general condition when he arrived, time would have to pass before the operation could take place. He was put on a strict diet, the necessary medications were started, and he was advised to take daily walks in the hospital yard.

On one of these walks The Hostess grabbed his hand for waiting photographers, and this photo travelled the newspaper syndicate lines around the world. She was given a wonderful opportunity to prove her devotion by staying by his side constantly and functioning in the role of a caring spouse. Andreas was captive and whatever he felt, he undoubtedly needed this "tender loving care" when his life was at stake. The hand holding made me remember with nostalgia our early days of romance when Andreas said that he would send me a message when we held hands with three short squeezes that meant "I love you."

My friends came by constantly to visit, those who were true friends and those who were waiting to see which way the power balance tipped. Although to most it seemed the die was cast, there were too many "ifs" in the picture, the most important of which was the disbelief that Andreas would choose a chorus girl type woman for a future partner.

Somebody dug up nude pictures of The Hostess and these were splashed on front pages for the eyes of the thirsty public.

(Diary entry) *September 30th, 1988, Kastri*

A most difficult day. Andreas underwent his by-pass and valve replacement, and at this point he is out of the operating room and in intensive care. I had no doubt about his surviving the operation. Although I am not into astrological predictions, when I heard he was scheduled for this event on my birthday, I relaxed, and the music in my head sang out, "He's going to be all right!" My greatest anguish was that I wasn't there; it seemed so unnatural not to be at his side at a time of a crisis. The children called frequently, giving me a running commentary on what was going on, knowing how much I wanted to be with him and them. Many of his friends and cohorts came by the house, wearing their emotions on their faces and in their body stances. Greeks express their emotions openly, and genuinely – a trait in the culture I much admire, given my own Anglo-Saxon temperament. Although there are developing doubts about his personality and emotional stability, he is very much loved.

Around 12:30, the first report came out from the Greek press secretary: "The Prime Minister has entered the operating room for preparations prior to the operation. This included the anesthetization. Shortly before entering the room, he showed optimism, courage and calm. By orders from the British authorities, the area around the operating room was put under tight security. Five Greek security guards were the only ones permitted but only in the hallway."

Early this evening Sophia read the report to me: "The Prime Minister of Greece underwent an operation today for the replacement of the aorta artery to improve the functioning of his heart. The operation, which began today at noon, lasted seven hours. The doctors involved in the operation are happy with the result and the condition of the patient."

I will try to sleep now. Sweet dreams, Andreas.

I turned my attention to preparations for the Pan-Hellenic meeting of EGE. I was curious about the atmosphere, about the outcome. The meeting of this group the year before on the island of Aegina had been conducted under the optimism of my knowledge of a reconciliation. This one was after a fait accompli. Nonetheless I was determined to continue my work on behalf of women.

Meanwhile, apparently orders from what was called "the new environment," that is, The Hostess and her affiliates, more items appeared in the newspapers to try to change the attitudes on the personal story swirling around the Prime Minister. Some papers dropped the name of Papandreou and referred to me as Margaret Chant, my maiden name. An alternative title for me acceptable to them was the "Amerikana." The biggest part of this campaign was to stress my political activities and compare them with the caring, loving, totally committed blonde at Andreas's bedside. *Avriani*, which had been a stalwart supporter of mine, but was first and foremost a PASOK newspaper, dropped occasional bits of information about my inadequacy as a housewife and companion. The buxom, brash and arrogant Hostess was described as tender and humble.

In the late summer before Andreas's trip to London, I had accepted an invitation to New York to speak at the UN Trusteeship Council Chamber in honor of the "Day of Solidarity with the South African Political Prisoners." With Andreas's convalescence at that time going well, and because of my need to test my new freedom and my capacity as a soon-to-be divorced woman. I informed the organizers I would definitely be present. My friends Lisbet Palme and Glynis Kinnock, wife of the head of the Labor Party of England, were speaking too, and I looked forward to seeing them. I informed Paul Olum of my schedule. Shortly after I did this, I received a phone call from Pierre telling me he would be in New York around the time of my speech. He had apparently seen the information in a UN bulletin because I hadn't talked to him since the early part of Andreas's trip to London.

I found myself in the enviable position of juggling rendezvous with two men. I used to do this when dating – and now, at my advanced age! What jolly fun! I spent Saturday and Sunday with Pierre, maintaining the platonic relationship I desired and when he left Sunday afternoon, I readied myself for a dinner at eight with the virtually unknown to me; Paul Olum. We were to meet in the lobby of the Plaza Hotel and walk to a nearby Italian restaurant. I barely remembered his physical features; remembering only his open and exuberant personality. As he walked toward me in the lobby, I experienced a pleasant surprise. He was good-looking, tall, broad shoulders, silvery white hair and flat-bellied. In my book of important characteristics for a man, this latter was high on my list. Since I knew nothing of his personal history, except for his career as a physicist, mathematician, and university president, I wondered if he was looking for an extra-marital adventure. My own extra-marital affair with Pierre seemed somehow alright in view of the fact we were both married and not looking for an intrusion by the other in our marital condition. Maybe that's just rationalizing infidelity.

The mystery was cleared up early at the dinner table. He had lost his wife to cancer several years earlier. He was the father of three children, one boy and two girls and apparently had a close and successful marriage. He was more serious than Pierre, less playful and teasing, less sophisticated. He seemed naïve to me, but by now all Americans seemed naïve. This latter observation comes from my contact through speeches with organizations anywhere from Kiwanis to Lions Clubs, to universities, to foreign affairs councils, or UN connected organizations and the peace and women's movements. In the movements I found more awareness of the forces operating in society and the world, although there were lots of do-gooders in the peace movement who could not give a sharp analysis of these forces. With Paul I found an honest, principled, straight-forward human being, one who gave a sense of stability and security. What was gone was the clandestine nature of the relationship with Pierre. I was free if

I so desired to walk with Paul anywhere, including taking him to my hotel room without looking back over my shoulder as I ascended.

We did not, however, go to my hotel room. We spent the evening talking, somewhat awkwardly at first, like teenagers on a first date. I was interpreting his restlessness and fidgeting – which I had seen in his office at Oregon – as tension, and it affected me. However, by the time we had finished a bottle of Italian Chianti, our talk became smoother and later, back at the hotel over an after dinner drink in the bar, I found myself easily describing my tortured inner world, my pain, my aching heart. Paul, with his understanding and sensitivity to my plight, including being angry at Andreas – something I was unable to do – had become my confidante, my therapist, my friend, in a short evening.

The next day I was almost embarrassed by my openness and verbal diarrhea. I was sure he would avoid further contact with me. At the end of five more days in New York, and no word from Paul, I assumed he had gone back to Oregon. I wanted to ask him to forgive me for loading him down with my troubles. I dialed his number in Oregon His rich voice came over the phone with a "how glad I am you called," and when I blurted out my concern about the evening, he laughed and said, "quite the contrary, it was a very special evening for me." His first letter to me had worked so well, he explained, that instead of a phone call, he intended to write me in Athens to tell me precisely that.

During the time Andreas was recuperating in London, the "sex and politics" tale became more and more a hot international scandal. Even as far as Japan, the Hostess's nude body was displayed in front page glory. I was sick of the story, sick of the ridicule of Andreas, sick of being described as "the American wife of forty years," sick of being sick. Upon my return I dove into EGE politics, making preparations for our Pan-Hellenic meeting in Athens.

(Diary entry) *October 21st, 1988, Kastri*

Tomorrow we start our proceedings for the Pan-Hellenic meeting. I go as president, about to be shorn of the title of wife of the Prime Minister, and of First Lady of Greece. We are having new elections for the Executive Board. Perhaps I am a little frightened to take on this struggle. I see so many aspects in my re-defined role which are ugly, which I never wanted in my life. Me against Andreas. Andreas against me. The truth of the matter is, even if I work at the political level, as president of EGE, it can be twisted to appear as if I am taking on Andreas as an opponent. It is difficult to see where this is going and how it is going to end. Although my cards seem good at the moment, and my prestige high, mostly from sympathy and compassion, if it boils down to a struggle, ultimately people will say, "What the hell does she want? Why is she doing this? Anyway, she's a foreigner." The people are committed to Andreas; their love him, and that is where their love belongs. I love this country, but that is not enough. And my popularity is not political power – only potentially.

Andreas was arriving back in Greece on the 23rd, the second day of our Pan-Hellenic meeting which was being held in Kalithea, close to the airport. The stalwart political party members who had become also members of EGE wanted to be present at his arrival. What they didn't know was his intention to present the Hostess as his new companion by waving her down the steps of the airplane after his initial appearance on the stairway. Kind of like giving the papal blessing. PASOK, in the meantime, told its members she was not arriving with him, but on a subsequent flight. The party wanted to guarantee a large crowd.

On the first day of the EGE meeting, I gave my usual opening speech, referring to the organization, our accomplishments in the past two years, our work for the three days of the meeting, etc. After much thought, I decided to refer to my personal situation.

"One last issue, not unimportant, is that I want to bring forth a personal issue that I intend to generalize. I heard and read that the manner in which I am handling my marital problem is not consistent with feminist ideology. What I understood by this was that after the way I was treated, my first reaction should have been to announce my intention to file for a divorce. I decided not to tell them that my mind was made up, and that I would take the initiative to announce it.

"First of all, I know of no specific feminist rules or formula for the dissolving of a marriage. Each case is different – such as responsibilities, children, length of marriage, the character of the marriage and the psychological world of each spouse.

"A divorce is the legal expression of a broken relationship. It is the official end of a marriage. It involves the process through which the two partners arrive at agreements concerning their lives, property, house, children and sometimes the form of relationship toward each other after the divorce. If the two persons agree, everything moves ahead normally. If they don't agree, other routes are available.

"My feminist friends would consider a statement of intent to divorce as an act of independence, dignity, defiance and perhaps anger. If a person, who tried to operate all her life with dignity, without fanfare, prefers not to express her anger or her defiance publicly, and to find the solution to the problem privately, what purpose will be served by a public statement? And if she has children whose feelings she respects and for whom she does not want to create new bitterness, why must she announce publicly her intentions?

"If there are feminist rules, feminist principles, they express the concern for others. A feminist must show understanding and solicitude. This includes caution not to throw oil on the fire to feed the serial. This means also that she continues with her work and actions, and with gusto. And those who are her feminist friends will support her right to deal with a painful problem in her own way."

The next day we called a break in the program to permit those who wanted to be present at the grand arrival to leave. Out of the hundred women present, five chose to go. They returned in tears. The big show had taken place. Applause greeted Andreas as he appeared in the doorway of the plane and while he was descending the stairs. After seven steps, he stopped, turned around, and dramatically raised his arm to gesture to a waiting figure inside the plane and abracadabra, presto, the Hostess was suddenly in the doorway. Absolute silence greeted her appearance. The crowd was stunned. Some gasped, "oh, no!" Then a loyal cheer leader from the PASOK movement, a lone soul, began applauding, and half the crowd, true to party discipline, clapped politely. The act was a fiasco, a total failure. Andreas was Zeus, hurling thunderbolts at the waiting crowd.

Andreas, the Prime Minister, was my lover, my husband, father of my children, partner in political action. His gesture was the final excruciating blow – a poison arrow into my chest, my heart. Yet I still loved him. He was my aetos and the bond could not be broken.

It was, nonetheless, my liberation.

Post-Script:

On April 23, 1991, a baptism ceremony was held for my grandchild, George's daughter, and she was to be named Margarita. The entire family was invited, including Andreas and his new wife. (I had not seen Andreas for almost two years except on TV and once at a distance while attending a funeral.) The family sat in the front isle separating us from the "couple" on the other side. While waiting for the ceremony to begin, I felt the closeness of Andreas nearby. I had no feeling of resentment or hostility. Mostly, I wanted to do just one thing – to stand in front of him with my hands on his shoulders, look him in the eyes and thank him for the voyage we had together. It was rich, giving me a deep relationship that could never be broken, full of romance, adventure, passion, and excitement. It also gave me the opportunity to explore the importance of duty, justice, equality, non-violence and spiritual values of caring in working for a better, healthier and just world. He would remain in history as one of the greatest leaders of modern Greece. And last, but not least, it produced four magnificent children.

The ceremony started and was soon over. Typically when a ceremony ends, the family members walk up to the altar to congratulate the parents, kiss the baby and thank the priest. We all waited for Andreas and the Hostess to go up first. I remembered it was the custom that coming back down Andreas would shake hands with the people in the front row. He headed for Sophia first while I tried to appear engaged in my own thoughts so he could ignore me – something similar to what I had done in my walk across campus the day we renewed our lost romance.

I heard him say "Margarita," and I saw an outstretched hand. I put mine out to meet his. He took it and pressed it three times. There was no renewal of the relationship, although I learned Andreas had regretted that we were apart, but the old hand shake of love stopped finally the lingering ache in my heart.